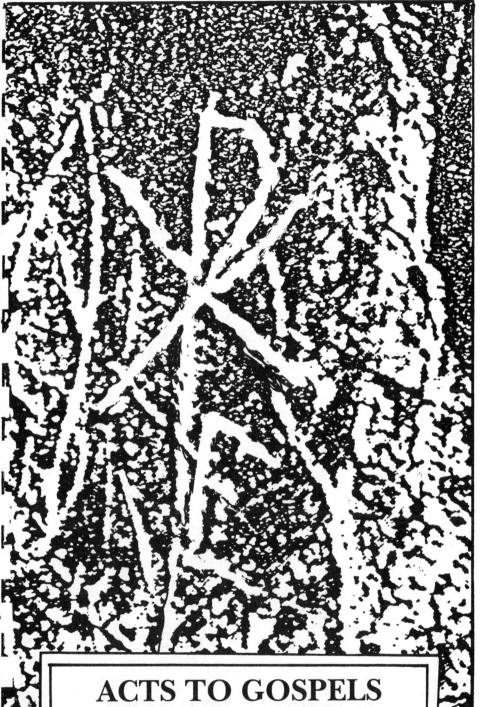

ACTS TO GOSPELS
A NEW TESTAMENT PATH

ACTS
TO
GOSPELS

A New Testament Path

John J. McDonnell, C.M., Ph.D.

UNIVERSITY
PRESS OF
AMERICA

Lanham • New York • London

Copyright © 1989 by

University Press of America,® Inc.

4720 Boston Way
Lanham, MD 20706

3 Henrietta Street
London WC2E 8LU England

British Cataloging in Publication Information Available

Library of Congress Cataloging-in-Publication Data

McDonnell, John J.
Acts to Gospels : a New Testament path / John J. McDonnell.
p.   cm.
Includes bibliographical references.
1. Bible. N.T. Gospels—Criticism, interpretation, etc.   2. Bible. N.T. Acts—
Criticism, interpretation, etc.   3. Bible. N.T.—History of contemporary
events.   I. Title.
BS2555.2.M38   1989   226'.061—dc20   89–36146 CIP

ISBN 0–8191–7545–5 (alk. paper)

The paper used in this publication meets the minimum requirements of American
National Standard for Information Sciences—Permanence of Paper for Printed Library
Materials, ANSI Z39.48–1984.   ∞

I am the way and the truth
and the life. . .
(John 14:6)

CONTENTS

Frontispiece The **symbol** on the frontispiece was found on a blue-plastered support-wall at right angle to a much larger red wall which, (sometime after his martyrdom in Rome about 66 A.D.), **identified** the grave of **St. Peter** among the surrounding pagan graves. Christians scratched memento symbols on the blue wall in prayer to Peter; it is known as the **graffiti wall.**

About two-&-a-half centuries later, after 312, Constantine liberated the Christians from the threat of further Roman persecutions. Then he commissioned the building of a basilica over this traditional site of Peter's grave. The famous slogan, "in hoc vince" (in this [sign = Christ's monogram], conquer) was found on the graffiti wall! The wall and grave were covered in the building process. The present **St. Peter's Basilica** is built over Constantine's original church; **the main altar is directly over this traditional gravesite.** Pius XII (1939 - 1958) permitted a special team under an archeologist (Fr. Kirschbaum S.J./1941) to excavate very carefully under St. Peter's in order to confirm the traditional data. Symbols like the special **chi/rho** (XP) identified the grave and confirmed the 19-centuries-old tradition.

Years later the patient detective work of epigrapher, Dr. Margherita Guarducci, deciphered the complex **Petrine chi/rho** symbolon the **graffiti wall**, and by a fortuitous piece of information discovered the actual bodily remains of St. Peter. The **chi/rho** is the monogram of Christ in Greek; the **Pe** is the start of Peter's name in Latin; the three prongs on the bottom not only form the **E** for Peter, but also form a **Key** to symbolize the Matthean text in which Christ says to Pater:"I will entrust to you the **keys** of the Kingdom of Heaven."(Mt 16:19) [John E. Walsh, The Bones of St. Peter, (Garden City: Image Books, Doubleday & Company, Inc., 1985), pp. 98-178.]

The Hebrew title, Messiah, is **Christos** Χριστός in Greek. The monogram uses the title's first two Greek letters, Chi/rho. The Chi has the rho superimposed on it and in this form was a commonly used ancient Christian symbol for Jesus Christ.

End Page   The letter **I** is the first letter of the name Jesus in Greek; the letter chi "X" (= **ch** in English) is the first letter of the title Christ in Greek; **th** = is the letter theta in Greek and is the start of the word Theou (= of God); **u** stands for uios which is the Greek word for son; and finally **s** is the first letter of the the Greek word soter which means savior. When these letters are put together thus: **Ichthus**, they spell the Greek word for fish. This ancient symbol, sometimes used as a secret sign among Christians thus meant Iesus Christ - of God (**th**) the Son (**u**) - Savior (**s**).

Common abbreviations of the N.T. books

Mt	=	Matthew	1 Tim	=	1 Timothy
Mk	=	Mark	2 Tim	=	2 Timothy
Lk	=	Luke	Ti	=	Titus
Jn	=	John	Phlm	=	Philemon
Acts	=	Acts of the Apostles	Heb	=	Hebrews
Rom	=	Romans	Jas	=	James
1 Cor	=	1 Corinthians	1 Pet	=	1 Peter
2 Cor	=	2 Corinthians	2 Pet	=	2 Peter
Gal	=	Galatians	1 Jn	=	1 John
Eph	=	Ephesians	2 Jn	=	2 John
Phil	=	Philippians	3 Jn	=	3 John
Col	=	Colossians	Jude	=	Jude
1 Thes	=	1 Thessalonians	Rv	=	Revelation
2 Thes	=	2 Thessalonians			

1 Thes 2:13 **is read** first Thessalonians, chapter 2, verse 13.
2 Pet 3:14-16 " second Peter, chapter 3, verses 14 to 16.
[The Front and End pages and some maps were designed and drawn by **Rev. Francis W. Sacks, C.M., Ph.D.**]

PREFACE

This brief **introduction** examines some books of the New Testament in light of the **Instruction on the Historicity of the Gospels** published by the Pontifical Biblical Commission (PBC) on April 21, 1964 and the Vatican II-document on Revelation, **Dei Verbum.** Attention is given to the fact that the teaching of the earthly Jesus was transmitted in preaching **before** the final production of the four Gospels. The study of the Acts of the Apostles **before** studying the Gospels helps to achieve the realization of how the written Gospels originated. The presentation has in view those who may be unfamiliar with the New Testament. These notes presume the simultaneous study of the parts of the New Testament being discussed.

The Gospel was **proclaimed** by the Apostles and their helpers for a number of years **before it was written down** by the evangelists (Gospel-writers) in the four relatively full forms in which we now have it, namely in the Gospels according to Matthew (Mt), Mark (Mk), Luke (Lk) and John (Jn). Of course, the words and deeds of Christ preceded the proclaiming which the Apostles did. The Apostles were the designated witnesses of what Jesus said and did. Thus, **three stages** are discernible in the genesis or production of the four written Gospel accounts. They are: first the stage of **Jesus' teaching and activity** in his public ministry, second the oral stage of the apostolic **telling** the significance of Jesus' words and deeds which is found in The Acts of the Apostles, and third the stage of the evangelists **writing down** the meaning of those words and deeds in the four Gospels to different groups of people in different parts of the world.

The New Testament book known as the Acts of the Apostles (briefly referred to as Acts) covers a very important section (but not nearly all) of the second period, that is, the time between Christ's doings and the evangelists' final writing. In view of the fact that the telling preceded the final writing, it seems clear that the telling-period formulated the framework of the Gospels and their contents before they were committed to writing. In other words stage two, the telling period, in the genesis of the Gospels prepared the way for the writing of stage three. Thus it appears useful to study stage two to get a sense of what happened in the telling-stage in order to appreciate more the elements contained in the writing stage.

One might object, "lets start at stage one[1] and take the stages in order." That's a good idea, but the fact is that almost all we know about stage one is contained in the writings from stage three. Jesus did the things and he picked particular men (later called Apostles) to proclaim his doings publicly, but Jesus didn't write about it; neither did the Apostles. To their utter amazement he rose from the dead after being crucified. After the risen Jesus convinced them of this and sent the Holy Spirit to strengthen them, then they first proclaimed it to Jerusalem and, later elsewhere, to all who would listen. The Apostles were so convinced of this new reality (Jesus' resurrection signified resurrection for everybody) that they set out to tell the good news everywhere (2nd stage). It cost most (if not all) of them their lives.

In the scattered places to which the Apostles and their evangelizing helpers went, certain people began to put some of the oral "Good News" (i.e. the Gospel) into **writing.** Those who later wrote the final Gospel accounts (3rd stage) are referred to as **the evangelists.** These evangelists wrote the Gospel account in the way that the apostolic witnesses believed it and taught it orally. Thus, it appears useful to study the apostolic stage (oral second stage) in the beginning in order to get a good grasp of the process which produced the four Gospel accounts.[2]

One scholar even thought that Luke himself, the author of the Gospel According To Luke and Acts, wrote Acts first. But the evidence does not sustain his position.[3] Nevertheless, the picture of Peter and his apostolic colleagues "shaping" the Gospel message is quite clear in Acts. As Jesus formed his Apostles into a unity, these Apostles, following his lead, formed those who believed in him into a community, (a **koinonia**) of believers. It is important to note that all the New Testament books are directed to this new community and its members by the believing leaders of this same new community. The books belong to this body of people, first emerging from Judaism, and in about a dozen years

1. Jerome Crowe, The Acts, (Wilmington: Michael Glazier, Inc., 1980), p.ix.
2. David E. Aune, The New Testament in Its Literary Environment, (Philadelphia: The Westminster Press, 1987 [paperback 1989]), p. 24 "Acts 10:34-43 is a crucial text for the hypothesis of the Gospels' kerygmatic origin, for it has **many similarities to the outline of Mark.**" [hereafter Aune, Literary Environment and page.
3. J.A.T. Robinson, Redating the New Testament, (Philadelphia: The Westminster Press, 1975), p.92.

becoming known to the world as **Christians.** The study of <u>Acts</u> leads easily into the world-famous four Gospel accounts according to Matthew, Mark[4], Luke and John.

Before doing <u>Acts</u>, however, we must first become acquainted with the New Testament as a whole and also the declining Greek world, the emerging, powerful Roman world and the Roman-dominated Jewish world into which the "Good News" appeared in action, speech and writing. Following the background material we proceed to examine the Acts of the Apostles and the individual Gospels for the purpose of gaining a sense of each book as a whole, some of its significant contents and an overview of the path along which the Gospels came into existence. The chapters are designed as follows.

First, **chapter I** identifies the 27 "books" which constitute the New Testament. **Chapter II** briefly focuses a wide-angle view of the Greek and Roman secular backgrounds during the New Testament era. **Chapter III** looks at the religious and philosophic atmosphere influencing the Mediterranean world.

Chapter IV narrows the focus to Palestine's Herodian dynasty and the prevailing groupings of people in the first-century Jewish world. Against this background **chapter V** examines the New Testament book, <u>The Acts of the Apostles</u> as it shows the oral tradition of and about Jesus Christ taking root in the Jewish heartland and moving out into the Greek and Roman worlds. In this book, <u>Acts</u>, the Apostle Peter's speeches provide the framework for the moving <u>Gospel According to Mark</u> which is closely studied in **chapter VI.**

At this point **chapter VII** introduces the recent history and theory of Gospel analysis. With the contents of <u>Acts</u> and the <u>Gospel According to Mark</u> known, the journey of Gospel analysis from literary criticism to more recent critical analysis can be better appreciated. Resting on the prevailing theory of the influence of Mark's account on the Gospel accounts of Matthew and Luke, **chapter VIII** examines something of the structure and contents of the didactic <u>Gospel According to Matthew</u> and **chapter**

---

4.   Aune, <u>Literary Environment</u>, p. 25 Mark's "primary function" as "the historical legitimation of the saving significance of Jesus." could very well flow from the **need** to give a solid historical base to the oral kerygma in the face of doubts arising from persecution and death.

IX looks at the framework and content of the compassionate Gospel According to Luke. **Chapter X** terminates the inquiry with the study of the Gospel (which soars like an eagle) According to John.

A number of **appendices**, significant for the understanding and appreciation of the Gospels (and the proper evaluation of the theology and history contained in them), were added to this brief study. Appendix **1** considers **what theology is**; literary and historical studies are needed to do theology, but are not themselves theology. Appendix **2** is the important **Instruction** on the Historicity of the Gospels published by the Pontifical Biblical Commission on April 21, 1964 between the second and third sessions of the second Vatican Council. Appendix **3** looks at significant excerpts of Vatican II's Dogmatic Constitution on Divine Revelation, known also by its shorter Latin title, **Dei Verbum** (Word of God). Appendix **4** briefly considers the belief-question: how can one explain **God's authorship** of the Gospels.

Appendix **5** presents Isaiah's most famous **Servant of Yahweh** song which is an Old Testament text of great influence in messianic understanding proclaimed in the Gospels. Appendix **6** presents some of the **papyri and manuscripts** which preserved the text of the Gospels and, indeed, of the whole New Testament through the centuries. the famous text problem of Luke 22 and its solution is looked at. Appendix **7** inquires into the question of "fundamentalism" as contrasted with the concept of "modified inerrancy" contained in Vatican II's "Dogmatic Constitution on Divine Revelation. Appendix **8** briefly sketches the idea of the classical **synoptic problem** and one approach toward its solution. Appendix **9** introduces 1,2 Thessalonians as the very first of the New Testament books which came into existence much as we now read it.

Appendix **10** studies all the "resurection accounts" together to gain a picture of their samenesses and differences. Appendix **11** is a synopsis of Cardinal Ratzinger's important 1988 New York lecture to scholars, entitled, "Crisis in Exegesis". Finally, Appendix **12** is a "Glossary" of terms, appearing in New Testament studies, which may be unfamiliar to some readers.

I am indebted to more scholars than I can even name starting with the careful teaching of Fr. James McGlinchey, C.M. who introduced me to the work of the famous Pere Lagrange O.P.

After Vatican II the enthusiastic teaching of Father Richard Kugelman, C.P. re-ignited my desire to know "the Sacred Scriptures" more fully. Fr. W. Harrington's publications guided me for years, not to mention the Jerome Biblical Commentary, and the very useful Dictionary of Fr. John L. McKenzie, S.J. A number of the books read or consulted and cited in the footnotes provided new insights and quotes.

I wish also to thank my many Vincentian Confreres who supported and encouraged me in this work: Father Gerard Mahoney, V.C.M., for his gracious approval and Father Thomas Concagh, C.M. for his kind assistance; Fathers John Freund, C.M. and Frank Sacks, C.M. patiently taught me the use of the computer; Fathers Michael Tumulty, C.M. and John B. Murray, C.M. painstakingly checked expression and theological content.

Any oversimplifications, shortcomings or errors in this **brief introduction,** of course, belong to me and not to the scholars whose classes were attended or whose works were consulted.

Chapter I: The New Testament

The **New Testament** consists of 27 pieces of writing, commonly referred to as "books". These books, which are like essays and letters, vary in length from one page to twenty-five or thirty pages. They vary as well from the point of view of each book's doctrinal importance.

It is very useful to learn the names of these "books" as soon as possible so that their contents, the class of writing to which clusters of the books belong, and the many the individual traits identifying each can be clearly distinguished from the beginning of the study.

1.The 27 Books The most important of the New Testament books are the **four gospels** which are focused on the **Person of Jesus Christ** and his words and deeds. These are: the gospels according to **Matthew, Mark, Luke and John.** The four gospels have been listed in this same order from the earliest times. References to Matthew (abbreviated **Mt**), Mark **(Mk)**,Luke **(Lk)** and John **(Jn)** refer to the gospels, not to the persons of the evangelists. Thus, Mt is referred to as the first Gospel, Mk as the second Gospel, Lk as the third and Jn as the fourth. Generally, when the person of a sacred author himself is intended, the context makes this clear.

The first three gospels, namely Matthew, Mark, and Luke, are also known as the **synoptic gospels** because their authors viewed the ministry of Jesus of Nazareth from a similar overall point of view and the finished gospels have a similar framework.

Another book is attributed to St. Luke, namely the **Acts of The Apostles.** This book was written in conjunction with Luke's Gospel but when, early in the second century, the four gospels were being gathered together to form a " collection of the gospels", the **Acts** book was separated from the collection, listed separately and as a piece of writing enjoyed a history of its own from that time on.

The next group of writings is a series of letters or **Epistles** whose teachings have **in a general way** been attributed to **St. Paul.** They are the epistles to the: Romans, Corinthians (two), Galatians, Ephesians, Philippians, Colossians, Thessalonians (two), Timothy (two), Titus, Philemon and Hebrews.

As the names suggest, some of these **epistles** were written to Christians who lived in certain cities, such as Rome or Corinth; others were addressed to particular persons, such as Timothy and Titus. This listing seems to indicate that Paul, through the services of a scribe, wrote or dictated all these writings. However, it was recognized from the time of their origin that such was not the case. The **Epistle to the Hebrews** is the easiest exception to cite, because some of the earliest local churches or Christian communities refused to accept it as a letter written by Paul. Yet, after some years, it was accepted that some of its content fitted in with the thoughts expressed in Paul's acknowledged letters, so for convenience sake, it was listed with this group of letters known as the Pauline "corpus" of writings.

The next group of writings is also a group of letters or EPISTLES. It is commonly referred to as the group of **seven Catholic Epistles**. They consist of writings attributed to James, Peter (two), John (three) and Jude. Whereas Paul's letters were addressed to particular individuals or communities, these latter epistles appear to be addressed more universally (or catholicly) to **all** the christian communities. The word in first century Greek which referred to the "whole" body of people addressed, or to "all", was **katholikos**. Hence, they are commonly referred to as the seven Catholic Epistles.

The book remaining to be named is the writing called the **Apocalypse** or **Book of Revelation.** this book is almost always listed last, but it was not the last of the 27 books to be written. The teaching of this book, along with his Gospel and three of the Catholic epistles, are commonly attributed to the teaching of the Apostle, **John** These five books are also identified as the Johannine corpus of teachings.

New Testament writings listed in summary form:

Gospels	Acts	Pauline Teaching			Catholic Epistles
		Romans Corinthians Corinthians			James
Matthew		Galatians Ephesians Philippians			1st Peter
Mark		Colossians Thessalonians 2Thes			2nd Peter
Luke	Acts	Timothy 2nd Timothy Titus			1st John
John		Philemon Hebrews			2nd John
					3rd John
					Jude

Apocalyptic Writing: Revelation (or Apocalypse)

The **first** epistle to the **Thessalonians** (usually identified by the abbreviation: 1 Thes) was certainly in existence in the year 50/51 A.D. By that year the convert-Apostle Paul had brought the Good News of Christ's resurrection to the town of Thessalonika and had started a new Christian community in the midst of the Greek and Roman pagans living there. Most scholars acknowledge that 1 Thes was the **first** one of the 27 books of the New Testament to come into existence in the content-form in which we now have it. This book as well as all the rest was written in **Koine** (i.e. common) **Greek.**

The **last written** of the 27 books is thought by some scholars to have been finished about 115+/-5 A.D.. The book is **2nd Peter** (2 Pet) whose teaching was attributed to St. Peter by the early Church. Peter had been martyred under Nero (54-68) but the principles of his teaching, repeated constantly by him over a 35-year period, were put into a final form of writing about the date given.

These 27 books were all produced by the convinced followers of Christ living in his Church. They were written to other followers of Christ living in that same Church to help them know Christ and live with ever-deepening faith in his believing community. Thus, they were written **by** believing members of his one Church **to** other believing members of that same one Church **for** the sake of the Christian faith and life. The evidence makes it very clear that Christ's new community, his Church, existed before any of the New Testament books were written and it existed and spread for nearly a century before the last New Testament book was written. Certain inspired members of Christ's Church produced the New Testament; the New Testament did not produce the Church. Further, the Church determined which 27 "books" were inspired. Thus, the New Testament alone and separated from Christ's Church can never by itself be a sole and exclusive norm for Christian living.

In general, those who didn't care about the Christian faith, which was seen as a **"new way"** or a new development within Judaism, couldn't be bothered writing about it. However, some pagan Romans, who dispised anything which didn't come from the all-powerful Romans, did in fact mention this new religion which came from Christ. **Tacitus,[1] Suetonius[2] and Pliny the Younger[3]** were three such authors. Although these authors did not like Christianity, their remarks have the value of indicating that even the pagans historically acknowledged this emerging group of people who proclaimed their experiences, beliefs and way of life in their 27 books.

2.The Canon   The foregoing data is common knowledge which requires a bit of research but no belief. The **element which distinguishes** the Christian, then and now, is **the belief** that these 27 books are different from, and enormously more valuable than, the secular books written in the same years. Christians believe that God inspired particular men such as Mark, Luke, Peter, Paul and the others to teach what He wanted human beings to know **for the sake of their eternal salvation.** Briefly, Christians believe that these 27 books are **INSPIRED by God** and are thus a norm (**canon**) for determining what God wants of us. Thus, if God is the inspirer and final determiner of the 27 books, He is also **their primary author.**[4] Further, if God has in this way told us things which we otherwise could not know or could not know with certitude, then this constitutes for human beings a divine revelation. The **belief** that God has specially inspired the twenty-seven New Testament books is what makes them precious to Christians. This belief strongly motivates Christians to read, study and reflect on New Testament's contents.

This business of God inspiring certain men to write what He wanted written about eternal salvation, and thus revealing things about Himself or about us to us, is critical for the study of theology.   Authors with no belief in God's inspiration and revelation may be engaged in what is called "religious study," but not in theology, strictly speaking. A "sine qua non" of theology is the fact of God's self-revelation and human belief in the content of that revelation. Christians, who accept as fact that God has revealed His wishes to us and that He has inspired certain men

---

1.   Tacitus,"Annals," Book XV p.380 <u>Complete Works of Tacitus,</u> ed. Moses Hadas, New York 1942
2.   Suetonius, <u>The Twelve Caesars</u>, tr. R. Graves, The Penguin Classics, Baltimore 1960, 1960 p. 197
3.   H. Conzelmann, <u>History of Primitive Christianity</u>, New York, Abingdon Press 1973 p.168
4.   Refer to the appendix entitled <u>God-Author of Sacred Scripture.</u>

to write what He wanted, identify those writings as **canonical** or Sacred Scripture.

The Church of the Apostles and the sub-apostolic Church (i.e. the Church led by the line of men appointed & ordained by the Apostles) determined which books came from the Apostolic teaching (in Greek: **didache**) and thus could be used for instruction and for the liturgy. Briefly, **the Church determined** which books contained and authentically developed the **Apostolic teaching** and were thus canonical or normative for Christian belief and practice.

Many other books for which some people and even local churches claimed inspiration were rejected. The Church **interpreted** their contents as in some way failing to present authentic Apostolic teaching. Those rejected books were termed **apocrypha.** The number of writings which the early Church rejected as apocryphal exceeds the number of the 27 books which were identified as authentic Apostolic teaching and thus, canonical. The Church's concern for the Sacred Scriptures continues into the present through the means of its Ecumenical Councils, Papal encyclicals, the ongoing attention of the Pontifical Biblical Commission commonly referred to as the **PBC.**

In early apostolic times the Jewish followers of Christ living in the **diaspora** (i.e. territory outside of Palestine) used the Greek translation of the Old Testament, known as the **Septuagint** for knowledge of the "Law and the Prophets". The Roman numeral **LXX** is the symbol used to represent the Septuagint. The New Testament authors take most of their Old Testament quotations from the **LXX** which the Catholic Church continues to hold as canonical.

Two important, relatively recent, **documents** which treat of the Gospels and Divine Revelation were published during the time of the Second Vatican Council (1962 -1965). The first was the April 21, 1964 **Instruction: Historical Truth of the Gospels**[5], put out by the PBC between the second and third sessions of Vat II. This document, synopsized in appendix II highlighted two important positions. First, it positively affirmed the **three stages** in the genesis or production of the Gospels: the primary stage in which **Jesus taught and did** the things described; the next stage in which

---

5.   Appendix: Instruction. . .April 21, 1964; it consists of 18 numbered, relatively brief paragraphs.

Peter and the other Apostles told people about it; and the final stage in which the **evangelists wrote** about it. Secondly, The 1964 Historicity Instruction also cautioned Catholics against the negative snags in the ways that some scholarly critics mistakenly applied useful but limited modern methods of interpretation to sacred Scripture. Four misinterpretations flowing from the faulty application of some inadequate methods were: 1)a denial of God's supernatural intervention in Scriptural miracles, 2)an espousal of a deficient notion of Christian faith, 3)an a priori denial of historicity to some N.T. data, and finally, 4)a giving of creative-authorship, not to individual persons, but vaguely to the community.

The second document was the very important **Dogmatic Constitution On Divine Revelation** (in Latin: **DEI VERBUM**[6]) promulgated by Vatican II itself on November 18, 1965.[7]

Dei Verbum[8] (appendix III) points out that God was pleased to reveal Himself and make known the mystery of His will to us through the teaching of **His Divine Word**; this "Word" is contained in the living teaching of the Church and the pages of Sacred Scripture. A **brief sampling** of the Document's thought, much taken from Scripture itself, follows. One readily notes: the modes of scripture and tradition by which the truths were transmitted; the unique relation of God himself to these inspired writings; the necessity of the Church as the preserving agency; and, finally, the matters of such great personal importance which they proclaim.[9]

---

6. Refer to the appendix headed by the same titles; this rather brief conciliar document consists of 26 numbered articles.
7. The English translation of this document is contained as an appendix under its own name.
8. Dei Verbum is composed of 26 numbered articles most of which are only one or two paragraphs long.
9. Paragraph indentation signifies direct quotation of the document; highlighting and bracketing, which are added for emphasis or information, are not contained in the Vatican II document. Also, one must consult a full copy for the official footnotes.

His will was that men should have access to the Father, through Christ,...and thus become **sharers in the divine nature**[10]

God wishes **to give eternal life** to all those who seek salvation by patience in well-doing (art 3).

...the apostles, in handing on what they themselves had received, warn the faithful to maintain the **traditions** which they had learned either by word of mouth or by letter;...in this way the Church [**ecclesia**], in her doctrine, life and worship, perpetuates and transmits to every generation **all that she herself is**, all that she believes....By means of the same **tradition** the **full canon** of the sacred books is known....(art 8).

The divinely revealed realities, which are contained and presented in the text of sacred Scripture, have been written down under the inspiration of the Holy Spirit....They have **GOD as their AUTHOR**, and have been handed on as such to the Church herself....[The sacred writings] TEACH **that truth which God, for the sake of our salvation, wished** to see confided to the sacred Scriptures (art 11).

The classical debate about **Scripture and Tradition** as sources of divine revelation is clarified by recognizing that **neither Scripture alone nor Tradition alone** is adequate in explaining the mystery of Christianity's origin. God Himself through Christ is the unique source of His own self-revelation. Scripture and Tradition are the living means (written and oral) by which revelation comes from the ONE divine well-spring. So intimately intertwined are Scripture and Tradition that they form essentially one sacred deposit of God's Word as Vatican II points out.

Sacred tradition and sacred Scripture, then, are bound closely together, and communicate one with the other. For both of them, flowing out from the same divine well-spring, come together in some fashion to form

---

10. Dogmatic Constitution on Divine Revelation or in Latin <u>Dei Verbum</u>, art 2. (Each document of Vatican II is divided into small thought-units called <u>articles</u>; the numbered articles facilitate reference. Emphasis is mine.)

one thing, and move toward the same goal. Sacred Scripture is the speech of God as it is put down in writing under the breath of the Holy Spirit. And Tradition transmits in its entirety the Word of God which has been entrusted to the apostles by Christ the Lord and the Holy Spirit. It transmits it to the successors of the apostles so that, enlightened by the Spirit of truth, they may faithfully preserve, expound and spread it abroad by their preaching. Thus it comes about that the Church does **not** draw her certainty about all revealed truth **from the Holy Scriptures alone.** Hence, both Scripture and Tradition must be accepted and honored with equal feelings of devotion and reverence (art 9).

Sacred Tradition and Sacred Scripture make up a single sacred deposit of the word of God, which is entrusted to the Church (art 10).

Questions

1. What does the **New Testament** consist of?
2. Which are the **most important** of the N.T.'s 27 books? Why?

3. In Theology, what is ordinarily signified by **the name** Mark? John? Luke? Matthew?
4. What is **the order** in which the Gospels are traditionally listed? Probable reason?

5. What is a **Gospel**?
6. In what **language** were the 27 books originally written?

7. What was the religious background of those who wrote the 27 books?
8. To whom and why were the N.T. books written?

9. Who is identified as the **author** of **Acts of the Apostles**?
10. Why was **Acts** separated from the **Gospel** according to Luke?

11. Name the writings generally listed under the name of Paul?
12. Which are known as the **Great Epistles**? Why called great?

13. Which are called the **Pastorals**? Why called pastoral?
14. Which are called the **Captivity Epistles**? Why captivity?

15. Which is **the first** of the 27 books to have been written? Date?
16. Which is thought to be **last** written of the 27 books? Date?

17. What is the **time–frame** in which the 27 books were completed?
18. Name the books of the **Pentateuch**?

19. **Compare** the N.T. time–frame to the O.T. time frame.
20. Why are certain epistles called **Catholic Epistles**?

21. Name the books of the **Johannine corpus** of writings?
22. Why is the epistle to the **Hebrews** called **deutero–canonical**?

23. Name the seven **deutero–canonical books**?
24. Scholars seem agreed that Paul directly and immediately composed **seven letters**; which ones are they?

25. **About when** were the **Epistles of Paul** being collected? **Evidence?** (cf 2nd Peter 3:16); The Gospels?

26.What is meant by **the Canon** of the New Testament? When was the N.T.Canon **"fixed"** or closed?

27. What is an **apocryphal book**? Name one apocryphal book.
28. On a map of the Mediterranian area **locate:**
    a)Rome, Corinth, Galatia, Ephesus, Philippi, Colossae.
    b)Thessalonika, Athens, Antioch, Cyprus,
    c)Malta, Judea, Samaria, Galilee, Jordan River.
    d)Jerusalem, Bethlehem, Nazareth, Capernaum

29. How can one explain that **God is the primary author** of Mark's Gospel? What about Mark's will, intellect, style.?
30. Name **2 documents** on sacred Scripture which were published during the 4 years of the 2nd Vatican Council ('62-'65)?

31. Identify **the source** which produced each document?
32. What **overall points** are made by the April 21, **1964 Instruction**?

33. **Why,** according to **Dei Verbum,** did God want the Gospels (& all the N.T.) written? (cf=[confer] articles #2 & #3)
34. **By what means** is the full canon of Sacred books known? [a.8]

35. Does **Dei Verbum** affirm that **God is the author** of the books of Sacred Scripture? [a.11]
36. Accord. to Dei Verbum **what truth** does Sacred Scripture teach **without error?** [a.11]

37. Does Dei Verbum affirm **T & S** (Tradition & Scripture) as **two separate and independent sources** of divine revelation?
38. How does Dei Verbum present **the relationship** of T & S? [a.9]

39. Does the Church draw her certainty about all revealed truth **from Holy Scripture alone?** [a.9]
40. Does the Church believe that the combination of **T, S & M [M** = the Magisterium = the living, teaching authority from Christ] is necessary to preserve the divinely revealed truths? [a.9]

Chapter II: Greek and Roman Background

The New Testament's 27 books were written by Christians immersed in a world in which a formerly dominant **Greek** culture was slowly yielding to the emerging dominance of the **Roman** Empire. These cultures seeped into the Jewish life in Galilee (sometimes called Galilee of the Gentiles) and even, but to a lesser extent, into the heartland of Jewish life in Jerusalem. As examples, the Jewish realities of **synagogue, pentateuch, and sanhedrin** are named with **Greek** words, not Aramaic or Hebrew words.

The Jewish sacred Scriptures, commonly referred to as the **Old Testament**, were translated from Hebrew **into Greek** between the years 200 B.C. and 50 B.C.[1] by Jewish scholars. The Jewish Scriptures were translated for the sake of the many Jewish people living outside of Palestine who could no longer read Hebrew. This Greek translation of the Old Testament is called the **Septuagint**; it is symbolized by the Roman numeral **LXX** (= 70, the number of scholars claimed by legend to have done the translating).

1.Greek background   The greek cultural or <u>hellenizing</u> influence was actively promoted by the Macedonian general, **Alexander the Great.** After he had conquered Greece, Asia Minor, Syria, Palestine, Egypt, ancient Persia (modern Iran) and the western part of India, he sought to impose both the Greek language and Hellenic customs on the conquered nations.

Having benefitted from the extraordinary teaching of antiquity's great Greek philosophers, Alexander, Aristotle's pupil, wished to change the world he conquered in the light of the **Hellenic ideals** he had imbibed. His initiative was so successful that Greek became the dominant and ordinary (koine) language of the countries in the Eastern half of the Mediterranean world. The New Testament books, all of which were composed between 50 A.D. and approximately 115 A.D., were written in this **koine Greek.** Even in the pre-christian period the Greek language was so pervasive that two of the Septuagint's (O.T.) books, namely the book of

---

1.   B.C. is commonly used to signify time Before Christ; A.D. from **A**nno **D**omini (in the year of the Lord) is generally used to signify time <u>after</u> Christ. Jewish scholars sometimes prefer to use B.C.E. meaning Before the Common Era, and C.E. meaning Common Era for time after the calendar's turning point.

Wisdom and 2nd Maccabees, were originated in koine Greek, probably about 50 to 75 B.C.

When in 323 B.C. Alexander died, his generals divided the conquered lands among themselves. General Ptolemy took Egypt; this started the long dynasty of the Egyptian **Ptolemies.** The Jewish territory (later named Palestine) came under their rule. General Seleucus, who became ruler of Syria, started the dynasty of the Seleucids whose capital was Antioch. The **Selucids** wrested Israel from the Ptolemies and about 170 B.C. tried to destroy the Jewish identity. The arrogant King Antiochus IV Epiphanes was the Syrian oppressor. The name 'epiphanes' was assumed by him to signify his status among the many greek gods. In pursuit of this arrogant assumption he demanded worship from the Jews.

The Jewish family of **Hasmon** rebelled at this false worship. The Hasmonian sons became known as the **Maccabees.** They led a rebellion against Antiochus and after 167 B.C. achieved freedom and independence for the Jews.[2] The Jews maintained this independence for about a hundred years. The Hasmonian dynasty governed the Jewish people during this century. Foreign domination over Israel started again when **Pompey**, leading a powerful Roman army, conquered the Judean and surrounding territories and subordinated them to the Roman authority of Syria headquartered in Damascus.

2.Roman Background   In 66 B.C., during the period of the Roman republic (509 B.C. to 27 B.C.), Roman General **Pompey** started his march of Roman conquest into the Greek-controlled territories conquered by Alexander. Pompey overcame and subjected to Roman rule all the countries bordering on the Eastern Mediterranean Sea. Pompey's military prowess reduced the Jews of Judea and Galilee to the status of a slave-people who thereafter were forced to conform to Rome's will under the constant surveillance of Rome's military power. Administratively, the Romans subordinated the Palestinian territories to the Roman province of Syria.

---

2. This successful rebellion is described in the Old Testament's first book of Maccabees.

-12-

Shortly after Pompey's conquests, **Julius Caesar** won similar military victories in Gallia, Helvetia (Switzerland), Germania and elsewhere. Some years after their triumphant returns to Rome, Caesar and Pompey challenged each other for the Roman supremacy. Caesar won. This victory gave Caesar control of the Roman military power which emerged as the master political force of the Mediterranean world. The Mediterranean Sea was characterized as "mare nostrum" (our sea). In 44 B.C. internal revolt simmered against Caesar's use of absolute authority. On the Ides of March in the senate forum over which Caesar reigned supreme, Brutus, Cassius and other conspiritors rose and stabbed Caesar to death. But some Romans strongly resented this violent betrayal.

Octavian, Caesar's adopted son, joined forces with General Lepidus and **Marc Anthony** to vindicate the murdered Caesar. In the year 42 B.C. their army pursued and defeated Brutus and Cassius and their troops in the battle of Philippi. Thereafter, the victors formed a rulership-of-three (a triumvirate) to govern Rome. The unsettlement in the capital loosened Rome's control of the conquered peoples. Marc Anthony decided to secure the East while Octavian and Lepidus took care of the North and West.

Anthony succeeded. While in Judea (40 B.C.) he placed a non-Jew, named **Herod** (later questionably called 'the Great'), in royal authority over Judea, Samaria, Galilee and Peraea. Continuing south, the victorious Romans established themselves in Egypt. However, Anthony was captivated by the fabled beauty of Cleopatra, Egypt's queen. Some years later **Anthony and Cleopatra**, seeking rulership over their whole world, challenged Octavian who had already superceded Lepidus in the West.

In the year 31 B.C. at the sea-battle of Actium, Octavian defeated the fleet of his challengers, Anthony and Cleopatra, both of whom committed suicide. Four years later the Roman senate conferred the title of supreme honor, suggestive of divine worship, on Caesar's son, naming him **Augustus**. Thus, in the year **27 B.C.** Rome, from its government as a republic, changed to that of "**Roman Empire**" with one absolute ruler, **Octavian Caesar Augustus.**

3.Octavian Caesar Augustus   Caesar Augustus, as commander of possibly the most powerful military force the world had ever known, maintained peace until his death in **14 A.D.** He divided the Roman world into about 30 provinces, while allowing the conquered peoples a measure of local independence under Rome's overall military authority. He built aquaducts, amphitheaters, bridges and extensive roads.[3] Many remnants of his enormous projects still exist. During his reign, **Jesus** was born in the little town of Bethlehem in Judea, about five miles south of Jerusalem, Judea's capital.

When (about 590 A.D.) **Dionysius,** the chronologer, was commissioned to change from the old Julian calendar of Julius Caesar to the new Gregorian calendar based on the life of Christ, he made a mistake of about seven years.[4] Thus, the year of Jesus' birth is calculated to be in the 20th year of Caesar Augustus' reign, i.e. **about the year 6 or 7 B.C.** of our present calendar.

On the death of Augustus, **Tiberius** became emperor (14 A.D. to 37 A.D.). Tiberius began his reign with the policies of his predecessor, but became more capricious in his later years, while ruling from his palace on the Isle of Capri. During his reign, probably in the year **30 A.D.,** the passion, death and resurrection of Christ occurred.

Following Tiberius' death on Capri, the young, self-centered **Caligula** took power. History has conferred the epithet "mad" on Caligula because of his debaucheries, arrogance and rule by whim. He demanded worship from his subjugated peoples. Among his mindless acts,and despite his close friendship with the young Jewish Herod Agrippa, he commanded the slaughter of all the Jews in Jamnia who refused to worship at his altar there. Caligula was assassinated in Rome before the order was executed.

Claudius (41-54), aided by the Jewish prince, **Herod Agrippa I,** took power following Caligula's death. Claudius re-instituted the sane governing policies of Augustus. Yet when trouble arose among the Jews in Rome, he exiled all of them without distinguishing among them the cause of the disturbance. Some scholars suspect that **belief in Christ** may have been dividing the members of the Roman synagogues as it had in Thessalonica.[5] Luke noted this division in his Acts of the Apostles (ch. 17). In any event, Claudius exiled all the Jews; he did not opt for slaughter as Caligula had done before him.[6] Two of the exiles,

---

3. In Italy you can travel on the Appian Way; in Philippi and Caesarea Marittima you can attend summer theater in the amphitheaters built by the Romans
4. R.A.F. MacKenzie, Introduction to the New Testament, (NTRG #1) Collegeville p.5
5. R. Brown and J. Meier Antioch and Rome
6. It should be noticed that the Roman Government here did not distinguish Christians from Jews.

Aquila and Priscilla, probably already Christians, befriend Paul in Corinth (Acts 18) during the (41-54) reign of Claudius.

4. Nero(54-68) **to Hadrian**(117-138) NERO'S reign is especially important in the story of Judaism and Christianity. The fire of Rome, state persecution of Christians and the massacres in Palestine identify his reign.

In July 64 fire broke out in Rome. Roman Historians, **Suetonius** and the more careful **Tacitus,** indicated that Nero engineered its continance for seven days. Rome boiled with reports that Nero was the culprit. To distance suspicion from himself, he officially blamed **the Christians** and initiated an **official persecution** against them. Whereas Claudius had exiled from Rome all Jews, Nero focused on those Jews who believed in Christ and also the believing Roman gentiles who had joined these believers in Christ. In the ensuing slaughter, **St Peter,** leader of the Apostles, was crucified and **St. Paul,** Apostle and a Roman citizen, was beheaded.

About the same time as the persecution of the Christians, Jewish Zealots started a rebellion in Judea. Nero sent his top general, **Vespasian,** to subdue the uprising. Vespasian bloodied Galilee's soil with the slaughter. In the process he captured **Josephus,** the governor of Galilee. Josephus narrates the vivid story in his book, The Jewish War. Vespasian led his powerful legions down the Jordan valley. At the head of the Dead Sea he destroyed the 'monastery' of the **Essenes** at Qumran.[7]

At this time back in Rome Nero's assassination ended the dynasty of the Julian House. Vespasian, placing his military son in charge of the Judean campaign, returned to Rome to overcome the three usurpers (Galba, Otho and Vitellius) and assume the powers of Emperor. **Vespasian** reign from 69 to 79 started the Flavian Dynasty.

In the meanwhile, The Roman army, now under General **Titus,** marched up from the Jordan valley (1200 feet below sea level) to the height (2400 feet above sea level) of Jerusalem. The

---

7.   These Jews had withdrawn from mainstream Judaism to live celibate religious lives of obedience, prayer and work. Among their works was the copying of the sacred Jewish Scriptures on scrolls. A few decades ago very many of these scrolls (called the Dead Sea Scrolls) were discovered.

Roman force surrounded Jerusalem. According to Eusebius[8] Jerusalem's Jewish-Christian community, forewarned of the Roman onslaught, had previously escaped to the trans-Jordan town of Pella in the Decapolis region.[9] In A.D. 70 **Titus** and his powerful Roman legions destroyed Jerusalem and its 585 year old Temple which to this day has never been rebuilt. The centuries-later Mohammed's Haram-esh-Sharif (Dome of the Rock) stands in its place. In Jerusalem's final moments about a thousand inhabitants escaped into the eastern desert and sought defense in the fortress on top of a 1200-foot mesa, named **Masada**. This 'fortress in the sky' stands on the southwest side of the Dead Sea. It took Titus three more years to mount Masada's sheer sides and finish the Judean campaign.[10] The Arch of Titus in the Roman forum depicts items like the gold menorah (the 7-branched candle holder) which he pillaged from Jerusalem's Temple.

Titus (79-81) ruled for only two years after his father's death. The next son of Vespasian, named Domitian[11], succeeded Titus. **Domitian** enforced the death penalty on Christians in a second state persecution against them. He ruled from 81 to 96 and was followed by Nerva, a capable leader, who reigned only two years from 96 to 98.

Trajan (98-117) next took over the imperial power. He ruled against seeking out Christians for punishment, but did not erase the law from the books. The younger Governor Pliny's letter to Trajan and Trajan's response are extant.[12] The law required a confessing Christian to: 1)adore the Roman gods, 2) worship the emperor, and 3)curse Christ, - or die.

Hadrian (117-138) concludes this period within which Christianity and its 27 New Testament books came into existence. He officially initiated the Empire's third persecution of the Christians and also tried to obliterate the Jewish nation. Hadrian responded to the Jewish uprising of 132 A.D. by again destroying Jerusalem. He changed its name to Aelia Capitolina and further,

---

8. Eusebius, The History of the Church, tr G.A. Williamson, (Baltimore: Penguin Books, 1967) p. 111.
9. Craig Koester, "The Origin and Significance of the Flight to Pella Tradition", The Catholic Biblical Quarterly, vol. 51, no. 1/ January, 1989, pp. 90-106.
10. The movie, Masada captured the last days of this bastian rather well.
11. Suetonius, The Twelve Caesars, tr R. Graves, (Penguin Classics, 1960) p.295; genealogy p.311
12. Primitive Christianity p. 168

legislated death for any Jew found within the city's walls. He built a temple to a Roman god and changed the name of the whole territory from Judea to the name which it still bears, today - PALESTINE.

5. The Herodian Dynasty   Mark Anthony had enthroned **Herod**, an Idumaean, over the Jewish people; the Roman senate officially supported his act in giving Herod the status of a subordinate but allied king withthe title, "**Rex Socius**". Roman support continued from 37 B.C. until the retirement of Agrippa II in 93 A.D.

Herod's scandalous life with many women placed many sons in line to take over their father's territory, power and authority.

Herod put aside his wife, Doris, in order to marry the Jewish princess, Mariamne. Historian **Josephus** says that Mariamne was very beautiful and that Herod loved her jealously. Her sons, Alexander and Aristobolus, qualified to continue the Jewish royal line. After some years, when Herod returned from a military expedition, Mariamne's enemies convinced Herod that she had been unfaithful to him. In a jealous rage, he killed her.

The next woman, Mariamne II, gave him a son, Philip; this son remained in Rome. Herod later took the Samaritan woman, Malthrace, whose son **Herod Antipas** will later, as Tetrarch, kill John the Baptist and mock Christ in a trial. Archelaus, the elder son of Malthrace, became King Herod's favored heir. Finally, Herod's Jerusalem wife, Cleopatra, gave birth to Philip, who later ruled the pagan territory named Trachonitis and its neighboring regions east of the Sea of Galilee.

The Herodian dynasty continues through the Jewish son, Herod Agrippa I, who grew up with Caligula in Rome and helped Claudius (41-54) to gain control of the Empire in the year 41. In return, Claudius gave this **Agrippa I** all the territory of his grandfath er with the same title of **Rex Socius**. Agrippa's sister, Jewish princess **Herodias** divorced her one uncle[13] by whom she had a daughter **Salome**, and became the wife of her other uncle, **Herod Antipas**, Tetrarch of Galilee & Peraea. This unsavory example of adultery and incest, especially on the part of **Herodias** who was of Jewish royalty, publicly flouted the **Torah** and evoked the public condemnation of **John the Baptist**. Herodias used the

---

13. Mark in his Gospel names him as Philip [of Rome?]; Raymond Collins, Introduction to the New Testament, (N.Y. 1975), p.319, thinks that Mark mistakenly named the wrong uncle.

-18-

occasion of Salome's sensuous dance which pleased Herod at his military stag party to ask for the execution of John the Baptist (cf. Mark 6).

Herod Agrippa I (ruler over Palestine from 41 to 44 A.D.) fathered three children whose lives entered certain N.T. events. Their names were: **Herod Agrippa II**, Berenice and Drusilla. **Drusilla** married the venal Roman Procurator **Felix** who as Governor of Palestine tried the case of Paul (Acts 24). **Bernice**, according to the Jewish Historian Josephus, lived with both General Vespasian and his son Titus during their conquest of Palestine, and later with her brother during his reign as king of Coelo-Syria. This kingship of Agrippa II, during which he along with Procurator **Festus** (Acts 25) heard the case of the Apostle Paul (Acts 26), ended the Herodian dynasty in the year 93 A.D.

The list of Herod's wives and children who enter the New Testament narratives follows:

Herod (40-4 B.C.)

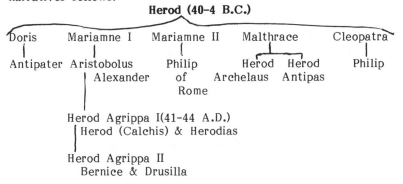

Doris	Mariamne I	Mariamne II	Malthrace		Cleopatra
Antipater	Aristobolus	Philip	Herod	Herod	Philip
	Alexander	of	Archelaus	Antipas	
		Rome			

Herod Agrippa I(41-44 A.D.)
Herod (Calchis) & Herodias

Herod Agrippa II
Bernice & Drusilla

-19-

Questions

1. In 30 A.D. **which city** was the heartland of Jewish life?
2. Into which Jewish territory (Judea, Galilee or Samaria) did Greek culture and language penetrate the **least**?

3. Give some **Greek words** which seeped into Jewish life language?
4. Which **Greek general** conquered most of the middle-east & cultivated Hellenism (Greek Culture & language) there?

5. Who was the Greek conquerer's **famous teacher**?
6. After Alexander's death who ruled the Syrian and Egypt?

7. About when did **the Seleucids** tke control of the Judea?
8. About 167 B.C. which **Jewish family** rebelled against **Antiochus IV**?

9. For **how long** did the Jewish freedom last?
10. **Which Roman General** subjugated the Jewish people to Rome?

11. Which Roman General conquered Pompey? When? What capable young man was **adopted** by Julius Caesar?
12. **Who** assassinated Julius Caesar? When? Where? Why?

13. Name the **triumvirate** which defeated Julius Caesar's assassins in the battle of Philippi about 41 B.C.?
14. After peace, what plan did **Mark Antony** follow? What alliances
    did he make? What happened at Actium in 31 B.C.?

15. In 27 B.C. what action did the Roman senate make which changed the course of Roman History for five centuries?

16. What are **the dates** of Octavian Caesar Augustus' reign?
17. What did Caesar Augustus achieve in his years of control?

18. What significant event occurred in **Bethlehem** during Augustus reign? Probably in what year?
19. **Who** produced the discrepancy in calandar dates?

20. Which emperor succeeded Caesar Augustus? For how long?
21. What significant **Christian events** took place in the time of Tiberius (14 A.D. to 37 A.D.)? Is Tiberius mentioned in the N. T.?

22. Who succeeded Tiberius? For how long? Why is he named "**mad**"? What did **Caligula** decree for Jamnia?

-20-

23. Did **Claudius** (41-54) distinguish between Jews & Christians? Which **official act** led to this conclusion?

24.**Nero** reigned from **54 to 68**; explain in detail why this was a **crisis period** for both Jews and Christians?

25. Who succeeded Nero from 69 to 79? Then, from 79 to 81?

26. In what way was **Domitian** (81-96) like Nero? **Nerva**?

27. **Trajan** (98-117): what did Governor Pliny's famous letter say to Trajan; what was Trajan's response?

28.During **Hadrian's** reign (117-138) the last N.T. book was completed. What did Hadrian do to both Christians and Jews?

29.In 40 B.C. **who** set up Herod (later called 'great') as ruler of the Jews? How long did the dynasty (started by Herod) last?'

30.Which **Son of Herod** ordered the death of John the Baptist & conducted a trial-hearing of Christ?

31.Which **grandson of Herod** grew up in Rome with Caligula, helped Claudius become emperor and later killed the Apostle, James?

32.In Mark (6:17) which **granddaughter** of Herod committed incest with her uncle Herod Antipas? Who was her previous husband?

33.Three children of Agrippa I enter the N.T. story: in what way?

Chapter III: Religious Context

Many polytheistic religions and two philosophies, among others, flourished influentially in the Roman Empire of the first century.

The **Golden Age** of the Greek philosophers, namely, Socrates, Plato and Aristotle, had passed. Their primary intellectual explorations still receive attention in the world's universities, but ancient attention waned with the death of Aristotle in 322 B.C. Although the school founded by Plato still flourished in Athens, and Aristotle's writings were still known, the age of painstaking metaphysics had passed. The philosophies of **Epicurus** and **Zeno,** whose young lives overlapped the end of Aristotle's career, were more significant in Christianity's first century of existence.

Philosophies[1] **Epicurus** (341-270 B.C.), founder of the Epicurean school, developed a philosophy highlighting the principle that **pleasure** is the **highest good of man.** Pleasure of the body may come first to mind, but by this term, pleasure, Epicurus intended to express **serenity of the soul.** An axiom such as "avoid pain and seek pleasure," readily testable by the senses, equates man with the animal kingdom if the axiom remains only on the sense-level. But Epicurus maintained that pleasures of the senses, if done wrongly or to excess as with food and drink, produce their corresponding pains. However, his totally **materialist world view** (gods, men, and animals were made of the material atoms envisioned by Democritus) failed to find an essential difference between man and beast.

His **ethics** focused on serenity of the soul; the habits which tend toward this serenity, he called virtues. He pictured the **Greek gods** as good Epicureans who went off to their own idyllic places and sought a serenity undisturbed by the incessant troubles of mankind. Roman Epicureans applied his analysis to their many Roman gods.

Epicurus had the idea that **man's soul** was made of very refined atoms which, at death, evanesced like a breath into the air; thus, death brought no pain and was not to cause anxiety or fear. This philosophy was attractive to the wealthy elite whose plush villas were far removed from the unwashed masses. It

---

1. A rounded picture of a philosopher's thought needs to look at his idea of **God**, his concept of **man**, and his view of **ethics** that relate man to God and man's final destiny.

amounted to a **calculating egoism.** St. Paul, in Athens, will argue with both Epicureans and Stoics (Acts 17:18).

Lucretius (97-53 B.C.), who glorified Epicureanism in his book, entitled On the Nature of Things, was his most well known follower.[2] Lucretius in his poetic work saw all reality in terms of atoms; his poem transmitted the term into Dalton's nineteenth century laboratory.[3]

Zeno of Citium (336-264 B.C.), the founder of **Stoicism,** on the other hand, developed a different worldview. To his students on the **stoa** (= porch), nicknamed Stoics, he pictured god as the "world-soul" which penetrates everything and produces the visible world order.

Man's soul is the physical part of god which inter-penetrates him. St.Paul quotes to his Athenian audience their own Stoic poet who said of their relation to the cosmic material god: "for we too are his offspring" (Acts, 17:28).

What man's soul is to the microcosm, man, so **Zeno's god** is soul to the macrocosm, the world. His follower, Heraclitus saw god as something like a great primeval intelligent fire interpenetrating everything.[4] Sparks escaping from this Great Primeval Fire (GPF) were plunged into the matter of earth and selectively became human beings.[5] Men and women were to purify this primeval spark, which humanized them, until it was perfect and escaped (at death) back to, and lost its identity in, the GPF from which it came. Thus, personal immortality could not exist.[6] Zeno had envisioned a great all-embracing, incessant, **cyclic pantheism.**

Zeno based his **ethics** on the principle of man's purifying the primeval spark which was his inner spirit. All selfishness and sensuality corrupted this flame. Integrity, restraint, sacrifice purified it. Each good Stoic realized he was a microcosmic part

---

2.   F.F. Bruce, New Testament History, (New York: Doubleday & Co., Inc., 1971), p.43.
3.   J. McDonnell, Is Dalton's Atom The Same As That Of Democritus?, (dissertation) New York: St. John's University, 1968.)
4.   F. Thonnard, A Short History of Philosophy, (Paris: Desclee & Cie, 1955), p.144.
5.   This concept seems to be borrowed from the "atmon escape from & return to the para-atmon" concept of ancient Hinduism.
6.   W. Harrington, Record Of Fulfillment: The New Testament, (Chicago: The Priory Press, 1965), p. 7.

of this great cosmos whose massive acts were nature's activity. Man, the microcosm, should act in harmony with the action of the cosmos (nature's action), of which he is a part; he should never oppose it. Rather he must remain calm in the midst of its most violent activity. If, after an earthquake, he stood alone on the ashes of Athens, he should neither rejoice nor weep. Que sera, sera!

Zeno's **ethics** dominated the Roman army's attitude, and had more influence on popular attitudes than any other philosophy of the day. Its basic sense of integrity and self-discipline helped pave the way for understanding the idea of Christian virtue. In its post-Christian stages Stoics replaced their GPF with a concept of a god, **Zeus**, which was about equal to fate. Some stoic terms sound Christian, but when examined closely, they are radically different concepts. Senator **Seneca**, uncle of Gallio and Nero's teacher, and emperor **Marcus Aurelius**, a persecutor of Christians, were well-known stoics.[7]

Mystery Cults   Mystery Cults flourished in the Roman Empire of the first century. Generally, they consisted of: a)**secret rites** which were supposed to open the secrets of a particular god, b)get his or her **protection** and, c)result in a **guarantee** of being among the gods forever. Men or women entering such rites were not required to change their morals or way of life at all. The mystery consisted of keeping secret the rites they performed. The popularity of the mystery cults manifested the widespread concern being felt about **human destiny after death.**[8]

The cults varied in each petty kingdom; conquering Rome did not destroy the local cults, but encouraged the provinces toward Roman ways. This added attention to Roman gods led to a decline in the popularity of the local gods. Intellectuals appear to have regarded the cults with cynicism. A thumb-nail sketches of some mystery rites reveal the personal worry about the afterlife. There were almost as many of these anxious pagan rites as there were inhabited towns. Refusal to participate in these or similar worship services at times led to the death sentence for both Jewish and Christian monotheists.

Elusinian Mysteries. A few miles to the west of Athens in the town of Eleusis stood the temple of Persephone, the supposed daughter of Zeus and Demeter. Hades, the god of the underworld,

---

7. F.F. Bruce, New Testament History, p. 48.
8. W. J. Bausch, Pilgrim Church, (Mystic, Ct.: Twenty-Third Publications, 1981), p. 16.

kidnaps Persephone every Fall; sorrowing mother Demeter searches for her daughter. Rejoicing Demeter finds her when the flowers come up from the underground every Spring. When the devotees of these gods reenacted this "lost and search rite", it was supposed to gain the protection of these gods for that person's life after death. No moral improvement was required of the rite-performer.

Isis and Osiris Sorrowing Isis searches for the dismembered body of her slaughtered husband. Meanwhile, powerful Osiris had become king of the underworld. Patrons reenacted a rite of helping Isis in her search for the parts of her husband's body to reconstruct him for Isis and thus gained the eternal favor of both these gods. This performance of the rite was supposed to eliminate the fear of facing them as enemies after death. No change in the moral practices of the devotees was thought necessary or even helpful.

Dionysian Mystery In this searching rite, attended mainly by women, quantities of wine were drunk at frequent intervals during the night. The achieving of ecstasy (?) was supposed to indicate that the participant was in communication with Dionysius who thereafter protected her in the next world. Moral improvement or decline was in no way connected with the guarantee which Dionysius was supposed to promise.

Ancient Historians   References to some of the foregoing can be found in the literature of the period. More profitable, however, are the references to the **actual historical events** found in the writings of Suetonius, Tacitus, Josephus and Pliny.

Suetonius (69-c.150 A.D.)[9] describes the period from Julius Caesar to Domitian. He says that Nero brazenly set fire to the City of Rome.   The destructive blaze raged for six days and seven nights.[10] After the great fire, Nero, to divert the blame from himself, declared that the **Christians** were the arsenists. Nero decreed the death penalty on them as a guilty and dangerous sect professing a new and mischievous religious belief.[11]

Concerning Claudius Suetonius says, "Because the Jews at Rome caused continuous disturbances at the instigation of **Christus,** he expelled them from the city."[12] Suetonius also mentions Josephus (p.277).

---

9.   Suetonius, The Twelve Caesars, tr. R. Graves, (New York: Penguin Classics, 1960.)
10.   Ibid., p.230.
11.   Ibid., p.217.
12.   Ibid., p.197.

Tacitus (55-115 A.D.)[13], more careful than Suetonius as an historian, says about the origin of the great fire of Rome: "A disaster followed, whether accidental or treacherously contrived by the emperor, is uncertain." and "no one dared to stop the mischief, because of incessant menaces from a number of persons who forbade the extinguishing of the flames..."[14] A bit later historian **Tacitus** writes: Nothing could banish

"...the sinister belief that the conflagration was the result of an order. Consequently, to get rid of the report,

Nero fastened the guilt and inflicted the most exquisite tortures on a class hated for their abominations, called **Christians** by the populace. **Christus**, from whom the name had its origin, suffered the extreme penalty during the reign of Tiberius at the hands of one of our procurators, Pontius Pilate, and a most mischievous superstition, thus checked for the moment, again broke out not only **in Judea**, the first source of the evil, but even in Rome...."[15]

Josephus (37-100 A.D.) in his book on The Jewish War[16] gives us the fullest view of Jewish life in the first century. He tells us that Marc Antony made Herod king of the Jews (p.58f), that Caesar Augustus retained him (p.73), that Herod murdered Mariamne and her sons (pp. 80-95), that Claudius elevated Agrippa I to the kingship (p.), that Titus captured Jerusalem and destroyed the Temple (pp. 321ff), that nearly 1000 Jews committed suicide on Masada, and many other inside items.[17]

The **Slavonic version** of the original Greek edition contains items about: John the forerunner and Herod Antipas (p.404), the ministry and crucifixion of Jesus (p.405), the early Christians (pp. 40-46), a temple inscription about Jesus (p.407), and other items. One or more of these items may have been inserted by a later Christian editor. In any event the material is from the first century.

---

13. Tacitus, Complete Works, ed. Moses Hadas, (New York: Random House.
14. Ibid.,pp.376 ff.
15. Ibid., p.380.
16. Josephus, The Jewish War (Penguin Classics, 1960 edition)
17. Josephus, The Second Jewish Commonwealth, ed. N. Glatzer (New York: Schocken Books,1971) [= bks XII to XX of Jewish Antiquities tr.W. Whiston] p.388 on **Jesus**; p.398 on John the Baptist.

Pliny/Trajan Exchange About the turn of the first century, Governor Pliny II wrote from the Roman Province bordering on the black sea to Emperor Trajan about the law mandating the death penalty for being a Christian. Pliny felt uneasy about an anonymous letter which identified and accused very many people in his province. Pliny publicly tested the accused with the requirements of: 1)worshipping Roman gods, 2)worshipping the Emperor's image, and 3)cursing Christ. Forthright Christians, he executed; problem cases he held over for the reception of Trajan's reply or sent to Rome. In due time, Trajan confirmed Pliny's trial procedure, but rejected the use of anonymous accusations as being "out of keeping with our [modern] times".[18]

18.   Hans Conzelmann, History of Primitive Christianity, tr.J. Steely, (Nashville: Abingdon Press, 1973), p.168.

Questions

1. Name **two** of the **philosophies** which flourished during the first century of the Christian era?
2. Name three of the religions known as **mystery-rite religions** which flourished in the 1st century Mediterranean world?

3. Name 3 **philosophers** from the golden age of Greek philosophy?
4. **Whose** school operated on the principle that "pleasure is man's highest good"? Did this mean pleasure of body or of soul?

5. What did **Epicureanism** say about "the gods"? Death? Did this philosophy cultivate virtue? Temperance?
6. In the final analysis what did **Epicureanism** amount to?

7. Which Epicurean authored a book about "atoms"?
8. Who founded the philosophy called **Stoicism** which pictured a god as the "world-soul" that penetrates everything.

9. How did **Zeno** view life as a great continuing cycle in terms of the **Great Primeval Fire**?
10. What was Zeno's **ethical principle**? How did he face disaster?

11. Were Zeno's ethics influential? Were any Roman leaders Stoics? What expression summarizes his philosophy?
12. What, in general, were the **mystery cults**? What concern among the people led to their growth?

13. Briefly describe **two** of the so-called **mystery cults**?
14. Name **3 first-century historians**, their ethnic backgrounds and one book of each? Did they favor Christianity?

15. From the book by **Suetonius** name 3 Roman leaders about whom he writes? In what way does he mention Christianity?
16. What does **Tacitus** have to say about Christ?

17. Who wrote the book entitled, The Jewish War? Name some specific items in this book? Does this book mention Jesus?
18. Who was **Pliny the Younger**? To whom did he write about the Christians? What means did the Romans use to test the Christians? Did the emperor approve all of Pliny's acts?

Chapter IV: Palestine and its People

The eastern coastline of the Mediterranean extends about 500 miles on an almost north-south line; it runs from Syrian Antioch in the North to the end of the Gaza Strip in the South. The **Palestine** of Herod the Great occupied approximately the bottom third of this coastline and extended inland to the Jordan River and a bit beyond it. The land rises gradually from the sea until after about 25 miles it becomes a mountainous range which runs parallel to the sea coast and the Jordan River. From its high point of about 2400 feet, where **Jerusalem** is located, the land to the east falls through barren deserts into the deep torrid but luxuriant, trench of the **Jordan Valley**. At its juncture with the **Dead Sea**, this deep trench is more than 1200 feet below sea-level.

First-century Palestine was divided into **Galilee**, its northern territory; **Samaria**, homeland of the Samaritans the central territory; and **Judea**, the heartland of Judaism, its southern territory. **Peraea**, in the trans-Jordan, also belonged to the Palestine of Herod, the Great. In the year 40 B.C. Marc Antony, with the approval of the Roman Senate, established Herod, who was a non-Jewish Idumean, in authority. The earlier **hellenization** by the conquering Greeks influenced the outer territories the most, but to a lesser degree, it even managed in both words and ideas to seep into **Jerusalem**, the capital city of Judea. Jerusalemites thought of the Galileans as sort of their Jewish country folk, but the Samaritans were regarded as hybrid Jews and despised.

Groupings   In first century Jerusalem, beside the general population of working folk and merchants, one might regularly encounter: **a Zealot, a Scribe, less frequently an Essene or a Samaritan, more commonly a Sadducee or a Pharisee.** Each of these belonged to a group well known at the time. Uniformed Roman soldiers of the dominant pagan Roman power would also be seen on the roads and at the market-bazaar.

Zealots, generally a younger crowd with older leaders, were those who hated the pagan Romans as violators of their God-given land and nation. The Zealots were **extreme nationalists** who openly dispised the Roman army of occupation. The **zeal** for their God-given patrimony made them reckless revolutionaries. Zealots were ready to use violent means to rid their country of the pagan Roman presence. They yearned to break the Roman domination

PALESTINE

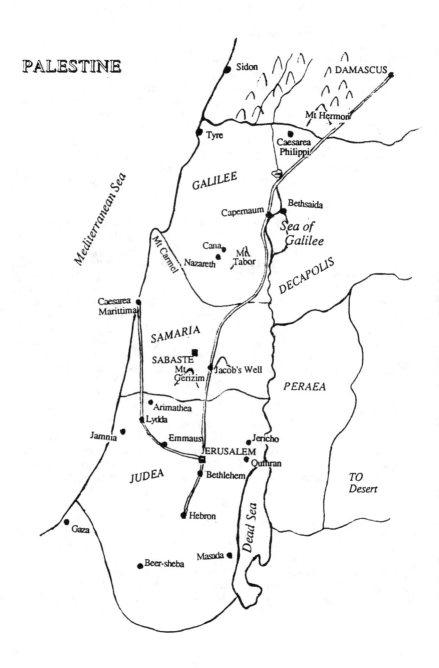

Sidon

DAMASCUS

Mt Hermon

Tyre

Caesarea
Philippi

GALILEE

Mediterranean Sea

Capernaum

Bethsaida

*Sea of
Galilee*

Cana

Mt
Tabor

Nazareth

Mt Carmel

DECAPOLIS

Caesarea
Marittima

SAMARIA

SABASTE

Mt
Gerizim

Jacob's Well

PERAEA

Arimathea

Lydda

Jamnia

Emmaus

Jericho

JERUSALEM

Qumran

JUDEA

Bethlehem

*TO
Desert*

Hebron

Gaza

Dead Sea

Beer-sheba

Masada

over their country as the Maccabees had destroyed the grip of their Seleucid conquerers almost 200 years earlier. Romans called some of the Zealots "**sicarii**", because they used a "sica" to stab isolated soldiers to death. Such zealot guerrilla violence would ultimately induce the Roman might to destroy Jerusalem.

Scribes were members of the ancient line of **skilled writers** who laboriously copied the Books of Sacred Scripture on **papyrus** (or for a much more expensive copy, on animal skin, like sheepskin referred to as **parchment**) for each succeeding generation. Over the centuries they had become very familiar with the Sacred Scriptures called the **Torah** (= Jewish Law or way of life), and they were acknowledged as instructors in the Law. Some scribes belonged to the Sadducee party, but most of them **belonged to the Pharisee party** (Acts 23:9; Mk 11:18). As a class of men they were strongly, but peaceably, opposed to the Roman occupation.

The **Essenes** were members of a hasidic (holiness-oriented) monastic-type body of men who had withdrawn from the mainstream of Jewish life probably because of leadership of John Hyrcanus (135-104 B.C.). Hyrcanus was the arrogant Hasmonian ruler whose secular mentality belittled the Temple worship. The monastery-type place at **Qumran**, on the northwest corner of the Dead Sea seemed to be their principal center. At Qumran, about 8 miles south of **Jericho**, they lived a very austere life dedicated to holiness, work and study while awaiting the eschatological or end-time moment God would choose to manifest his power in a magnificent and even cosmic day of judgment.

Josephus[1] describes the austere three year routine undertaken by candidates who entered this community. At Qumran between the Dead Sea and the barren western hills, the main body of Essenes shared their property, food and talents in a tightly disciplined and celibate community life. Apparently, those who left and married could have homes nearby and participate in some of the community's activity.

Beside intense study and prayer, the Qumran community members spent long hours copying their sacred texts. The discovery of their manuscripts, **the Dead Sea Scrolls**[2], in 1947 and thereafter, constituted one of the greatest ancient literature finds of all time. Parts of almost every O.T. book were found in the hill-

---

1. The Jewish War, p. 371, Excursus I.
2. Theodor Gaster, The Dead Sea Scriptures, (New York: Doubleday & Co, Inc., 1964), p. 3.

caves near Qumran. Scholarly knowledge leaped 1000 years closer to the Hebrew textual formulations of the O.T.[3]

No Essene, as such, appears in the pages of the New Testament; but a few concepts[4] are common to both the Scrolls and the New Testament. One in particular is the method of "fraternal correction" found in Matthew's Gospel (18:15-17). Scholars are generally convinced that this common material found in both the Dead Sea Scrolls and Matthew's Gospel is present in each text, not from a copying either way, but from the ongoing flow of the overall Jewish tradition.

Samaritans, living in the territory, named **Samaria**, between Galilee and Judea, were the remnant of the Jews left in Palestine at the time of the Babylonian Captivity (587 - 538 B.C.). This remnant married local or transplanted pagans and thus mingled their practices and their blood with the pagan Gentiles (goyim, in Hebrew) who entered their territory. For this reason the Judean leadership despised them as sort of half-Jews; **Samaritans** returned the hostile feelings. Galileans traveling to and from the Temple in Jerusalem would generally avoid Samaria unless they traveled with a group. The Samaritans had preserved the **Torah** (Pentateuch) and expected a Messiah whom they referred to as the **"Taheb"**.[5]

The New Testament mentions **Herodians**[6] on occasion. These people were the political supporters of the Herodian dynasty; their services were useful to the opponents of John the Baptizer and Jesus, who were influencing the lives of the people in a religious way. When Rome displaced the Herodian dynasty with governors after the time of Pontius Pilate (26-36), their influence diminished sharply, except for a brief period from 41 to 44 when **Herod Agrippa I** was established as "Rex Socius" (i.e. as Allied King like his grand-father) over the Jewish people.

Sadducees comprised a very significant group during the public ministry of Jesus. The Jewish priestly families, in general, and the wealthy and aristocratic Jewish families belonged to this group. The heads of these families apparently had an influential

---

3.   Roland Murphy, The Dead Sea Scrolls and the Bible, (Westminster, Md.: The Newman Press, 1963.), p. 39.
4.   Mt 18:15-17, fraternal correction
5.   A study at mid-century said that there were about 450 Samaritans of the continuous line still living in Samaria. On a visit to Jacob's Well or Mount Gerizim you may meet some of them. They still sacifice a lamb at Passover time.
6.   Mk 3:6, 12:13; Mt 22:16.

voting-block in the Jewish **Sanhedrin**, the highest official interpretative and judicial body for all Jews everywhere. The Sanhedrin was composed of about 70 men plus the High Priest as its president and leading authority. Heads of the Priestly families, heads of the aristocratic families and some scribes constituted its membership.[7] The **Sadducees** believed that the **Torah** consisted of Genesis, Exodus, Leviticus, Numbers and Deuteronomy **exclusively**. This five-book presentation of the **Torah**, known as the **Pentateuch**, was to be intrepreted literally only. This belief put them in the position of denying final judgment, immortality, resurrection of the body and the existence of angels. Since the Pentateuch did not explicitly declare these realities, even though they be implicitly contained there, the Sadducees denied their existence. Their interpretation of the Pentateuch was fixed; they did not sufficiently adapt the Torah to meet the changing circumstances of Jewish life.

Politically, the Sadducees, the **more wealthy** elite among the Jewish people, supported the **status quo** with the Romans and Herodians. Their **control of the Temple** seemed to have engendered a superior and disdainful attitude toward the common Jewish people. The ordinary poor Jewish people, generally uneducated yet respectful of the Torah and its way of life, were referred to as the **anawim**. Joseph, Mary and Jesus in their ordinary domestic and work life would have been classified as "anawim".

Opposing the Sadducee stance was the group known as **Pharisees**. This sect within Judaism probably originated from the same **hasidic** (= holy or pious) background as the Essenes, but this group stayed in the mainstream of Jewish life. The name **Pharisee** seems to mean "the separated ones". Their devout convictions separated them from the Sadducee leaders while their learning separated them from the lower classes ignorant of the Torah. It has been estimated that there were **about 6000 Pharisees** in first century Palestine. They opposed the Roman occupation, but rejected violence as a solution to the oppression suffered from the Roman occupation. The Pharisees were more sympathetic than the Sadducees to the anawim. Although holding an attitude of superiority over the anawim, the **Pharisees** nevertheless sought to instruct them in the proper understanding of the full Torah.

They were, in general, among the most learned students of the Torah. Contrary to the Sadducee position, they held that the

---

7. 30 priestly members, 25 aristocrats, & 15 scribes, as **assumed numbers**, might help to make an image of the Sanhedrin more concrete.

full Torah consisted of the Pentateuch, the Prophets (of whom Isaiah, Jeremiah and Ezekiel were the major prophets, twelve others were minor prophets) and the Writings (such as the Psalms, Job, the books of Samuel and Kings etc.). Until about the year 95 A.D. the Pharisees probably held as sacred all the books of the pre-Christian Septuagint.[8] As a middle class **their influence** was based not on blood or wealth, but rather on their learning in the Law and their efforts to instruct the Jewish people in the Torah.

Differing with the static posture held by the Sadducees, the Pharisees actively searched the Law & the Prophets for adaptation to new situations. This active study of the Sacred Scriptures convinced them of the doctrines of human **immortality, personal judgment, resurrection and the existence of angels.** These four doctrines distinguished the Pharisees from the Sadducees. The Sadducees could not find these four beliefs explicitly stated in the Pentateuch, consequently they refused to profess them. Such convictions on the part of the Pharisees, plus their investigative flexibility, enabled the Pharisees to **adapt** their lives on the basis of the full Torah after the Roman onslaught. The Jews who came to believe in Christ were strengthened in these beliefs which they already had.

On the side of weakness, however, was this business of multiplying new obligations from the study of new cases. Through this casuistry (case by case study of the Torah's moral implications)

---

8. The Septuagint is the Greek translation of the Old Testament; the translating appears to have been done by about 70 scribes [hence septuagint or the symbol LXX] in the pre-christian years between 200 and 50 B.C. in Egypt for the sake of the displaced Jews who could no longer read the Hebrew Sacred Scriptures.

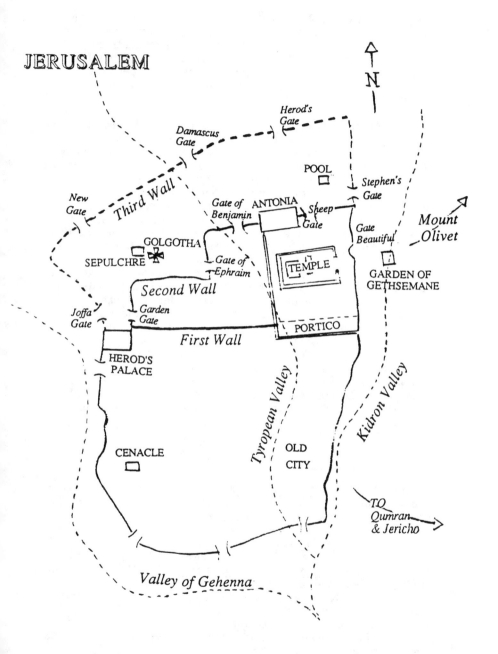

they derived **613 obligations**[9] in the Law, of which honoring the Sabbath, observance of the ritual purity and tithing were the most important. They taught as **traditions of the ancients** that there were 39 ways in which Jews could violate the Sabbath. Jesus would charge them with multiplying peoples' burdens with man-made rules, while neglecting the laws of God which were far superior.

Recently, greater effort has been made to distinguish among the Pharisees of the first century: the School of **Shammai** (Bet Shammai) from the School of **Hillel** (Bet Hillel). In his recent book Harvey Falk, an orthodox Rabbi, thinks that Jesus was perceived as close to the School of Hillel. The judgments of Rabbi Shammai were regarded as very severe and harsh on the people, whereas those of Hillel were held as more gentle and compassionate. The opposing positions of these schools of thought clashed in the **Sanhedrin** which was the supreme judgmental body for the Jews in first century Jerusalem.[10] The **Torah** was the **basis of all the rules** of living for the Jews. The Sanhedrin interpreted the Torah's meaning for all cases; religious law and secular law were not formally distinguished in the Jewish way of life; both were governed by the Law of God, the Torah. Beth Shammai appears, in the view of Harvey Falk, to have controlled the Sanhedrin in the years during the public ministry of Jesus and up until the destruction of Jerusalem.[11]

Shammai's disciples unbendingly rejected dealings with the **goyim** (= non-Jews, gentiles, other nations). They supported the extreme position of the Zealots, which precipitated the bloody confrontation with the powerful Roman forces.[12] On the contrary,

---

9. Harvey Falk, Jesus The Pharisee, Paulist Press, New York, 1985. In this recent book by an Orthodox Jewish Rabbi, the 613 precepts are frequently mentioned; cf. pp. 4, 20, 85. [Hereafter, Falk, Jesus The Pharisee and page.]
10. Falk, Jesus The Pharisee, passim.
11. Daniel J. Harrington, "The Jewishness of Jesus: Facing Some Problems", The Catholic Biblical Quarterly, vol, 49, no. 1, Jan. 1987. Whereas one extreme immerses Jesus exclusively in his Jewish context, other authors have him become totally transcendent to his Jewish context. p.10.
12. The Oxford Dictionary of the Christian Church, (rev.) eds F. Cross & E. Livingston, Oxford University Press, 1983, p.1268 (hereafter quoted as Oxford Dictionary).

the position of **Hillel's disciples** was much more conditioned to the demanding circumstances of daily life in both home and marketplace; separation from the **goyim** was more tolerantly phrased.

After the destruction of Jerusalem, Bet Hillel's position guided the Jewish people in the reconstruction of their lives.[13] **The Pharisees** of Hillel's school of thought **preserved the Jewish people,** as a distinct people, despite the Roman Empire's efforts to destroy them. "**Gamaliel** was the most distinguished disciple of Hillel and succeeded him as the head of the school which bore his name."[14] Gamaliel flourished in Jerusalem between 25 and 50 A.D.[15] He is mentioned in the New Testament as the teacher of Paul and as exercising a restraining influence on the Sanhedrin's hostility to the Apostles (Acts 5:33-40).

Sanhedrin   This supreme ruling body of the Jews consisted of just over seventy men and the High Priest was its president (Mt 26:57; Acts 24:1). **Its composition** appears to have come from the: a)heads of the priestly families; b)heads of the aristocratic families; c)Scribes. The first two groups were generally **Sadducees** by conviction; whereas the Scribes, writers of, and teachers of the Torah, were for the most part **Pharisees** by conviction. The Sanhedrin's meeting place was in Jerusalem; it judged all cases including capital-punishment cases. The Oxford Dictionary of the Christian Church notes that this body "pronounced the death penalty on Christ."[16]

When the Temple was destroyed by the Roman army under Titus in the year 70 A.D., the Sanhedrin ceased to exist. Soon after the fall of **Masada** and the withdrawal of the major military force of the Romans, the Pharisees started the restructuring of their Jewish way of life at **Jamnia** which lies about 35 miles to the West and slightly south of Jerusalem.

---

13. Ibid., p.650.
14. F.F. Bruce, New Testament History, (Garden City N.Y., Doubleday & Co., 1980) p.236.
15. Bruce, New Testament History, p.187.
16. Oxford Dictionary of the Christian Church, article: "Sanhedrin".

It was this restructuring work of the Pharisees on the basis of fidelity to the "Word of God" in the Torah (as they defined it) which enabled the Jewish people to retain its identity and continue in existence as a distinct people through the repeated, traumatic crises of the high-powered Roman annihilation tactics.

Questions

1. Briefly locate and describe Herodian **Palestine**?
2. Name the **4 territorial areas** ruled by Herod the Great?

3. How did Jerusalemites regard people in the other three Palestinian territories?
4. Who were the **Zealots**? Did Roman troops like them?

5. Who were the **Scribes**? How did their skills elevate them? Were they mostly Sadducees, Pharisees or neutral?
6. Where was **Qumran**? Who lived there? What happened to this place and its writings about the year 69? Which 1st century author describes **the Essenes**?

7. Who were and are the **Samaritans**? What provoked the hostility between the Jews and the Samaritans? What sacred book do the Samaritans follow? Did they expect the Messiah?
8. Mark mentions the **Herodians**; who were they?

9. What was **the Sanhedrin**? Who were its members? What was the extent of its authority
10. Identify and contrast the leading groups known as the **Sadducees** and the **Pharisees**?
    a)How did each group define **the Torah**?
    b)How did each group regard the ordinary poor Jewish people ("the anawim")?
    c)Were they equal in **authority**?
    d)How did each group regard the Romans?
    e)Which group placed great emphasis on **learning**?
    f)Name four doctrines which distinguished Pharisees from Sadducees?

11. How many **obligations** did Pharisees derive **from the Torah**? Which were **most important**? How many ways of **violating the Sabbath** had they determined?
12. Which was the more gentle of the **two schools of thought** which flourished among the Pharisees? Which school had more influence during the time of Christ?

Chapter V: Acts of The Apostles

Acts of the Apostles,[1] commonly referred to as Acts, was written by St.Luke (about 85 +/-5) as a sequel to his Gospel. It covers the time period from the resurrection and ascension of Christ (probable year: 30 A.D.) to the house-arrest of the apostle Paul in Rome (probably up to 62 A.D.)

Overview Luke quotes the risen Christ (1:8) as commanding Peter and his other apostles to be **witnesses** of the Good News in Jerusalem, Judea, Samaria and to the end of the world (= Rome). Using this command as the framework of his narrative,[2] Luke describes key events in Jerusalem, under the leadership of **Peter** (chapters 1-7) to show the start of its fulfillment. Influenced by the Holy Spirit, the infant community (**koinonia** is Luke's Greek word) develops **its structure** with Peter leading the apostolic community in meetings, prophetic speeches and judgment.

Peter's speeches are the key to the meaning of the events. The core of each speech or proclamation is "the Passion, Death and Resurrection of Christ for all"; Luke's Greek word for this proclamation is **kerygma**). The risen Jesus gave them no command to write; his command was to be his witnesses to the ends of the earth starting from Jerusalem; Matthew 28:19 expresses the cammand thus, "Go and make disciples of all nations." The Apostles did not scatter at once; with **Peter defining** the meaning of Christ's death and resurrection and the meaning of the events occurring to themselves (Pentecost, miracles, punishment from the Sanhedrin), they grew from the size of a "mustard seed" to become the **first sizable Christian community** in Jerusalem itself.

Peter's definition of **an apostle** was: **one who** walked with Jesus "from the baptism of John until. . .he was taken up from

---

1. The early study of Acts yields an extended view of Christ's infant community; this provides a sense of the 30-year historical context (although at times idyllic) in which the testimony of the Apostles shaped the narratives about Christ and his words for the later writing of the Gospels. It anchors the New Tesament writings in time and place; it helps in the appreciation of the flesh and blood reality of Jesus and the dailyness in the lives of his followers.
2. Jerome Crowe, The Acts, (Wilmington: Michael Glazier, Inc., 1979), p. xxiii.

us [to] become with us a **witness to his resurrection.**"[3] God added public miraculous events to the witnessing of Peter and John in the very Temple area itself! God gave Peter the miraculous power to cure a well-known cripple. Soon arrested, Peter and John courageously **witnessed to Christ** before the Sanhedrin. Beaten for witnessing to Christ as risen Lord; they rejoiced! Peter judged for the community what God wanted of them.

Luke clearly shows Peter to be the spokesman and leader of this first community of believers in Christ. This leadership, the teaching of the apostles and a new form of worship bound this community firmly together together. The community grew. For a couple of years all the new believers in Christ were Jews; many spoke Aramaic. Some were greek-speaking Jews from the diaspora.

The continuing growth strained the abilities of the Aramaic-speaking Apostles to care for the religious and other needs, – especially of the new greek-speaking believers. With the other Apostles, Peter decides to add the service-rank of **deacons** to the structure of the infant church. In a service of prayer and imposition of hands (ordination?) **Peter and the Apostles** incorporate, as subordinate assistants, Stephen, Philip and five others into the work of serving, baptizing and proclaiming the Risen Christ. **Stephen**, giving witness to Christ, will be killed at the hands of the Sanhedrin, – the young community's first martyr.[4] **Philip**, driven from Jerusalem, will take the kerygma **to Samaria**. Many Samaritans, despite ancient hostility to Jews, join the Christ-believing Jews in the conviction that Jesus is the risen Messiah. Thus, Christ-believing Samaritans join Christ-believing Jews in extending this new community. The naming of the group is getting awkward! When Christ-believing Gentiles join the growing community of believers in Antioch, it will be more awkward still to name the origin of the new believers.

Then, Luke shows (chapters 8-12) the spread of the Gospel (by the power of the Holy Spirit) to and beyond Samaria and the countryside of Judea; the spreading faith goes as far as **Damascus** in Syria. Then, it travels 350 north up the coastline to **Antioch** (Acts 11:26) where the followers of Christ are, for the first time, simply named **Christians** without reference to the belief-positions

---

3. Paul will experience some rejection of his work because his witnessing was to the resurrection; he had not walked with Jesus in the flesh.
4. As the proto-martyr, the first witness to shed his blood for Christ, Stephen is honored with the celebration of his heroic act each year on December 26, the day after Christmas.

from which they had come to praise God in the new way learned from Christ.[5]

Then, (chapters 13 to 28/end) Luke depicts the complete fulfillment of the Divine command. He narrates this through the medium of three missionary journeys and one final journey traveling with Paul who, as a "prisoner for Christ", proclaims the Gospel in the last great city (= Rome, the new Babylon) at the end of the western world.

The following **outline** emerges from Luke's account; some of the dividing lines occur near the ends of preceding chapters.

I.   Chapters 1-7 = In Jerusalem
II.   "   8-12 = Judea and Samaria
III.   "   13-end = To the end of the world
             a)13-14 = 1st missionary journey
             b)15   = Jerusalem Council
             c)15:36-18:22 = 2nd journey[6]
             d)18:23-21:26 = 3rd journey (end: Jerusalem)
             e)21:27-26 = Paul's trials
             f)27-28 = to Rome & in Rome

The first missionary team, led by Barnabas, takes the **new way** of Christ beyond the confines of Palestine and Syria into the territories of Asia Minor (chapters 13-14).[7] The team, of

which the convert Saul (= Paul) becomes the dominant member, departs from and returns to Antioch as its home base. Chapter 15 looks in on a very important **Jerusalem Meeting** (probable year: 49) which forestalls the dividing of Christ's new koinonia into a Jewish-Christian Church and a Gentile-Christian Church.

Following this Apostolic Meeting in Jerusalem, two teams embark on further missionary journeys: one, Barnabas and John

---

5. F.F. Bruce, New Testament History, pp.213, 232 the title **Christian** did not spring from a Jewish milieu, nor did the early Jewish-believers use it of themselves; they thought of what they believed and did as "the Way" (Acts 9:2, 19:9,23).
6. **Chapter divisions and numbers** were inserted by Rev. Stephen Langton, professor at the University of Paris; Langton was later made a cardinal. He died in 1228. **Verse numbers** were inserted over three centuries later by a printer named Robert Steven; his numbering of the text was completed in 1555.
7. Lebanese scholar, Farid Jabre, C.M., has uncovered evidence of Christian missionaries moving East toward India and beyond.

Mark, the other, Paul and Silas. Luke, possibly a convert of Paul's, chooses to narrate **Paul's** bold missionary exploits on this second missionary journey. In fact, it appears that Luke actually joins the team of Paul, Silas, and the newly recruited young Timothy as they sail from Asia Minor to take the Gospel **into Europe** (chapters 16-18:22). This missionary venture takes about three years during most of which time Luke apparently stayed on at Philippi, while the team went on to Thessalonika, Boerea, Athens, and Corinth before returning to their home base at Antioch. During this trip Paul wrote his first letter to the **Thessalonians** (50/51 A.D.).

The same missionary team (Paul, Silas and Timothy) took off on the third missionary journey which covered a period of about five years; they visited many of the places of the first and second journeys (chapters 18:23-21). During this period Paul wrote his **letters to** the Christian communities in **Galatia, Corinth and Rome** (years: 56/57); this latter community (already Christian!) Paul had not yet visited. Paul terminated this third trip in Jerusalem where he is arrested and jailed.

Chapters 22 to 26 narrate the dramatic episodes of the widening gap between the Jews who have rejected Jesus as the Messiah and the Jews who have become Christ's disciples.

Under trial, Paul, as a Roman citizen, appeals to Caesar (the supreme court in the Roman legal structure). As a prisoner he is sent to Rome (ch.27). Luke closes his narrative with Paul under house-arrest freely (ch.28) proclaiming the Gospel in Rome (= end of the world), the Babylon of the West.

Purpose   Acts is the main source of our knowledge about the history of the early Church. St. Luke wrote it as a **Theology of Salvation History** (heilsgeschichte). His **main purpose** was to describe the spreading of Christ's new koinonia through

Acts of the Apostles

1 Ascension; "Upper room" & Peter leads; defines "Apostle"

2 Pentecost; Speech: Peter plus 11 speak; 3000 baptized

3 Beggar at gate; Peter: Portico speech

4 Sanhedrin arrest; Peter's speech

5 Spectrum of living Barnabas <---> Ananias & Sapphira

6 Problem: Hebrews/Hellenists: "diakonein": Stephen, Philip, etc.

7 Stephen, synagogue, Sanhedrin, speech [XP>T & T], stoned, Saul

8 Philip: Samaria Peter and John; Gaza/convert

9 Paul: Damascus Peter: Lydda; Joppa

10 Peter: centurion/ convert=Gentile

11 Peter: rationale for receiving Gentiles; name: Christians

12 Agrippa I: James martyred; Peter arrest/escape

13 1st journey: Barnabas/Saul/ Mark;

14 install presbyters

15 Jerusalem "Council": Peter speaks; James clause

16 "WE" passages;

17 Areopagus: Kerygma to Gentiles; "soma-sema" problem;

18 1-2 Thess.

19 Gal
Co
2nd Co

20 Ro

21 "breaking of the bread"; Didache to presbyters

22 Temple events

23 Before Sanhedrin Resurrection Q

24 Trial before Felix

25 trial before Festus

26 Paul: Festus & Agrippa II

27 to Rome; shipwreck

28 in Rome.

the action of the Holy Spirit.[8] He was also interested in the persons and events through which the Holy Spirit moved the new community into the pagan Roman world.

As a **secondary purpose** Luke wished to document the influx of the pagan Gentiles (Luke had been a Gentile or goy) into this originally all-Jewish community of Christ. Note that the Jewish practices of circumcision, observance of ritual purity, sabbath rest and temple taxes are not imposed on the gentile converts. These four practices were distinguished by the Pharisees as the most important of the 613 precepts of the Torah. **Thirdly,** Luke also seemed intent on showing that this new way of the Christians is not a threat to the Roman Empire despite charges to the contrary. In their court cases neither Gallio (ch.18) nor Felix (ch.24) nor Festus (ch.25,26) find Paul guilty of breaking Roman Law. The Apostles were intent on the religious mission of proclaiming the good news of Christ's awe-inspiring resurrection. In this resurrection God revealed to everyone his divine intention to raise all human beings to a new kind of life after earthly death; this was an exciting ingredient of the enormously **Good News (= Gospel)** that the kerygma proclaimed!

Extended Kerygma   The briefest content of the **kerygma** may be expressed as "the passion, death and resurrection of Christ for all". This minimum statement is naturally more extended in the Apostles' proclamation of it. Luke uses the speeches of Peter in Acts (2,3,4,5,10) to show the context in which the kerygma was proclaimed.[9] This petrine expression may be referred to as the **extended kerygma;** it enlarges the core kerygma into six points. They are:

1)   Now is the time that God has chosen to establish his reign.
2)   Jesus of Nazareth is the Messiah who proclaimed that reign at the cost of his **passion and death.**
3)   The Father showed his approval by Jesus' **resurrection.**
4)   As promised, the Holy Spirit has come.
5)   Christ will come again to judge the living and the dead.
6)   Repent (metanoia) and be baptized.

The Passion Death & Resurrection (PD&R) are the nucleus of the extended kerygma. Also the persons of Jesus, his Father

---

8.   Luke's work has with reason been termed "The Gospel of the Holy Spirit".
9.   C.H. Dodd, The Apostolic Preaching (New York: Harper & Row, 1964), pp. 21ff.

and the Holy Spirit (= a very early reflection leading to the doctrine of the **Trinity**[10]) are all engaged in bringing human beings into the divinely established **Reign of God** which issues in eternal life.[11] The Apostles experienced the words and deeds of Jesus; they experienced what happened at Pentecost. Thus, their proclaiming is not done on the basis of theories but on the solid basis of their experiences. Peter's reply to the Sanhedrin, "better for us to obey God than men," (5:29) was based on what he had personally suffered and thrillingly experienced. Peter later suffered martyrdom rather than deny what he knew to be true from personally-experienced conviction.

In fulfilling his specific purposes Luke also indicated how Christ's new ecclesia (= church) was structuring itself, in summaries he indicated what was holding the new group together and also problems it faced in growing. His account suggests some community growth in its understanding of Christ (Christology) and data-points in the oral kerygma which will provide a framework for the written Gospels. In Acts, Luke also shows the opening to the non-Jews (= Gentiles) and he stresses the conversion of Saul (= Paul), the tireless opponent of the infant ecclesia.

Ecclesial structure   In Acts' early chapters Luke shows how the new koinonia (Paul in 1 Thessalonians calls it an **ecclesia** [= church]) of Christ is **structuring** itself. **Peter** is the chief speaker in chapters 1,2,3,4,5,6,10,&15. He is clearly the spokesman and leader of the Apostles and of this original Christian community. He defines the criteria for filling Judas' place among "The Twelve"; he judges in the community in ch.5; he decides with the other apostles in ch.6; he pronounces the overall decision in ch.15. Thus, Luke's narrative shows that Peter stands in the midst of the other apostles and the community as the foundation **rock (= petros in Greek)** of Christ's new koinonia. In ch. 6 Peter, with the other Apostles, decides to add a new order to the structure of the koinonia. With prayer and the imposition of hands, they establish seven men to serve (= diakonein, Luke's word) the new community. The community will call them deacons.

---

10. Dictionary of the Christian Religion, eds F. Cross et al. cf. Acts.
11. The Nicene Creed, from the Council of Nicaea in 325, is structured on these doctrines of the Trinity and the Passion death and resurrection of Christ.

In a take-it-for-granted way, Luke (14:23) simply notes the installation of men called **presbyters** charged with overall responsibility for the local community. Their responsibility to oversee (= episcopein) emerged as greater than the service of the deacons. Thus, there emerges the structural triad of apostle, presbyter and deacon. As the community grew, an apostle chose an episcopos (bishop comes from this word) to fulfill his function in the community.

In Antioch before the year 100 A.D., the structural triad consisted of **episcopos** (= bishop), **presbyter** (= elder, the word, priest, comes from it) and **diaconos** (= deacon)[12]. The development of this structural triad in the early Church was more fluid than this brief mention suggests. But this pattern emerges early and almost universally in the sub-apostolic period. About the year 110 **Ignatius, the Bishop of Antioch,** suffered martyrdom in Rome for his Christian faith. On his way as a prisoner from Antioch to Rome, he wrote seven letters. In his letter to the Trallians, he said this about the three orders:

> Without these three orders you cannot
> begin to speak of a church.[13]

Summaries In reading Acts, Luke's major summaries 2:42ff, 4:32ff and 5:12ff are noteworthy. In these three **Lukan summaries** the inspired author gives the reader a sense of the elements which served to unite the first Christians and to identify them as a community of Christ. For example, in ch.2 Luke notes that the community is made one in faith by the **Apostles' didache** (= teaching), by the **breaking of the bread and prayers** (= the eucharist), by some kind of shared or **community life**, and, by going daily to the temple. These four activities and some others characterize the new Jerusalem community (Luke's word = **koinonia**) of Christ's disciples. The temple attendance, of course, was only in Jerusalem where the one temple of the one God was located. However, the common purse of communal life did not seem to spread beyond this first Jewish-Christian community in Jerusalem, whereas collections for local and missionary needs of Christians remain a Christian practice to the present day.

Problems/Growth In certain places, (ex. Antioch and Galatia) some Jews who became Christians tried to impose

---

12. R. Brown & J. Meier, Antioch & Rome, (New York: Paulist Press, 1983), pp. 76ff.
13. William Jurgens, The Faith of the Early Fathers, (Collegeville: The Liturgical Press, 1970), pp.20f.

kosher laws (and the Torah in general) on the new Gentile-converts. Such Jewish-converts were known as **Judaizers.** Acts refers to them in a pejorative way; the trouble they caused among the Galatians evoked Paul's most emotional letter. Undoubtedly, the demand by the Judaizers for the preservation of the full Torah contributed to the need for the historic Jerusalem Apostolic Meeting to resolve this problem.

Although St. Luke generally describes the new community's early years in an idyllic way, he nevertheless indicates some of the trouble spots which surfaced; for example, the Hebrew/Hellenist problem (ch.6), and the problem of whether Gentiles had to become Jews to reach Christ (ch.15). In overcoming such problems the Apostles perceived that the world's boundaries of language, geography or nationality were not barriers for Christ's love and salvation. Luke saw from hindsight that living Christ's new way dismantled boundaries and deepened the vision of a **unity in Christ** that transcended man-made barriers. The persons who came to Christ from the most diverse countries were in some new way made one. Jerusalem Christians were not to be different from the Christians in Antioch; nor were the Christians in Athens to differ essentially in doctrine and practice from the Christians in Rome. There was one Christ who established only one koinonia.

The community grew in the understanding that their new ecclesial unity transcended their former cultural and linguistic diversities. In their language differences they had to probe more deeply into the **meaning of Christ.** To the Jews the word Christ was enormously significant, but to the Gentiles, unaware of its divinely authoritative connotation, it sounded merely like the remainder of Jesus' name.[14]

Christology   Similarly, in living and experiencing the Christian life, a growth or development in theological thinking about Christ himself was also taking place. The Apostles perceived deeper ways of explaining the meaning of Christ. They reflected on the meaning of Jesus' resurrection, after that they probed the mystery of his suffering and death, and after Pentacost the Holy Spirit led them to perceive and proclaim the mysterious unity of Father and Son; the Holy Spirit's relationship was somehow discerned before the finishing of the Gospels of Matthew (Mt 28-18-20) about 85 A.D. and John (13-17) about 95 A.D.

The Apostolic explanations appeared from the start to emphasize **(a) Christ's resurrection** (which overcame the universal

---

14.   Bruce, N.T. History, p.279.

corruption of death); this is manifested in the speeches of Peter to his fellow Jews in the Upper Room speech, the Pentecost speech, the speech at Solomon's Portico, his speeches to the Sanhedrin, and to the Gentiles, Cornelius, and his household.[15] The aramaic underpinning (Peter's native tongue) of these speeches suggests that Greek-speaking Luke had based his account on some very early documentation. C.H. Dodd declares, "I cannot resist the conclusion that the material here presented existed in some form in Aramaic before it was incorporated in our Greek Acts."

The emphasis seems to proceed from Jesus' Resurrection[16] to his fulfillment of the role as **(b) Suffering Servant of Yahweh** (Isaiah 52/53 and passim). The Ethiopian, met by Philip (c.8), asked to whom Isaiah was referring. Philip's instruction reveals that the Isaian "Suffering Servant" image was perceived as having been fulfilled by Jesus at this level of Christian understanding. This Servant of Yahweh was the one whose suffering was **for others** (= vicarious suffering).

It appears that the Holy Spirit next led the Apostolic insight further to express **(c) Christ's unique relationship with his Father** without diminution of his stature as man. As Acts proclaims: in his name sins are remitted (2:39); in none other is there salvation (4:12); God exalted him at his right hand to be Prince and Savior (5:31). The prophetic expression, "The **Lord** said to my **Lord**, sit at my right hand..." is seen as an application of a divine title to the exalted Christ.[17] The study of this progressive development or growth in understanding something of the mysterious nature of Christ is called **Christology**[18]. It was after Jesus rose from the dead and they received the Holy Spirit that the Apostles began to perceive his divinity, and thereafter saw Jesus' earthly career in a new light, and "...passed on to their listeners what was really said and done by the Lord with that fuller understanding which

---

15. See Peter's speeches in Acts: Pentecost 2:14-59; Portico 3:13-26; first to Sanhedrin 4:10-12; second to Sanhedrin 5:30-32; to Gentiles 10:36-43.
16. C.H. Dodd, The Apostolic Preaching, p. 10 footnote.
17. Psalm 110:1; cf. also Dodd, The Apostolic Preaching, p.15.
18. The development from Resurrection to Suffering Servant to Unique Divine Sonship must be taken here as merely a suggested development; at what point which Apostle so perceived it, or which sacred author so wrote it, is itself a book-length hypothesis beyond the scope of this brief introduction. R.A.F. MacKenzie, Introduction to the New Testament, (Collegeville, 1965) p. 17, suggests a somewhat different order.

they enjoyed"[19] In interpreting the Gospels, the reader must take care to recognize that different passages were verbalized during the different periods of this developmental process in Christology just examined.

Gospel structure The contents of Acts constitute the middle stage in the genesis or production of the yet-to be written Gospels.[20] This middle or Apostolic stage is that in which the Apostles, the new deacons and others who joined in the Apostolic work proclaimed the "Good News" **orally.** In this oral transmission of the extended kerygma, the starting point appeared to be the life-changing experiences which penetrated the consciousness of Peter and the other Apostles following **Jesus' Resurrection:** Peter's speeches in chs.2,3,4,5,10. To answer the questions about why he died, and the events before he died, the Apostles reviewed Jesus' **ministry in Jerusalem** (10:39) up to his suffering and death.

As these reflections became fairly complete, believers, wanting to know more about Jesus, inquired about his **ministry in Galilee** (10:37). In the light of Jesus' resurrection, all of the events which the Apostles shared with him took on new and deeper meaning. On occasion they would review Jesus' parables, then his miracles, then his conflicts with authorities. Soon the picture of his public ministry began to take an overall shape. The episode of Jesus' Jewish life that started this public ministry was his coming to **John the Baptizer** (10:37) the prophetic figure like Elijah before him.

In this analysis, based on the Petrine extended kerygma, the telling of the events worked from the climactic point, the Passion, Death and Resurrection (PDR) **backwards** to the historic starting point of the public meeting with John the Baptist. As the Gospel message was repeated over and over again in new places to new faces, these four points were turned around and presented in their time-order. In Acts, the risen Jesus commissioned Peter and the eleven to tell the world the Good News. This turn-around then provided the overall ordered framework for that telling of the Gospel. **Mark,** frequent hearer of that telling used its framework for his **Gospel** in the following sequence:

1. John the Baptizer and Jesus,

---

19. Pontifical Biblical Commission, The Historical Truth of the Gospels, art. 8.
20. Pontifical Biblical Commission, The Historical Truth of the Gospels, Rome: April 21, 1964, articles 6-9; cf appendix five.

-53-

2. Jesus' Galilean ministry,
3. Jesus going to Jerusalem and ministry there,
4. Jesus' passion, death and resurrection.

According to **Papias**, the bishop of Hieropolis who wrote five books on The Exposition of the Oracles of the Lord, Mark became Peter's interpreter. Without question, Peter, eagerly desiring to fulfill the commission given to him by Jesus himself, told the story of what happened whenever he got the chance. How many times would that be from the year of the resurrection (30) until Peter's martyrdom for this faith probably in 66/67? Since Mark served him as interpreter for some time Mark heard the account often, and undoubtedy often told it himself.[21] **Papias** characterized Mark's account as accurate. These statements of Papias, contained in his books which are no longer extant, are recorded in the book by Eusebius, entitled Historia Ecclesiae (The History of the Church) written by 325 A.D.[22]

Opening to Non-Jews

Up through chapter seven Acts keeps it attention on Jerusalem. The narrative is focused only on Jews; not a gentile (goy, plural: goyim) has entered the picture except for **Deacon Nicholas** who, before believing in Christ, had previously converted from paganism to Judaism. Surprisingly, the Sanhedrin's persecution (c.7) initiated an active missionary movement carried on by the believing Hellenists who were driven out of Jerusalem. Instead of stopping the movement, persecution deepened it and spread it.

When, according to Luke, the Sanhedrin killed the **Deacon Stephen** (c.7), it started a persecution against the Greek-speaking Jews who had become followers of Christ. **Deacon Philip** escaped to Samaritan territory, the land of originally Jewish people who had mingled their blood through marriage with the "unclean" goyim. They still followed the Pentateuch (= Torah = Genesis, Exodus, Leviticus, Numbers and Deuteronomy). Philip exercises his new functions of proclaiming the Gospel to the Samaritans and baptizing those who believed that the risen Jesus was the Messiah.

The invocation of the Holy Spirit on the new converts was apparently the function of an Apostle. Philip sent to Jerusalem to get Peter and John to perform this function. The event had

---

21. Martin Hengel, Acts and the History of Earliest Christianity, (Philadelphia: Fortress Press, 1980), p. 29
22. Eusebius, Historia Ecclesiae, tr. G. Williamson, (New York: Penguin series, 1960), p.152

the appearance of a "**little Pentecost**". The author next highlights the passage of the Good News through time and space south to the Gaza Strip. Philip meets the Treasurer of Ethiopia, a goy (=a gentile, a non-jew). Yet the man is a "**God-fearer**" (= one who is monotheist and follows the ten commandments, but refuses to be circumsized to become a Jew). The man is reading the prophet Isaiah (52-53) on the vicarious suffering of the **Servant of Yahweh.** Philip explains how Jesus had fulfilled this Isaian prophecy and was indeed the expected messiah and much more. **The Ethiopian** asks to become a follower of Christ; Philip baptizes him. A Gentile, a goy has entered the all Jewish-Christian community! The first!

Shortly thereafter, when Peter, sojourning in Joppa, is staunchly affirming his rejection of non-kosher food as unclean, he is given to understand that he must no longer call anything that God has made unclean! In conjunction with this, a Roman military officer, named **Cornelius**, asked Peter to visit him. To enter a Gentile's home meant "uncleanness" for Peter. He suddenly realized his recent instruction forbade his calling **this Gentile** unclean.

Peter traveled to **Caesarea Marittima**, Rome's military headquarters in Palestine, and entered the Centurian's home. They talked. As Peter explained Christ's Passion, death and Resurrection, a "Pentecost-like event" occurred. Peter understood that he could no longer reject Gentiles. He baptized all present who believed that Jesus had risen, was the Messiah, and had utterly transcended the prophetic-expectation of him. Luke, himself a Gentile who had come from paganism, had shown that the "new way" of Christ was open to all persons of good will, not merely to the Jews who, nevertheless, were still the privileged first-called.

In the meantime, the new movement had already claimed believers in the synagogues of **Damascus.** The young Saul, who had encouraged the killing of Stephen, was commissioned by the Sanhedrin authorities to go to Damascus in order to root the Christ-believing members out of the synagogue there. His commission was to bring them back to stand trial before the Sanhedrin in Jerusalem.

Saul's Conversion Supported with Sanhedrin guards, Saul, "a Pharisee and Hebrew of the Hebrews"[23], "breathing murderous threats against the Lord's disciples"[24] headed toward ancient **Damascus** to bring the baptized believers in Christ

---

23. Philippians, 3:5f.
24. Luke, Acts, 9:1.

back to trial before the Sanhedrin. After crossing the Golan Heights and nearing Damascus, Saul fell as he was suddenly confronted by a person in a blinding light. The person demanded:

Saul, Saul, **why do you persecute me?**
Who are you sir, asked Saul.
I am Jesus, the one you are persecuting.
Get up and go into the city, where you
will be told what to do.[25]

Saul's companions stood speechless. They led the now-blinded Saul to a house in Damascus where, three days later, he was contacted by **Ananias**, a Jewish convert to Christ. Ananias, probably the head of the Damascus synagogue, was suspicious of this Sanhedrin-agent with police powers of arrest. Nevertheless, Ananias greeted and placed his hands on Saul; immediately his sight returned. Saul (whose Greek name was **Paul**) asked to be baptized into the community of Christ, the new community he had, until then, been trying to destroy!

One may wonder how long it took Paul to reorient his life and rearrange his thoughts after being confronted by the Risen Christ. But before he finally left Damascus he was confounding the Jews there by strongly proclaiming and even proving [perhaps from the fulfillment of Old Testament prophecies] that **Jesus is the Messiah.** Luke may be suggesting that Paul's early proclaiming even transcended the Jewish concept of messiahship.

Luke, a later convert from paganism and perhaps converted by Paul, was deeply impressed with this dramatic conversion. Despite the confinement of his limited and expensive scroll[26], Luke told this episode three times (chs 9,22,26): once here, once to his fellow Jews in the Temple area, and, finally, before Jews and Gentiles in a Roman court hearing at Caesarea Marittima.

On the road to Damascus, Saul, the Jewish persecutor, became Saul/Paul the tireless Apostle of the risen Christ. Paul saw an intimate connection between the risen Christ and his baptized followers. Paul was focused on Christ's followers; Jesus had said: "Why do you persecute **ME**? Later, Paul will conclude **Jesus (somehow) = one with his baptized disciples.** Paul's first letter, in a take-it-for-granted way identifies the baptized followers as

---

25. Ibid.,9:4-6
26. Hengel, Acts and History, pp.6-8

being **in Christ.**[27] He perceives that this new union with the risen Christ transcends mere corporate, human unities. Later, he will proclaim that Christ's baptized followers mysteriously form **one body** with their glorified savior. Surrounded by the brilliant light which Paul intuitively understood to be the **divine glory,** Jesus' statement: "I am Jesus, whom you are persecuting" could only mean two things: "Jesus is Lord; the Church is [mysteriously] Jesus"[28]

27. 1 Thes. 2:13, 3:4. (Cf. Joseph Fitzmyer's article "Pauline Theology", Jerome Biblical Commentary, (Englewood Cliffs, N.J.: Prentice-Hall, 1968), p. 823. Also, Fitzmyer estimates that "Paul's theology was influenced most of all by his experience on the road to Damascus", p.803.
28. George Montague, The Living Thought of St. Paul, (Milwaukee: Bruce Publishing Company, 1966), p.4.

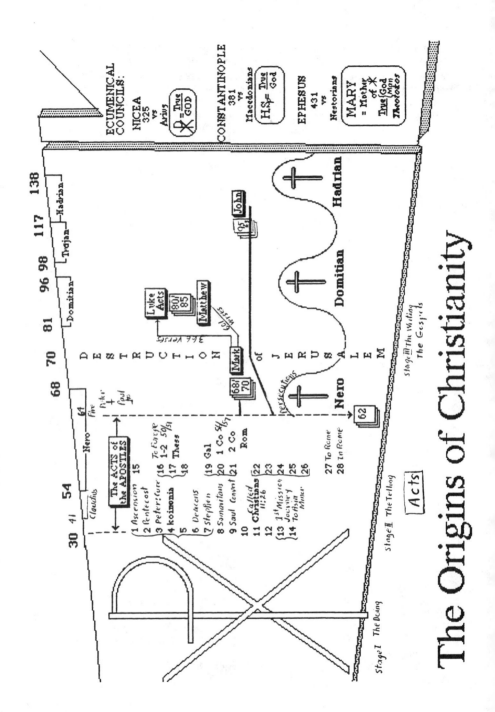

The Origins of Christianity

-58-

Questions

1. When was the book, **Acts of the Apostles** written? Who is its author? Of what is it the sequel?
2. What time-frame does it cover? Probable dates of that time frame? Overall Opening and closing events?

3. Acts 1:8 is used by St. Luke as the **overall outline** of his book: What was the **commission** given to the Apostles? by Whom? What are the Apostles commissioned to be?
4. What word does Luke use to speak of this group?

5. What **driving force** develops and extends this new community?
6. Who is this infant community's spokesman and **leader**? Is Luke presenting a **living, teaching authority** operative in this Apostolic community [= magisterium]? Who defines the criteria for being "one of the Twelve [Apostles]"?

7. Is the group Christ founded growing structurally? How?
8. Who gives the **Pentecost speech**? Who speaks at Solomon's Portico? Who responds to the Sanhedrin's inquiry? What is at **the core** of Peter's speeches? What is the **Kerygma**?

9. What drives the Gospel-message beyond Jerusalem?
10. **Where** is the Gospel proclaimed immediately after Jerusalem? By whom?

11. In Acts **what functions** are the new deacons carrying out?
12. As in Chs 1-7 Luke shows the Gospel-community in Jerusalem, so in 8-12 he shows Christian leaders going beyond Jerusalem.

13. From Chs 13 to the book's end Luke shows the words of **Acts 1:8** being fulfilled, - explain this.
14. Where did the **missionary work** extend after Palestine and Syria? Who led the 3-man team? What towns did they visit? 15. Discuss the very serious problem which evoked the **"Council of Jerusalem"**. Its solution? What did the **James Clause** say?

16. **What team** embarked on the **2nd missionary journey** from Antioch? Why different; what happened? What **new territory** did the missioners go to? Name the chief towns? Identify some event with the major places? Any **epistles** written during this 2nd journey? Does Luke describe all this in the 3rd person?
17. What were the starting and ending points of the **3rd missionary journey**? Probable years? Same mission team? Where did they go? Identify major events with places? Any **Epistles** written?

18. Why was Paul arrested in the Temple area (c.21)? What did Paul say which upset the Jewish crowd there?
19. What happened in Paul's **Sanhedrin hearing**? What in Paul's response divided the Sanhedrin? What saved Paul's life?

20. How **Governors Felix & Festus** react to Paul? **What is Luke showing** by this Roman trial of a Christian Apostle?
21. Compare responses to Paul given by Festus & Agrippa II.

22. Give 3 highlights of Paul's **sea-journey**, toward Rome?
23. What happened during Paul's house arrest **in Rome**?

24. What are **Luke's purposes** in Acts?
25. Briefly state **the kerygma**? What <u>six points</u> are included in the **extended kerygma**? Is the kerygma extended on the basis of speculation or experience? How did Peter express his option at the Sanhedrin inquiry? Was Peter convinced of his position?

26. How is the **structure** of the new community manifested in Acts? What data point to the community's structure?
27. What assertion from Bishop **Ignatius of Antioch** confirms the ecclesial structuring starting in Acts?

28. Give 4 points from Luke's **summaries** 2:42ff, 4:32ff, 5:12ff?
29. What problems surfaced in the primitive Jerusalem community? What was the **Hebrew/Hellenist** problem? How was it solved?

30. Did <u>growth in understanding</u> about **Christ** occur in this early community? Cite 3 apparent steps in this growth?
31. In the **oral transmission** of the Gospel (esp. in Luke's Petrine speeches) the **four-point framework** of Mark's Gospel can be found: a)what are the 4 points? b)what is meant by development backwards?

32. Discuss briefly from Acts the first three **Gentiles Converts**
33. How did **Saul's conversion** occur? What had Saul been bent on doing? What was the Risen Christ's initial question to Saul? To whom was he sent in Damascus? **What act** was performed to make him a follower of Christ? What did Saul soon realize about the **relation between** the risen Christ and His baptized followers?

Chapter VI: The Gospel According to Mark

Preceded by the stage of Christ's public ministry and the oral stage of the Apostolic preaching, the **third stage** in the genesis of the gospels was the stage of the actual writing of the Gospels. They were written in Greek which, in the **fourth century copies**, became a major source of the English translations that we are reading. Each one of these copies is an ancient manuscript in book-form called a **codex**. Very famous are the fourth century Codex Vaticanus and Codex Sinaiticus; the fifth century Codex Alexandrinus and Codex Ephramensis are also highly regarded. Textual critics examine these ancients manuscripts and all related papyrus and parchment copies for purposes of dating them, looking for copyists' errors, and searching for linear, parent-like relationships to discover the earliest copy.

Ancient **papyrus** scrolls and flat sheets to make a codex were expensive; **parchment** (such as sheepskin) was very expensive. and these materials could be rather limited in the quantity of written matter they could hold.[1] **Papias**, the Bishop of Hieropolis, wrote five scrolls (each scroll was called a book) on the <u>Sayings of the Lord</u>. Irenaeus, Clement, Origen, Tertullian and Eusebius were other very early Christian authors (there were many more) who commented on first century New Testament happenings in their writings. Among these writings the Gospels are listed as the ones according to: 1)Matthew, 2)Mark, 3)Luke and 4)John. From antiquity until now, this remains the **order of listing** of the Gospels.[2]

Concerning the gospels, these ancient authors (compositely) said that **Matthew**, writing **in Aramaic**, was **first** to compose a gospel. Matthew's <u>Aramaic text</u> is no longer extant. If it were written on <u>papyrus</u>, its 'life-expectancy' would have been much shorter than if it had been written on parchment such as sheepskin. All of the extant hand-written copies of Gospels (not the autographs) that we do have are in Greek, and the first of these, i.e. the first in existence **as we still have it**, seems to be **Mark's.**

Historic Tradition   Christian authors, such as Papias (+ca. 140), Irenaeus (140-204), Clement of

---

1. M. Hengel, <u>Acts and early Christianity</u>, pp. 6-8.
2. Some centuries later, Matthew and John, as Apostles, were listed up front; but this rearrangement did not prevail.

Alexandria (150-215), Tertullian (160-225), and Origen (180-255), make comments both about the Gospels and quote from them in their still-extant writings. These works constitute a source of information outside of the New Testament. This information, frequently referred to as **tradition** (i.e. historic tradition), constitutes evidence which gives scholars needed assistance in determining the date, place, and ambience of all ancient books. They do not answer all the questions we have, but they frequently give our inquiries decisive information, and also further leads. Checking the correspondence between the <u>outside</u> information and the data <u>inside</u> the N.T. is a constant scholarly pursuit. Literary and also archeological correspondence with the scriptural text is a steady source for articles in learned journals.

Papias says that John Mark was **Peter's interpreter** and that he **wrote carefully.** In general, the early Church unanimously attributed the traditionally second Gospel[3] to Mark.[4] **Origen,** who identifies Matthew's Aramaic gospel as first, speaks about the Peter/Mark relationship in a passage on the Canon of the New Testament; thus:

"I accept the traditional view of the four gospels which alone are undeniably authentic in the Church of God on earth. **First** to be written was that of the one-time exciseman [= tax collector] who became an apostle of Jesus Christ - **Matthew**; it was published for believers of Jewish origin, and was composed in Aramaic. **Next** came that of **Mark**, who followed Peter's instructions in writing it, and who in Peter's general epistle was acknowledged as his son: Greetings to you from the church in Babylon [= Rome], chosen like yourselves, and from my son Mark. **Next** came that of **Luke**, who wrote for Gentile converts the gospel praised by Paul. **Last** of all came **John's**"[5]

---

3. The order of the gospels is always as: 1st Matthew, 2nd Mark, 3rd Luke, 4th John; this listing seems to imply the time order of their first appearance. If the Aramaic Matthew text pre-dated Mark, then the Greek text of Matthew may post-date Mark as many scholars hold.
4. W. Harrington, <u>Mark</u>, (Wilmington: Michael Glazier, Inc., 1979), pp.xi ff.
5. Eusebius, <u>The History of the Church</u> (in Latin: Historia Ecclesiastica, or sometimes, Historia Ecclesiae) -abbreviated hereafter <u>HE</u>), tr G. Williamson, (Baltimore:Penguin Books, 1965), <u>HE</u>, p.265.

The earlier traditional information from Papias is contained in the Historia Ecclesiastica (History of the Church) written by Eusebius in 325.[6] Eusebius quotes Papias thus:

"Mark who had been **Peter's interpreter**, wrote down **carefully**, but not in order, all that he remembered of the Lord's sayings and doing. For he had not heard the Lord or been one of His followers, but later, as I said, one of Peter's. Peter **used to adapt** his teaching to the occasion, without making a systematic arrangement of the Lord's sayings, so that Mark was quite justified in writing down some things just as he remembered them. For he had one purpose only - to leave out nothing that he had heard, and to make **no misstatement** about it."[7]

Irenaeus indicates that Mark's gospel comes **from Rome.**[8] And many scholars have concluded that Mark's account was finished before the destruction of Jerusalem (Temple and all) in the year 70 because Mark seems to contain no evidence or hint that the destruction had occurred;[9] further, Mark (the name alone identifies the gospel unless the context indicates otherwise) seems less mindful of the developing Church than the other gospels.

The New Testament itself yields some **data about Mark.** Col 4:10 calls him a cousin of Barnabas, and 1 Peter 5:13 identifies him as "Mark, my son". This is interpreted as indicating that **Peter** brought him into the new Christian life through baptism. Mark is known too by the readers of Acts; he is the young man who abruptly abandoned the Barnabas/Paul team on their first missionary journey. Paul's refusal to take him on the second journey broke up the team! Barnabas went back to his native Cyprus with Mark while Paul started a new team with Silas and later added Timothy. After Paul had reevaluated Mark's maturity some years later, he asked for Mark's assistance (2 Tim 4:11; Phm 24).

---

6. G. Williamson, "introduction", The History of the Church, p.20.
7. Eusebius, HE, p.152.
8. R. Brown & J, Meier, Antioch & Rome, (New York: Paulist Press, 1983), p.197; "...the internal evidence is **not unfavorable** to the tradition that Rome was the place of provenance for Mark; cf. also H.E., p.210 and p. 254.
9. David E. Aune, The New Testament in Its Literary Environment, Philadelphia: The Westminster Press, [paperback ed.] 1989), p. 61; A "shortly after A.D. 70" date and a Galilean background are briefly suggested in a differing interpretation.

Gospel Framework: Acts 10:34-43

As younger companion to Peter, Mark must have heard him proclaim the gospel-data many, many times. Peter was the chosen intimate and number one witness of Jesus' public ministry and resurrection.[10] Surely, Peter tried to tell as many people as he could about the events that changed his life and in witness of which he would die in Nero's persecution. Analysis of the extended Petrine kerygma in Acts (especially Peter's instruction to Cornelius, Acts 10:34-43) can yield this overall **place framework** for Mark's Gospel; (overall time-sequence seems implied):

1. John and Jesus: baptism in the Jordan
2. Jesus' ministry in Galilee
3. Jesus' journey to Judea & ministry there
4. Jesus' death and resurrection: Jerusalem

These four points, culled from Luke's account of Peter's oral kerygma to the Jews (Acts 2,3,4,5) and especially to the Gentiles (Acts 10) supplied a **framework** within which Mark could place the parables, miracles and controversies of Jesus' public ministry. One readily finds the four points in Mark's Gospel, thus:

1. Mk 1:9 = John and Jesus: baptism in the Jordan
2. Mk 1:14-8:30 = Jesus' Galilean ministry
3. Mk 10:1-13 = On to Judea & ministry there,
4. Mk 14-16 = Jesus' death and resurrection (Jerusalem)

Although these points frame Mark's account and suggest its main content, they fail to convey the urgency and dramatic thrust of his Gospel. Peter and the other Apostles proclaimed the "Good News" **orally** as the Risen Christ had commanded them. Surely, notes or memory-aids were written down by the Apostles or others. Should a whole account be written? Roman Christians said: **"yes!"** Was Peter still chained in Rome's prison? Or was he already martyred by 67? The suffering Christians pressured **Mark** (Peter's interpreter) to write the Gospel.

Why write it? To whom? Mark's account keeps moving; it has an urgency about it. It looks conflict and suffering right in the eye; it doesn't blink. Mark's "encouragement is addressed **to Christians** who are themselves

---

10. 1 Cor 15: 4-6, Jesus "...rose on the third day; that he was seen by Cephas [= Peter], then by the Twelve. After that he was seen by 500 brothers at once..."

suffering."[11] Among the Roman addressees are **many non-Jews** for whom Jewish customs need a parenthetical explanation. Their serious suffering and even death seem to be described in Mark's chapter 13. It advises implicitly: face it! Don't flinch! Dont run away! Jesus didn't. Follow Christ; his way leads to Divine Glory. Mark reworked (redacted = the technical word) the traditional data; his overall plan appears thus:

1:1 Topic sentence **Content** of the Scroll[12]

I   1:2-1:13   Prologue
II   1:14-8:27   Who is this Jesus???
III   8:28-16:8   The mystery goes deeper:
                   What kind of a Messiah is He???
IV   16:9-20 The Markan ending?[13]

The shadow of the cross seems to hover over Mark's **Portrait of Jesus.** One scholar sees the "manifestation of the suffering Son of God" as the central theme running through the account.[14] With **Rome** as the site in which this Gospel was written, and the time **between** Peter's imprisonment or death **(67)** and the destruction of Jerusalem **(70)** as its date, then the focus on the courageous Suffering of Jesus would carry great conviction for the Roman Christians suffering the violence of Nero's butchery.

Nero's persecution martyred the great Christian leaders, Peter and Paul. It entrapped gentile-Christians as well as Jewish-Christians. Undoubtedly some quit Christ rather than lose their lives. All Christians needed powerful encouragement. Was Peter already crucified? Paul beheaded? If these terrifying events were past, then the needs of the suffering Christians of Rome would have given Mark a **powerful motive** to put Peter's teaching into writing. His theme, his selection of conflicts, and his development through the transcendent reality of **resurrection to eternal glory** fills a gnawing need. To meet this need, Mark wrote his stark account. The Gospel, written in commonplace **(koine)** Greek and formerly thought of as unsophisticated, is only recently recognized as having a structure carefully designed to emphasize it **meaning.**

---

11. R. Brown, The Church The Apostles Left Behind, (New York: Paulist Press, 1984), p.28; (hereafter: Church/Apostles Left).
12. David E. Aune,The New Testament in Its Literary Environment, Philadelphia: The Westminster Press, [paperback ed.] 1989), p.17; "Ancient literary parallels indicate that Mark 1:1 is not a book title ('beginning' means the point at which the narrative starts)."
13. Cf. Fitzmyer, Luke p.1536.
14. W. Harrington, Explaining the Gospels, (N.J. Paulist Press, 1963) p. 86.

A **summary** of introductory data seems to indicate that the second Gospel was written in Rome by John Mark, the interpreter of Peter. Mark wrote or dictated his Gospel account in koine Greek for Greek-speaking Roman Christians of mostly non-Jewish background to support and encourage them in severe trials suffered for being Christians.[15] Mark's focus on the misunderstanding and suffering of Jesus seems to have its greatest force if read by Christians who are undergoing or had recently undergone persecution themselves. The Gospel's date appears to be after the start of Nero's persecution of the Christians in Rome and before the destruction of Jerusalem in the year 70. However, some scholars have recently leaned toward an immediate post-70 date with the suggestion that Mark's eschatological discourse (13) implies a confirmation of some historical data.

Structures in Mark's Gospel

Mark uses introductory summaries, inclusions and triads, (i.e. series composed of three units or items) to structure his Gospel significantly.[16] These elements are clearly noticeable within the major section of the Gospel identified with Galilee (1:14-8:30). This Galilean ministry section is composed of a **triad** of sub-units, each of which is introduced by a **summary** (1:14-15; 3:7-12; 6:6b). Not all of the introductory summaries are equally extensive, but they are there. In each of the three units, labeled [A],[B] and [C], the summary is followed by Jesus' action concerning his disciples whom he will later commission and **send out** [= apo + stello (apostle)] to proclaim the Gospel to the world. Jesus' action with his future **Apostles** is itself a significant development: initially he **chooses** his first disciples, then he **institutes** them as **the twelve,** finally he **missions** them out to the surrounding towns in what looks much like a small-scale missionary enterprise still under his watchful eye.

---

15. David E. Aune, The New Testament in Its Literary Environment, Philadelphia: The Westminster Press, [paperback ed.] 1989), p.25; Aune identifies the "primary function" of Mark's Gospel as "the **historical legitimation** of the saving significance of Jesus".
16. Ellis, Patterns, p.94.

Mark follows each of the three statements about the chosen disciples with a narrative complex which appears to be in the form of a literary picture having two parallel panels; such a two-panel literary picture is called a diptych. If the picture has three panels it is termed a triptych. These and the ongoing designs of Mark's Gospel are much easier to discern in the composite outline which follows.[17]

---

17. Peter Ellis,"Patterns and Structures of Mark's Gospel" Biblical Studies in Contemporary Thought, (Burlington,Vermont:Greeno, Hadden & Company, Ltd), pp.88-103; this outline was designed for teaching purposes; it owes elements to the works of W. Harrington and the Jerome Biblical Commentary.

Structural Outline
1:1 Gospel synopsis; (some call it a title)
1:2-13 Prologue: a)Baptist; b)Jesus baptized; c)Temptations.

[A] 1:14-15 Summary of Jesus' activity
  1:16-20 "Apostles" chosen: first four
  1:21-3:6 Narrative complex:

Cure (CCSS)	Descent through roof
" Peter's m-in-law	Eating at Levi's
Cures & exorcisms	Fasting question
Teaching & praying	Grain on the Sabbath
Leper cured	Hand healed (CCSS)

[B] 3:7-12 Summary
  3:13-19 Institutes "The Twelve"
  3:20-6:6 Narrative Complex

[Rejection]	Sower & Seed	(Storm at sea)
Family:Crazy?	Lamp	Geresene man
Scribes:Beelzebul!	Measure	Jairus' Daughter
Who is family?	Seed & Weeds	Hemorrhagic Woman
	Mustard Seed	[Rejection in Nazareth]

[C] 6:6b Summary
  6:7-13 Apostles missioned
  6:14-8:27 Narrative complex (diptych):
  H.Antipas:**Who is he?** [flashback:Death of Baptist]

Feeds 5000	Feeds 4000
Crosses sea(Gentiles)	Crosses sea (Gentile territory)
Conflict:defilement	Confrontation: Demand a sign!
Tyre & Sidon	Warning contra Pharisee leaven
Deaf & dumb man	Cure of Blind man (Bethsaida)

Jesus: Who do YOU say that I am?

[A] 8:31ff	[B] 9:30ff
1st Prediction of the PD&R	2nd Prediction of the PD&R
Obtuseness of disciples	Obtuseness of Disciples
Discipleship/Insight	Discipleship/Insight

  [C] 10:32ff 3rd Prediction/Obtuseness/Discipleship

[A] 11:1 Summary;11:2-6 Apostles;to 13:37 Narrative complex

Judgment in act	in word	Apocalyptic
Triumphal entry	Vineyard tenants	On
tree:barren	Image of Caesar	Jerusalem &
Temple clearing	Resurrection?	Temple
tree:dead	Great Commandment	Judgment: it will
Authority?	Origin of Messiah	be destroyed

[B] 14:1-2 Summary

Burial prep.	Judas/Apostles/Passover	Pilate
Anointing	My Body/My Blood = Sacrifice	Thorns
at Bethany	Foretells:betrayal & denial	Via Crucis
	Agony/arrest/Peter's denial	Crucifixion
	Trial:**Are you Messiah & Son???**	Death
	Yes//	Burial

[C] 16:1-8 The tomb. He is **risen**. The empty tomb

16:8-20 Longer Ending: Magdalen; the Two; the Eleven.

-68-

Following his triple focus on the future Apostles, Mark in each instance presents a **narrative complex** composed of a literary frame with two panels (diptych) or in the [B] section, possibly three panels (triptych). The panels themselves appear to be designed as parallel structures. The end of the last panel in each section parallels in some noticable way the beginning of the first panel of that section. This literary device is known as **inclusion**. We today would probably call it "sandwiching" because the meaty-content of the two or three panels is sandwiched in between the two inclusion verses as if they were slices of bread.

Identifying **chapter numbers** were written into the whole bible by teacher Stephen (later Cardinal) Langton who died in 1228. **Verse numbers** were placed in the books by a printer, Robert Stephen, who in 1555 introduced the verse numbering into the Latin text of both the Old and New Testaments.[18] Mark and other scroll composers identified the ends of their composition elements by means of **inclusions.**

The inclusion enclosing the first narrative complex is the event of a "Cure in Capernaum in the Synagogue on the Sabbath" [CCSS] (1:21-28); this same sequence terminates the second panel [CCSS].

The second narrative complex starts with the **rejection** of Jesus by his own familial tribe at Capernaum and ends with the **rejection** of Jesus in his own family hometown of Nazareth.

Considerations of structure, as such, may be concluded with the view of the third narrative complex. Mark starts this section with Herod's question concerning Jesus: **Who is he?** To which his advisors respond: John the Baptist, Elijah or one of the Prophets. It ends with the climax to this section and to the whole first part of the book by Jesus asking: **Who do men say that I AM?** to which his disciples reply: John the Baptist, Elijah, or one of the Prophets. After which Jesus asks the crucial question: **Who do YOU say that I AM?** Peter answers for the chosen disciples then, and for all Mark's anxious, suffering Christians in Rome, with a formal affirmation of faith: **You are the Messiah!** W. Harrington, in his book entitled, Mark declares

...It is evident that among all the occurrences of the title, [Messiah], 8:29 stands in high relief. Here Jesus is **formally**

---

18.   William G. Heidt, Inspiration, Canonicity, Texts, Versions, Hermeneutics, (Collegeville, Minnesota: The Liturgical Press, 1970, O-N.T.R.G. # 31) p.40.

acknowledged as the Messiah of Jewish expectation and as the Christ of Christian worship because the narrative is concerned with **Christology.**[19]

Messiah-models Immediately, the entire tone of the Gospel changes and Mark moves into the **triple** prediction (a major triad) of Jesus' foreseen passion, death and resurrection. Jesus must strip his disciples' concepts of "Messiah" and "God's Kingdom" of all political connotations or even suggestions. Mark is zeroing in on "who Jesus is" and "what kind of a Messiah or Christ is he" (= Christology). In Mark's conviction Jesus is the Messiah (THE CHRIST) and much more than that. He is showing the suffering Roman Christians the struggle of the Apostles to reach this conviction and the further struggle the Apostles had yet to undergo to grasp the full reality of Jesus' person which transcends all the prophecies of the Old Testament.

Jesus was **not** a military, political messiah **like David**; his messiahship even went **beyond** the unifying leadership of **Moses** their most extraordinary leader. These leaders constituted **models** of what the messiah might be like. Jesus' messiahship was totally religious; its model was deliniated in **2nd Isaiah** (= chapters 40-55),[20] formulated in the exilic suffering of the Babylonian captivity (587 to 538 B.C.). Before his uncomprehending disciples, to whom he had clearly but privately confided his **startling intent**, Jesus was fulfilling the will of his Father,[21] depicted by Isaiah as the **"suffering servant of Yahweh."** The disciples eagerly looked for a triumphant Davidic-model messiah. Jesus had to change their mind-set glued to the Davidic model to focus on the suffering **Isaian-model messiah.** The disciples were reluctant (then and still) to make the change.

Christology in Mark For his mainly gentile-Christian readers Mark had (1:1) identified Jesus as **Christ** and **Son of God.** At Caesarea-Philippi, about nine months before Jesus' passion and death, Jesus' future Apostles had at last expressed the conviction that he actually was the long-awaited Messiah (= Christos in Greek). But a bigger step still awaited their struggling understanding.

---

19. W. Harrington, Mark, (Wilmington: Michael Glazier, Inc., 1979), p.120.
20. See Appendix: Isaiah 52:13 to 53:12.
21. Donald Senior,"Crucible of Truth: Passion and Resurrection in the Gospel of Mark", Chicago Studies, v 25, 1, April 1986, pp.21-34.

Step by step through his account Mark reminds the anxious Christians of the Apostles' gropeing to understand Jesus' predicted death and hard-to-comprehend rising afterward. Recalling that Mark is writing from **full Christian belief**[22] of about the year 69, one must recognize that the title <u>Son of God</u> on Jewish lips in the years 28 to 30 **before** Jesus' **Resurrection and Pentecost** was entirely lacking, but open to, the divine meaning it carried **after** those crucial divine events.

Crescendo on Christology

Mark proclaims "the **theological meaning** given to it in Christian faith."[23] The formal aspect of the assertions seems to increase, like a crescendo in music, as the Gospel advances. In 1:11 he notes the Father's identification of Jesus: "This is my beloved son." In 2:1-6 Mark shows the Jewish leaders manifesting indignation when Jesus "forgives sins" which only God can do; their anger turns to calculating determination when Jesus claims "power over the Sabbath"(2:28) which God alone possesses. Mark allows the hesitant Romans Christians (and us) the privilege of viewing Jesus' awe-inspiring transfiguration (9:7), [with Moses (= **the Law**) and Elijah (= **the Prophets**) witnessing to Jesus' person and path], for his specially chosen three disciples. Faithful hearers and followers of **Moses and Elijah** throughout their Jewish lives, Peter James and John are now instructed, **"This is my beloved Son. Listen to him."**

The climax proclamation for Mark occurs in the hearing before the Sanhedrin led by the high priest. This Sanhedrin was the highest judgmental body on earth for Jews. Jesus did not reply to false charges. Jesus' silence under trial served to magnify the moment of speech. Finally, the high priest, with the right to question, demanded: "Are you the **Messiah**, the **Son of the Blessed One**? To this, in Mark, Jesus answered **I AM;...**" (14:61f).

Mark terminates his highlighting of the "Son of God" motif by noting the very same title for Jesus from the mind of a **gentile**, a goy, the centurian who was the agent of Jesus' death. Thus,

---

22. Mark does not give witness of the incarnation with an "infancy account" as Mt and Lk do; nor does he contemplate the Son's eternal preexistence with the Father as John does, but Mark clearly proclaims Jesus' divine reality which utterly transcends human capability.

23. Xavier Leon-Dufour, <u>The Gospels and the Jesus of History</u>, tr J. McHugh, (New York: Desclee Company, 1968), p. 134; (hereafter cited as Leon-Dufour, <u>Gospels</u>, & page.)

however briefly, Mark is picturing the belief in Jesus Christ, Son of God which started in Judaism, is now opening to the gentile world. Mark is not looking at history to be an historian, rather he is looking at it to tell the **theological meaning** of it. As noted scholar, Xavier Leon-Dufour, says "...the purpose of Mark's Gospel [is] to reveal...that Jesus was the Son of God."[24] Although much remains to be considered here, a brief introduction must move on.

Messianic Secret The expression "messianic secret" is used to focus the presence in Mark's Gospel of **instructions** by Jesus **to remain silent** about his miraculous acts. Mark 1:44 quotes Jesus as telling a leper whom he has cured, "not a word to anyone, now, go off and present yourself to the priest and offer for your cure what Moses prescribed." Disregarding this instruction, the man went off and publicly broadcasted it. Mark continues:

> "as a result of this, it was no longer possible for Jesus to enter a town openly. He stayed in desert places; yet people kept coming to him from all sides."

Untimely publicity about this miracle led people to seek Jesus not for instruction about **the Reign of God** he came to establish firmly, but rather for relief of individual pains and aches. More publicity of this kind could prevent him from accomplishing what he came to do! Such broadcasting had to be put into context or quieted. After the miracle of the **daughter of Jairus,** Mark shows Jesus enjoining "them strictly not to let anyone know about it,..."(5:43).

On the other hand, after going into non-Jewish Geresene country and healing the demonic man, who then wanted to remain with his healer, Jesus instructs him: "Go home to your family and **make it clear** to them how much the Lord in his mercy has done for you." (5:19). Yet again, after his transfiguration, Mark says Jesus "strictly enjoined them **not to tell** anyone what they had seen, **before** the Son of Man has risen from the dead", (9:9). It appears that Mark has cited the command of secrecy <u>at times</u> when it was not able to be kept. At other times, he put a limit on it, or even urged the telling of the source of the amazing act. The secrecy seems to be **confined** to the pre-resurrection period and to the territory under Sanhedrin authority.

We may wonder if Jesus could have openly proclaimed that he was the long-awaited Messiah. He had come to establish the

---

24. Leon-Dufour, Gospels, p.134.

reign of God (1:14f). He had to form the men he was going to commission to carry on the work. He kept striving for internal conviction in his hearers. Would his work have been established for all time if he had openly publicized his status as "The Messiah"?

1) As a result of the broadcasting by the cured leper, the people who heard it apparently swamped Jesus for miracles, for good things for themselves, i.e. for favors instead of attending to the **Reign of God** which Jesus came to establish. 2) Also, he set about fulfilling the function of the Isaian "suffering servant of Yahweh", rather than proclaiming his status. 3) If the people hungered for a military, political **messiah like David** to get the hated Romans off their backs and establish them as the most noble among the nations, then an **Isaian-model messiah** who loved, taught and suffered for them would struggle against waning enthusiasm, especially if the constituted authorities moved against him. A conflict of concepts was clearly present here; Jesus' hearers also faced a conflict of priorities. 4) It appears that Jesus even used the expression "Son of Man" to embed his messianic claims in scriptural terms which responsive hearers were forced to consider and reflect on in the light of their regular Sabbath scripture readings.

Son Of Man   Mark uses this title as Jesus' **self-identification.** Some scholars think that Mark used this title, (which is **bar enash** in Aramaic) in his writing, but that Jesus didn't. However, it is in all the traditions, and when time-&-place separated traditions coming from the same ultimate source all use the same title, one must go back to **Jesus himself** to find the original source of the expression **Son of Man** as a public identification for Jesus. This Hebrew idiom suggested and carried much more significance for the Jewish-Christians than for the Gentile-Christians. Thus, it lapsed into disuse as the "Good News" spread further into Gentile territory. Acts uses it only once (7:55).

Mark uses the title **14 times**: 2 times before Peter's confession in 8:29, and 12 times after this. The two early times (2:10; 2:28) are within the framework of the five Galilean conflicts. This five-conflict passage is a well-knit literary unit. It seems that it was already a rhetorical unit in the oral-tradition period before Mark incorporated it into his narrative. If this be so[25], then it appears that Mark did not wish to eliminate the self-identifying title, even though he seems to prefer to confine its use to the roles of suffering and glory which Jesus identifies as messianic.

---

25. W. Harrington, Record of Fulfillment, (Chicago:The Priory Press, 1966), p.127, (hereafter, Harrington, Record and page.)

In the post 8:29 section of his writing Mark uses the title 12 times: 9 times in the passages on **suffering**, and the remaining 3 times in the parousia (the Son of Man will come again in power and glory) texts. The Old Testament sources of these passages imply that the messiah is both **an individual person** - and also, very importantly, the **representative** of all the people. He is the one who suffers in the place of his people. His **vicarious suffering** relieves the burden on the backs of his people. This representative suffers silently; but he bears it for others, - willingly.

The **Suffering Servant of Yahweh** passages should be read in the light of Isaiah 52:13-53:12. These passages occur pointedly in Mark's account of the three predictions (8:31, 9:30, 10:33) of the passion, death and resurrection of Christ. In 8:31 Mark writes:

> He began to teach them that the **Son of Man** had to suffer much, be rejected by the elders, the chief priests, and the scribes, be put to death, and rise three days later. **He said these things quite openly.**

The three **Risen-Lord-Coming-in-Glory** passages (8:38, 13:26,14:62) are related to the **End-time** (= eschaton in Greek). Mark quotes Jesus as telling the Sanhedrin, sitting in judgment on him, "You will see the **Son of Man** seated at the right hand of the power and coming with the clouds of heaven." This risen, glorified Son of Man will judge the living and the dead.

In this brief reflection on the "**Son of Man**" use, it appears that Jesus gathered the personal and representative messianic functions announced by the prophets, especially Isaiah's emphasis of vicarious suffering, and used this as **his self-identification.** One exegete acknowledges this as Jesus' self-identification, but thinks that Jesus' use of the "son of man" title goes beyond the Old Testament meanings directly to Jesus' relationship to God the Father.[26]

---

26. W. Harrington, Mark

Forming Apostles It is remarkable to note in our first extant Gospel how much attention is given, mostly in passing, to the **formation of the future apostles.** Of course, in the three large sections of the Gospel's first half, Christ's **choosing** them (1:16-20), **instituting** them as "The Twelve" (3:13-19), and **missioning** them, i.e. instructing them and sending them out on missions to the surrounding towns, (6:7-13) are well-noticed because of Mark's triadic development.

However, there are many other places where Jesus gives them his special attention. In fact, when the instruction they receive is highlighted, it becomes clear that the development of the future apostles is a **serious intentional theme** in Mark's Gospel. This implies that Mark, writing from the hindsight vantage point of forty years, is concerned to show the continuous authoritative influence coming from Christ through the Apostles to his readers.

In 4:10 Jesus explains his parables to **them.** In 4:34 he identifies them as **his own disciples.** In 6:31 Jesus takes them aside **for private instruction.**

In 7:17 distinguishing them from others who hear him, Jesus remarks that **they** are so **slow to understand,** indicating that he wants them to comprehend as much as they can of his teaching. In 7:24 as the pressures of the authorities are mounting against Jesus, and of course against their cooperation with him, Jesus **takes them aside,** -- outside of their own country into neighboring Tyre and Sidon.

In 8:13 Jesus **warns them** of the leaven (i.e. the false teaching) of the Pharisees on certain matters. In 8:27 Jesus **travels with them** away from their usual haunts to bring them to a new high point of their relationship with him. It is at Caesarea Philippi that Jesus tests their conviction with the question: **"Who do you say that I am?"** Peter speaks for the future apostolic group when he affirms: **"You are the Messiah".** Matthew identifies this as a divine revelation.

After this Jesus warns them that there is a serious confrontation ahead; he speaks only to them about his coming passion and death (8:31). Later, he gives confidential answers to their questions (9:28ff). In 9:30 Jesus wishes to remain incognito while teaching them.

As the account moves toward Jerusalem they continue to turn to him for understanding (10:10). Shortly after this he again forewarns them of his passion and death (10:32) but assures them of his resurrection. In 10:42 Jesus instructs them in how to exercise authority.

After Palm Sunday's heady excitement, Jesus takes only them with him. In Mark's apocalyptic account, Jesus answers their questions and prophesies to them about the destruction of Jerusalem and its unique 550 year old Temple to the only God.

With them alone Jesus formally initiates the New Covenant (14:17ff) and changes their most precious Passover meal into the formal act of his own total self-sacrifice. In the accounts of Luke and Paul Jesus **commissions them alone** to do this which he has done for them and with them. He warns them of their defection, denial and desertion.

The study of these elements in Mark's account beget a conviction that a major Markan interest was to show how **Jesus** focused much of his effort on **forming his core community** in the persons **his chosen Apostles**; he would commission Peter and the ten to lead it after his utterly generous and courageous sacrifice and his awe-inspiring resurrection for all. What parent has striven so much to form her child? What teacher has labored so much to form his pupils?

Portrait of Jesus   Mark's portrait of Jesus is rather **stark!**
        Suffering, rejection, lack of understanding are sounded again and again through Mark's account. Jesus is pictured as **the suffering Son of God.** In 2:7 opponents charge Jesus with blasphemy; in 3:6 they plot his death. His own town rejects him as a prophet (6:3-5). His specially selected disciples are slow to understand his parables; they are so slow to move from material things to spiritual meanings; so very slow to reach conviction about his divinely-given work and his own person. After Peter and the eleven acknowledge that **he is** the promised **Messiah,** Jesus tells them of the suffering and death that await him in Jerusalem (8:31ff). Concerning his death and then his forthcoming resurrection - his future apostles were obtuse; they did not understand! Mark says that Jesus said these things quite openly (8:32). He told them again in 9:31 and they didn't understand Isaiah's portrait of the **Suffering Servant of Yahweh.** But they grew fearful. Again, he forewarned them in 10:32f; their incomprehension added to his suffering. At the Last Supper he made the **formal self-offering,** body and blood, simultaneously instituting his followers' eucharistic offering. The agony of Gethsemane was followed by a night hearing which charged his revelation to them (in Mark) with blasphemy. Scourged and mocked as **King of the Jews,** Jesus endured a **stark crucifixion** in repayment for his transcendent claims despite his public life of generous

self-giving. In Nero's persecution Jesus' persecuted followers needed to know that Jesus went through it **before them and for them.** He loved them that much! Pliny's letter showed that Christians could have saved their lives by denying Christ. Those who suffered martyrdom **had to love Jesus more** than they loved their lives on this earth.

Questions

1. What is the **3rd stage** in the genesis of the Gospels; are any of the **autographs** (the original manuscript copies) extant?
2. Name 5 **early Christian writers** who comment on the first century Christian events and writings?

3. **Who** wrote 5 scrolls (books) on the <u>Sayings of the Lord?</u>
4. Which Gospel was **first?** Explain.

5. Name some of the Gospels' **earliest manuscript** codices still in existence. [Cf. footnote 1]
6. **Of what value** for our knowledge of the Gospels are the early Christian writers?

7. In what **order** does **Origen** place the origin of the 4 Gospels?
8. What does **Papias** say about John Mark? In **what ancient text** can this **external evidence** by Papias be found?

9. Where did Mark's Gospel-account originate? Who said so?
10. What **internal evidence** suggests that Mark was written: a)before 70 A.D.; b)prior to the other Gospels?

11. What **data about John Mark** is present in other N.T. books?
12. From whom did Mark get information about Jesus? Evidence?

13. Which **Petrine speech** mentions Jesus' 1)contact the Baptist, 2)Jesus' ministry in Galilee, 3)in Judea, & 4)in Jerusalem?
14. What is the **4-point place framework** of Mark's Gospel? Name a likely **source** of Mark's framework.

15. Mark's readers, apparently suffering persecution, urgently needed encouragement. **Where** were Christians suffering such persecutions? **When? Under whom? Why** write a Gospel? Is it **for** Jewish-Christians or Gentile-Christians?
16. In terms of **content** (not place) what is the brief, overall **outline** of Mark's Gospel? Which are the two major parts? What **question** does each major part answer?

17. What **literary devices** (like repetition of sequences) can you find in the structural outline of Mark's Gospel?
18. Who numbered the **chapters** and **verses** of Mark's Gospel?

19. What is a literary **inclusion**? Can you find three inclusions in the fuller outline of Mark's Gospel?
20. What is the line which corresponds as an inclusion with the line of Herod Antipas: **Who is He?!?!**

21. What is **Christology**?
22. What is the **thought-content** of Peter's confession of faith at Caesarea-Philippi? (Extraordinary man? Messiah? Son of God?)

23. Is Peter's idea or **model of Messiah**: a)Davidic; b)Isaian?
24. What is Mark himself affirming **here**? What in 1:1? To Mark is Jesus only the Jewish Messiah or is he more than this?

25. What are the **steps** in understanding of "who Jesus is" by which Jesus' disciples (later to be Apostles) grew?
26. **What** must be **subtracted** from the disciples' idea of the Messiah **before** they can proclaim him? **What** must be **added**?

27. Give 4 places where Mark implies **Jesus' transcendence**? Which is the formal **highpoint**? Who on Calvary identifies Jesus?
28. What is the **messianic secret**? Was everyone told to keep it?

29. What in Mark does Jesus set out to do in his public ministry? Does premature **broadcasting** of his miracles help to establish "the Kingdom of God"? [cf.Mk 1:45]
30. What **reasons** urge a restraint of publicity concerning his messiahship? Is the **secrecy motif** equally distributed in Mark?

31. How many times does the title, **Son of Man**, occur in Mark? Before 8:27; after 8:27? Related to: **suffering**? **glory**?
32. What is **vicarious suffering**? What O.T. **source** provided this model of the **suffering "Servant of Yahweh"**?

33. What O.T.**source** provided Mark with a descriptive image of Jesus' 2nd coming in power and glory?
34. What **portrait of Jesus** emerges from Mark's Gospel?

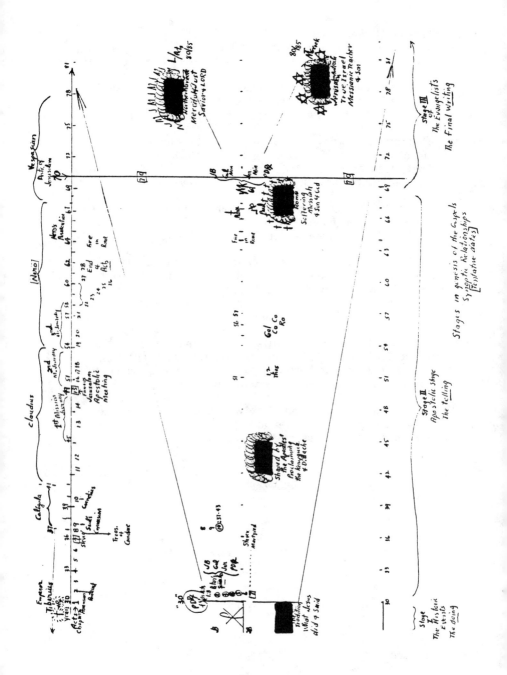

Stages in genesis of the Gospels
Synoptic Relationships [Tentative dates]

-80-

Chapter VII: Synoptic Relationships

It appears clear that the **three stages** in the genesis or production of the written Gospels were: **first,** the actual, historical words and deeds of Jesus, especially those during his public ministry; **second,** the Apostolic, mostly-oral stage during which the commissioned Apostles and their helpers proclaimed Jesus' words and deeds, especially the Resurrection to everyone who would listen; **third,** the writing stage in which certain members of Christ's new community were inspired to put into writing much of the "Good News" (= Gospel) which the Apostles were proclaiming.

The re-discovery of these **production stages,** which, of course, were known by all Christians in the first century, took place in the last half of the nineteenth century especially in German universities.

Over the centuries, claims and denials concerning the Bible's miracles and other contents have led scholars ever more deeply into the analysis of the sources of each book's contents, the relationships between the writings, and other such questions. A German scholar, **Hermann Gunkel** critically studied **Genesis** from the point of view of **literary analysis** and very sucessfully distinguished and separated whole passages or **strands** marked by different characteristics (words, phrasing, concepts, contexts, etc.) which had been woven together by the inspired author to produce the text we have. The words and concepts in these passages revealed something about the history of the group in Israel from which the different strands had originated. Similiar **literary analysis** was applied to the Psalms and about the 1890's to the New Testament.

Up to about 1915, New Testament scholars, doing literary analysis **only from the Gospel texts,** had concluded that **Luke,** taking advantage of the fact that "many had undertaken to compile a narrative of the events" before him, **had used** about 366 verses of **Mark's Gospel** to write his own account. Further, there were about 601 verses common to Mark and Matthew. They **assumed** that Matthew had gotten them from Mark. Thus, putting Mark first, they constructed this picture:

Mk
Lk   Mt

Next, they noted about **235 verses** common to Luke and Matthew, which Mark did not have. Since they could not have come from Mark, and some scholars judged that neither Luke nor Matthew had ever seen each other's work, the German analysts concluded that the 235 verses came from another source. The German word for source is **Quelle**, so it became known in English as **Q** or redundantly as **the Q Source**. The analysts then constructed the following diagram:

Q   Mk
Lk   Mt

This set of **synoptic literary relationships** is known as the **Two Source Theory**, i.e. that the two sources needed to explain the production of Mt and Lk are Mark's Gospel and Q. This analysis is only a theory, but it is rather widely held and it is a very useful tool for analyzing possible literary relationship among the Synoptic Gospels and for highlighting the remaining data as proper to, or special to, each author. If it is a valid insight, rather than merely a theory (and some scholars treat it almost as a fact) then Matthew's and Luke's adaptation or **redaction** of the Mark and Q material tells the attentive reader something about the thinking and theology of each Gospel. [The **primary target of biblical interpretation** is to determine the sense intended by the sacred author.] Most scholars think that this "two source theory" by itself is inadequate and needs many refinements. Others reject it totally and construct a theory based on Matthew's primacy. After some years of comparing the texts of the Gospels, scholars felt that this comparative literary analysis of the synoptic texts seemed to have arrived at a dead end. A new analytic path was sought.

During World War I two German scholars, **Rudolph Bultmann** and **Martin Dibelius** (B&D), working independently **tried to imagine** how a little episode or parable, (called a "**Form**" in German) would be heard and talked about among the Jewish people. In a word, they tried to imagine the history (**Geschichte** in German) of each little episode or parable from its origin to its place in one of the Gospels, say Mark's (since B & D thought it was first). Hence their method of analysis was called the **Formgeschichte** method. In England it was called the **Method of Form Criticism**, possibly because the method was clearly more suited for literary analysis than for determining **what actually happened**, i.e. for historical analysis.

Dibelius, in his 1919 book, started off from the a priori position that the narratives in the Gospels had been spoken[1] before they were written down by the evangelists. In other words, an oral stage had preceded the writing stage in the production of the Gospels. This is true! But overemphasis on oral stage (the proclaiming) tended to neglect the actual historical stage that gave rise to and empowered the oral stage.

In his 1921 book, **Bultmann**, whose work was more influential than that of Dibelius, started from the a posteriori position by isolating every episode, parable or saying and putting the isolated forms into classifications or groupings. The classifying work turned out to be moderately useful. However, because undue skepticism[2] was incorporated into the work, the method turned out to be a **mixed bag**, like a bag of jelly beans in which some good jelly beans were mixed with some brightly painted pebbles, i.e. the "Form Critics" arrived at some indefensible positions (B more than D) but also uncovered some good new insights. Unfortunately, some of the form critics failed to distinguish skepticism or even non-belief from their work of literary and imaginative analysis. A very brief sketch of starting questions and evaluation follows. The starting-point questions may be worded in this way: Were the evangelists true **authors**? Are the Gospels **biographies**? Did the **community** produce the Gospels?

B & D, in an overall way, answered the questions thus:
Authors?   1. Evangelists = collectors, not authors.
Biographies? 2. The Gospels are not biographies.
Community?   3. Communities produced the Gospels.

---

1. Dibelius' principle was: Am Anfang war die Predigt! (In the beginning was the preaching; Dibelius' text actually reads: "At the beginning of all early Christian creativity there stands the sermon . . ." cf. N. Perrin, What is Redaction Criticism, p. 15, footnote 19.
2. Gunther Bornkamm, Jesus of Nazareth, tr I. and F. McLuskey with J.M. Robinson, (New York: Harper & Row, 1960), p. 10. To those who suggest that the Gospels yield practically no history about Jesus, Bornkamm (a student of Bultmann) says: "I cannot myself share this extreme skepticism, . . ."

The starting-point answers must be distinguished. As is often the case with necessary pioneering work, the initial answers contain some valuable insights and implications and some invalid and unacceptable implications. Bultmann introduced a greater degree of skepticism into his assumptions than Dibelius.

On #1: it is true that any author must **collect** his material before he writes his book. But he must also put his material in some kind of a rational **order**. His own integrity and reputation depends on the **known** integrity of his sources (cf.Luke 1:1-4). He must **emphasize** what he judges to be very important. He must **select** what fulfills his purpose among the data available to him. If you do these things in writing a life of Lincoln, and you must do all of them and more, you will be identified as the author of a new Life of Lincoln. Most exegetes have on these bases rejected the first starting point above. Recall that Papias said of Mark that he was Peter's interpreter and that he wrote accurately. Interestingly, some exegetes are today writing commentaries about single gospel accounts and viewing Mark and Luke **as authors** and the disciples who finished Matthew and John as authors and/or final editors.

On #2: Most scholars have distinguished this second point. It is true that the Gospels are **not biographies in the modern sense.** They are not strict time/place narratives from birth to death. If you now write your own biography, you will probably start with the day, month and year of your birth, your parents' names, your place of birth, the address you lived at, the schools you went to, etc. On the other hand, if you are asked to write about the most frightening (or worst, or best etc.) thing or episode that ever happened to you, you may write a couple of paragraphs about it and never mention a date, or an address, or a city, etc. This latter narrative is not **a biography**, but it is **biographical**, and nobody denies this. Thus the Gospels are a relatively ordered sequence of **biographical episodes**, while not being biographies in the modern sense.

It must be realized that writing biography with internal coherence and psychological growth of the person is a modern development; to require this of a first century writer is an anachronism. Too many scholars apply modern criteria in judgeing ancient biography and history. David Aune, in his recent book, The New Testament in Its Literary Environment, which analyzes the Gospels as to the generic features of their form, content and function, says,

An analysis of the constituent literary features of the Gospels situates them comfortably within the parameters of ancient biographical conventions in form and function.[3]

Noting that Mark [as other ancient authors] has his own time framework and vagueness in the time-links of his episodes, David Aune affirms, "Formally the Gospels are indistinguishable from Greco-Roman biographies."[4]

Reflect on how many biographical episodes, or how much of a biography, you may be able to compose of one of your deceased grandparents, say the one whose name you bear. Such a reflection helps us to see in perspective how much, in fact, we know about Christ. There are very few first-century people about whom we know more episodes and more details. Regarding the episodes it must be added that the evangelists are **primarily interested** in the **meaning** of the episodes, not their precise time/place historical circumstances. Yet, David Aune defends the position that "the Gospels are a subtype of Greco-Roman biography, [which] assumes that the Evangelists wrote with historical intentions."[5] Although the ancient way of writing history is not the modern way, nevertheless the overall time/place framework of the Gospels is generally, but seldom in a detailed way, historical. Luke is clearly more historically explicit and is interested in locating Jesus' overall public ministry within the framework of world history.

On #3: Exegetes again distinguish in answering the question of the community's influence on the Gospels. The receiving community to whose needs the writing is addressed, does not produce the Gospel. No one would claim that the audience of the St. John's theater produced last year's play. Such a claim would be considered absurd! At the same time if the audience did not enjoy or respond to the play, it would not be used again by this university theatre group. The author would still be the author, but the response and interest of the local community kept it alive. Thus in some analogous way the Christian community **did have some influence** in the production of the Gospels. But the Gospel

---

3. David E. Aune, The New Testament in Its Literary Environment, (Philadelphia: The Westminster Press, 1989) p. 46. [Hereafter, Aune, N.T. . . . Environment, and page.]
4.   Aune, N.T. . . . Environment, p. 47.
5.   Aune, N.T. . . . Environment, p. 64.

content is much more important because eternal salvation of both writer and hearer is critically related to its truth.

It seems easiest to see this **influence point** in the Gospels of Matthew and Luke. The community **Matthew** addressed was clearly Jewish, thus he chose Jewish customs, prophecies and data from the Mosaic Torah to present Jesus as the fulfillment of their sacred history and more. **Luke**, on the other hand, emphasized those elements about Jesus which would most help Theophilus (and other Gentiles) to understand who Jesus was and is, and what he wants of his followers. The message has to be proportionate to the understanding of the receiver, or it is liable to be no message at all.

Deficiencies The problems embedded in some presentations of form criticism come rather from positions adopted by the individual critic, rather than from the method itself or the scriptural data being studied.[6] These were the "painted pebbles" of the jelly bean analogy. For example, some form critics have started by denying that anything **supernatural**, such as a miracle, is possible. Of course, once a commentator adopts this position, then he has ahead of time negated the New Testament proclamation of Christ's miracles **before** carefully evaluating its data. Such a position **classifies the Gospels falsely as if** they were legal briefs **forced to prove** in court what they set out only to narrate. The Gospels are written by believing Christians to believing Christians for the sake of encourageing their common Christian belief. They were not written to prove something to hostile or skeptical pagans; yet even a skeptic must wonder at the multiple witnessing in such separated places of the phenomenon of Jesus' Resurrection! The position which denies divine causality cannot adequately explain why Christianity spread so rapidly, so widely and so perseveringly against such powerful persecuting forces.

The **nature of faith** was also misunderstood. Some Christians make faith so vague that they think it can exist without any relation to the flesh and blood, real, matter-of-fact Jesus of Nazareth and his terribly real passion, death and resurrection. Christian faith is based on the reality of who he is and what he

---

6. cf. PBC's Instruction on the Historicity of the Gospels, April 21, 1964

did. Jesus' question: **"Who do YOU say that I am?"** is addressed to every Christian as well as to Peter and the original disciples.

Further, An **a priori** denial of properly qualified historicity can vitiate the form critical method. The New Testament contains history, poetry, hymns, teaching, polemics etc.; each item must be examined in its own right. Prior denial of all historicity without examination simply frustrates any method. Finally, as noted, some form critics **gave too much authorship power to the community**; limited influence, yes; Gospel composition, no.

Bultmann and Dibelius separated considerably in their conclusions. Dibelius was far less skeptical than Bultmann. "The general outline of the passion story is viewed by Dibelius as trustworthy." Further, Dibelius is "confident of the trustworthiness of the sayings."[7] Without a doubt the debate started by Bultmann and Dibelius totally undercut the position of "Fundamentalism" and introduced decades of argumentation and fruitful research concerning the background, settings and meanings of the Gospel texts. Fruitful insights were gained. When careful understanding of the Gospel text prevails,

> the person and work of Jesus, in their unmistakable uniqueness and distinctiveness, are shown forth with an originality which again and again far exceeds and disarms even all believing understandings and interpretations. Understood in this way, the **primitive tradition of Jesus is brim full of history.**[8]

Good Insights   The form critics uncovered sequences of material in the synoptics which appear to have been orally formulated in a rhetorical or literary form **before** they were included in the final Gospel. The Galilean conflicts appear to be this kind of a unity, i.e. a pre-existing **oral unit** before inclusion

---

7. Edgar V. McKnight, What is Form Criticism, (Philadelphia: Fortress Press, 1969) p.34. On pages 35-37 McKnight indicates the pervasive skepticism which infected Bultmann's exegesis, although, assuredly, Bultmann "does not doubt that Jesus lived and did many of the **kinds of works** attributed to him in the tradition." (p.36)
8. Gunther Bornkamm, Jesus of Nazareth, tr I. and F. McLuskey with J.M. Robinson, (New York: Harper & Row, 1960), p. 26; the highlighting is mine.

in Mark's Gospel. The collection of the seed-parables appears to be another example. The **Evangelists** were more free in their composition of the Gospel in its final form than was formerly realized. The **Apostles** did influentially shape the message orally during the years before the evangelists put it in writing. The risen Christ had commanded them to proclaim the Gospel, he had not told them to write it. The light of the **Resurrection** and Pentecost pervades all the Gospel accounts. Finally, the **needs** of the communities addressed did influence the data which the evangelists chose to select and emphasize.

Redaction Criticism   Form criticism had focused its attention mainly on the oral stage (2nd Stage) in the transmission of the original traditional material of what Jesus did and said. Its indefensible positions led scholars to a closer examination of the writing stage (3rd stage), i.e. how Luke and Matthew in their presentation of the Gospel account used their **assumed sources: Mark, Q and tradition.** Did they modify them, edit them, rework them? The Latin-root word for rework = **redact.** One of Bultmann's students, **Gunther Bornkamm,** who receded from the undue skepticism in his professors's analysis, discovered that Matthew had somewhat modified Mark's account of the "Storm at sea" episode to emphasize the note of discipleship in the story more than Mark did.[9] Briefly, Bornkamm thought that the later Matthew (c.85 A.D.) had reworked the often-before heard Mark's (c.69 A.D.) account to highlight the theme of **faithful discipleship** in his narrative. The narrative is essentially the same, but Mark keeps his focus on Jesus and tends to downplay the disciples, whereas Matthew tends to note their continuing fidelity; he interprets the episode to highlight discipleship.[10] Matthew's account seems to be set in the **liturgical reliving** of an experience which the Apostles later came to understand more deeply, namely the expression, **"Lord, save us!"** of the event; Mark's focus seems to be the blunt retelling of Jesus' awesome power over nature **to strengthen** the faith of his suffering hearers/readers.

Another German exegete, Willi Marxen, named the foregoing work Redaktionsgeschichte (= redaction history). In England and the USA it is called **Redaction Criticism.** This method of analysis

---

9. Bornkamm, Jesus of Nazareth, p. 151.
10. Norman Perrin, What is Redaction Criticism, (Philadelphia: Fortress Press, 1969) p. 26-27.

assumes that Lk and Mt are dependent on **Mark and the already assumed Q.** It examines every word and line to see how, and if possible why, the evangelists redacted (re-worked, edited) their sources. The method seeks to discover: any slight shift of emphasis; any clue as to a community problem being addressed; and any insight into the theological perspective of the inspired author.[11] **Use implies approval.** Thus, Mt's and Lk's use of material from Mark implies their approval of that data and the decision that the material taken is also useful for the different insight each author has in mind. A new insight can mean a theological advance.

Q = a working hypothesis   Although the **Q** document does not exist as far as anybody knows, it is a useful working tool which encourages exegetes to examine every word and line of the synoptics and other books of the Sacred Scripture as well to uncover hitherto unnoticed connections. Many scholars work with it. Daniel Harrington, in his Interpreting the New Testament, points out the significance of **Q** for most New Testament scholars.

"The vast majority of New Testament scholars today have accepted it as an adequate working hypothesis. Its usefulness has been confirmed by form-critical and redaction-critical studies. Its **validity is assumed** . . . ."[12]

---

11. D.Harrington, Interpreting the New Testament, (Wilmington: Michael Glazier Inc.,1980), p. 98; (hereafter, Harrington, Interpreting, and page.)
12. Harrington,Interpreting.

Questions

1. What leads scholars to probe into the Bible's contents?
2. On what **basis** did H. Gunkel analyze Genesis? **What** did his literary analysis **discover?**

3. By 1915 what had certain German N.T. scholars concluded about the literary relationships of the **Synoptic Gospels?**
4. What led them to the **assumption** symbolized by the letter **Q?**

5. Draw a **diagram** illustrating the synoptic literary-relationships known as the **two source theory.** Explain it in words. **Why** is it called a **theory?**
6. What is the **value** of the two source theory? What is the **primary goal** of scriptural interpretation?

7. **Who,** in analyzing Scripture, developed the **Method of Form Criticism** (heilsgeschichte)? About when? How did this method seek to probe beyond the prior literary-analysis method?
8. What factor of **uncertainty** entered scriptural analysis with this pioneering method?

9. What were the **starting-point questions** which the form-criticism   proponents asked of the the synoptic gospels?
10. Were the Gospel-writers merely collectors of data about Jesus **or** were they **authors?** What actions go into authoring a book? Did the evangelists have to do what an author does?

11. Are the Gospels, in fact, **biographies** of Jesus? Are they **biographical?** How can the difference be shown?
12. Who authors a book: **a person or a community?** If the evangelist is unknown does that make the community from which he came the author of his book?

13. How does the **need** of the community influence the production of a book? **In which Gospels** can the **needs** of the community being addressed be clearly seen?
14. In the method of form criticism, the critic tends to impose his own beliefs &/or non-beliefs into his analysis of texts. The April 21, 1964 Instruction on the Historicity of the Gospels **cautioned** against four **assumed-positions** of some form-critics: what are the four assumptions?

15. Form criticism uncovered some valuable **new insights**; name and briefly describe five of them.

16. On **which stage** in the genesis of the Gospels does form criticism focus its attention? In **what kinds of activities** and settings did the Apostles shape their presentation of the Gospel events?

17. One of Bultmann's students, aware of the skepticism in his teacher's analysis turned his attention back to the writing stage. He realized that in narrating the miracle of the **storm at sea** that Mark and Matthew had focused on **different reactions** in the disciples: **which reaction** did each evangelist emphasize?

18. In what **context** does Mark (chs 4&5 = **Who is He???**) narrate the **storm at sea** episode? Where does Matthew fit it into his overall schema? Mt 5,6,7 = **Messiah in word**; Mt 8&9 = **Messiah in deed**. What point is each evangelist making in telling this episode? What kind of a hearer would be helped by Mark's narrative? By Matthew's?

19. What is the **name** of the study which examines **how** each evangelist presented or re-worked the traditional material which came from Christ's words and deeds? What is its name in German?

20. What does the **redaction-critical method** assume about the literary-dependency relationships of the synoptics?

21. How does Daniel Harrington assess the status of the assumed **Q document**? What has highlighted its usefulness? In general, how do many American scripture scholars regard **Q** ?

22. The 2-document theory works chiefly from the literary analysis of the synoptic texts; **what theory insists** that any theory must account for **all** the historical data?

23. Give the **historical data** that speaks about: a)Mark? b)Matthew? c)Luke?

24. With what data does the **Vaganay theory** start its analysis of the synoptic problem?

25. As a matter of fact for any theory, about how many **verses are common** to: a)Mark & Luke?_____; b)Mark & Matthew?_____; c)Matthew & Luke?_____.

Chapter VIII: The Gospel According to Matthew

In extending his saving gifts to mankind God chose Abraham (c. 1850 B.C.) and especially Moses (c.1250 B.C.) to form a people who, despite surrounding polytheism, would tenaciously preserve the revelation of the one, true, living God in the inspired books of the Mosaic Covenant called the Old Testament. The New Testament books including the Gospels **reflect** in varying degrees the precious heritage of the Jewish sacred books.[1]

Of the four Gospel accounts, the one according to **Matthew** is the most **Jewish**.[2] John Meier, in his study entitled Matthew, judges that the community being addressed was "stringently Jewish in origens".[3] This Gospel uses **Aramaic** words without always bothering to translate them for Gentile (i.e. non-Jewish) readers. It frequently and explicitly quotes **Torah** texts (= the Law, the Prophets & the Writings) to show their fulfillment. The overall structure of its central section (chs 3-25) may have been intended to suggest the **pentateuchal** (five-fold book) form[4] of the Torah (the principal part of the Mosaic law for the Jewish people). It is quite emphatic about the issue of which community (the one that accepts Jesus, not the one which rejects him) is the **true Israel**.[5] These data and others indicate that hearers from a Jewish background would be more at home with Matthew's presentation than Gentiles would.

Before considering the structure and content of the Gospel, however, one needs to answer the questions of **who** wrote this

---

1. Vatican II, Dei Verbum, IV:14
2. John L. McKenzie, Light on the Gospels, (Chicago: The Thomas More Press, 1976), pp.19f, (hereafter quoted as McKenzie, Light, and page.)
3. John Meier, Matthew, (Wilmington: Michael Glazier, Inc., 1980), p. xi.
4. John L. McKenzie, "Matthew" Jerome Biblical Commentary, (New Jersey: Prentice-Hall, 1968), p. 66, "the commonly accepted scheme of five books"; (hereafter quoted as McKenzie, JBC and page). Refer also to John Meier's Table of Contents in his Matthew.
5. Peter Ellis, Matthew: his mind and his message, (Collegeville: The Liturgical Press, 1974), p.3. (hereafter, Ellis, Matthew & page.). On p. 130 Ellis notes that Matthew is the most Jewish of the Gospels.

account, **when, to whom, where,** and even **why** it was written, although this last question can be rather difficult to answer with certainty if the writer has not spelled it out explicitly.

Preliminary questions It may seem strange to ask **who** wrote Matthew's gospel when the name of someone who was known as one of the original twelve apostles is so firmly attached to it. The attachment of Matthew's name to the gospel was already fixed before the time (about 100 A.D.) when it was gathered with the other extant gospels to make a collection of the gospels. The name Matthew ordinarily means the written Gospel itself rather than the person unless the context makes it clear that the writing is in fact about the actual person whom Jesus chose as an apostle, as the following consideration is.

However, many scholars **date** Matthew's Gospel from about the year **85 +/-5**, and, if Matthew himself had been about 30 years old at the time of Christ's resurrection in the year 30, then he would have been about 85 years old when the gospel, written in Greek, whose translation we are reading, came into existence. This, of course, is quite possible, but, if it happened in the time-frame suggested, then some early Christian writers (like Papias, Irenaeus, Clement, etc.) would surely have enjoyed mentioning Matthew's still-being-alive to confirm this Gospel's completion during the lifetime of a primary Apostolic witness.

Further, Matthew would not have used Mark's Gospel as a source (accepted as fact by many scholars) especially about his own personal invitation to follow Christ. But all we can find is the account of **Papias** (in Eusebius) that "**Matthew** compiled the Sayings [of the Lord] in the **Aramaic** language, and everyone translated them as well as he could."[6] Eusebius finds a time reference for Matthew's Gospel from a comment by **Irenaeus** that

"Matthew published a written gospel for the Hebrews in their own tongue, **while** Peter and Paul were preaching the gospel in Rome and founding the church there."[7]

Both Peter and Paul were martyred by the year 67 thus dating Matthew's Greek Gospel to a time which most modern

---

6. HE, p.152.
7. Eusebius, HE, 7.4.8 (text used p. 210.)

scholars estimate as too early, but allowing for a Matthean **Aramaic account** which is no longer extant.

Thought by some to have been sort of a catechism-like text for the Jewish-Christians in Jerusalem, this **Aramaic** text was apparently translated into Greek many times[8] according to Papias, but neither the original nor even one of the translations is any longer extant. The Greek text we do have shows no signs of being a translation, but appears instead to be a text directly written in rather good Greek. The Apostle Matthew, the basic authority for the Gospel's content, was a Jew; some commentators think that the **Scribe** of 13:52 is possibly an auto-biographical remark. The unknown disciple who gave us the finished product was also probably a Jew who believed and followed Jesus, Messiah and Son of God.

This Gospel seems too **pervasively Jewish** to have come from a Gentile convert's mind; yet the Gospel toward its end opens completely to the Gentile world. Consequently, some scholars feel forced to conclude that this extant text was probably freshly rewritten by one of **Matthew's** very capable but **unnamed** Jewish-Christian disciples. The apparent reliance on Mark's text, even for describing Matthew's own call as a disciple, persuades exegetes that a fresh hand rewrote the Gospel,[9] even though **the authority** which supported the account was Matthew's apostolic teaching. Unbroken continuity of the attribution to Matthew from antiquity requires that this Gospel be identified by the name of the Apostle, **Matthew**.

Meier thinks that it was completed just about as it is in the mixed Jewish/Gentile-Christian community of **Antioch**.[10] This Gospel exhibits a greater concern about the founding and the authority of Christ's new community (ekklesia = word used) than Mark does. Questions about the founding and the authority of the **ekklesia** (= Church) do not arise so explicitly in Mark's Gospel.

---

8. Ibid., 10.3.10 (p. 214 of text used) Eusebius cites a certain Pantaenus (c.180) as reaching India and finding that An Apostle who had reached there had left behind "**Matthew's account** in the actual **Aramaic** characters"
9. "Introduction" to the Gospel according to Matthew, New Testament of the New American Bible, revised edition, 1987 pp.6-10.
10. Meier, Matthew, xii.

Matthew's attention to these later-type problems is another indication to scholars that Matthew's Gospel was written **later** than Mark's. Matthew's Gospel probably flourished in and around Antioch during the 90's; **St. Ignatius of Antioch** familiarly quotes Matthew's gospel in the still extant letter he wrote to the Smyrnaeans on his way to martyrdom in Rome **about 110.**[11]

Matthew's "seven woes" (c.23) reveal a very strong opposition to, and condemnation of, the Pharisees and Jewish leadership. Many scholars interpret this to mean that a strongly felt opposition was levelled by the Pharisees against the community in which this Gospel was completed. This opposition may have contributed to the **why** this Gospel was written. About this same time a "prayer against heretics", Birkath ha Minim (minim = heretics) was introduced into the services of the post-war Palestinian synagogues.[12] The prayer, directed against Jews who, while still attending their local synagogue, believed Jesus was the Messiah, read:

> "For persecutors let there be no hope, and the dominion of arrogance do thou speedily root out in our days; and let **Christians and minim** perish in a moment, let them be blotted out of the book of the living and let them not be written with the righteous."[13]

Structure Chapters 1-2, the infancy account, constitute an **introduction** for this gospel. Chapters 26, 27 and 28, containing Christ's passion, death and resurrection, are its **climax.** The Chapters between this beginning and end are divided by sharp inclusion lines at 7:28,11:1,13:53,19:1 and 26:1. The inclusion line,

---

11. Ignatius of Antioch,"Letter to the Smyrnaeans" (c. 110 A.D.) The Faith of the Early Fathers, ed W. Jurgens, (Collegeville: The Liturgical Press, 1970), pp.24f. Cf. also John Meier, The Vision of Matthew.
12. John 9:22 footnote in N.T. of the NAB, revised edition, 1987, p.160
13. Ellis, Matthew, p.5; Ellis is quoting W.D.Davies, The Setting of the Sermon on the Mount, pp. 275ff.

in general, says: 'and it happened that when Jesus finished these words he went to another place.'[14]

When these cut-off lines are applied to the remaining chapters of this gospel, the text can be placed in five parallel columns, each of which is composed of a **narrative** of events and a **discourse** to reveal the significance of the events, thus:

$$
\text{Prologue} \left\{
\begin{array}{ccccc}
\text{I} & \text{II} & \text{III} & \text{IV} & \text{V} \\
3,4 & 8,9 & 11,12 & 14\text{-}17 & 19\text{-}22 \\
\text{N} & \text{N} & \text{N} & \text{N} & \text{N} \\
& & & & \\
\text{D} & \text{D} & \text{D} & \text{D} & \text{D} \\
5\text{-}7 & 10 & 13 & 18 & 23\text{-}25
\end{array}
\right\}
\begin{array}{c}
\\
\text{Climax} \\
26,27,\&28
\end{array}
$$

Even if the inspired author did not allude to it, the closely-knit, five-fold **structural design** readily discoverable in these five small books[15] (identified with the Roman numerals) suggests the pentateuchal unity of the Mosaic Torah. Jewish commentator **Samuel Sandmel**, in his book A Jewish Understanding of the New Testament, notes concerning Matthew's five blocks of discourse material: "The Law of Moses is in five books; perhaps the five blocks are a conscious imitation of the five books."[16] The Torah's pentateuchal form provided a ready-to-hand model for framing the material in Matthew's gospel. The **Mosaic Torah** would then be viewed as reaching its highest fulfillment in the **Messianic Torah**. Matthew shows Jesus contrasting his teaching with that of Moses in the Sermon on the Mount with the repeated antithetical formula: "You have heard it said to them of old..., **But** I say to you....". This antithetical "**But**" formula suggests that Jesus is "displacing and supplanting the Law of Moses".[17]

---

14. 13:53 reads "kaì egéneto óte etélesen ò Iesoûs tàs parabalàs taútas, metêren ékeîthen." This cut-off line identifies the discourse given as one composed of parables. 26:1 identifies the end of all Jesus' speech-making with the expression, "pántas toùs lógous toútous" = "all these discourses" as it leads into the climax of this gospel.
15. John Meier structures his whole commentary Matthew on this design; cf. his Table of Contents.
16. Samuel Sandmel, A Jewish Understanding of the New Testament, (New York: University Publishers Inc.,1957), p. 158; (hereafter, Sandmel, A Jewish Understanding and page).
17. Sandmel, A Jewish Understanding, p.145.

However, on closer examination Matthew is, for the most part, showing that Jesus is underlineelevating and underlineinteriorizing the Mosaic teaching. The doctrine of Jesus is pushing beyond that of Moses to higher and more difficult terrain. The **Torah** says, 'dont commit adultery'; **Jesus** says,'do not even contemplate it.' The **Torah** says, 'dont return an injury more than you have been injured; **Jesus** says 'forgive him who has injured you'. In these texts Matthew shows Jesus elevating and fulfilling the law, as he presents Jesus saying "Do not think that I have come to abolish the law and the prophets. I have come, not to abolish them, but **to fulfill them**"(Mt 5:17).

John McKenzie maintains that Jesus fulfills the Law when he brings it to its divinely-designed fullness.

"The fullness of the reality of the reign does not annul the Law any more than mature manhood annuls childhood; but to remain in childhood would annul mature manhood. One must move beyond the Law when Jesus comes to reveal the full reality of the reign which was not revealed in the law."[18]

Matthew is leading the Jewish-Christian hearers to recognize that Jesus, who legislates beyond and above Moses, is indeed the Messiah. One is reminded of Stephen's speech in Acts (c.7) that Jesus is greater than the Torah and the Temple, and Mark's Transfiguration episode where Moses (promulgator of the Torah all must listen to) recedes from the scene after which Peter, James and John are instructed, "This is my beloved Son, listen to him."(Mark 9:1ff). The Sermon on the Mount and the other four discourses constitute **a great collection of Jesus' teaching** (didache in Greek; doctrina in Latin) in which this first Gospel is intensely interested. A common theme threads these discourses, and each discourse is also distinguished by a specific theme (or a specific character) in a plan which unfolds from beginning to end.

Common theme   Matthew identifies the theme common to all these discourses as the **Kingdom of Heaven.** This expression is noted as a circumlocution used by devout Jews to avoid pronouncing or writing (and thus in some way cheapening) the sacred rarely-to-be-pronounced name of **God (Yahweh)**, as in the expression, "Kingdom of God". When the name Yahweh was

---

18.   McKenzie, Light, p.24.

read in the sacred text, the name Adonai was to be said in its place.[19] The Jewish scholars translated Adonai into Greek as Kyrios, which came into Latin as Dominus, and into English as Lord. This sensitive avoidance of the common use of **God's name** reveals another facet of Matthew's Jewishness.

The editors of "New Testament" of The New American Bible (**1987** revised edition) chose to translate the **"Kingdom of Heaven"** expression literally as Matthew has it. The **1970** edition had translated it as the **Reign of God** because the sense of the phrase is focused on God's loving rule or **reign** in the hearts of his children rather than on a kingdom in the territorial sense. This living under God's **reign** will then identify the community or kingdom of people which is made one by its loving response to his rule. The **1987** editors chose to preserve Matthew's Jewish sensitivity regarding the too common use of the name "**God**".

Outline of structure

Introduction: 1-2 Infancy account:

Bk I *Promulgation* {3-4 Narrative: Triptych; Galilee
   K of H   {5-7 Discourse: Sermon on the Mount

Bk II *Spread* {8-9 Narrative: Ten miracles
   K of H   {10 Discourse: Missionary instructions
                  to the Disciples

Bk III *Mystery* {11-12 Narrative: Hostility increases
   K of H   {13   Discourse: Seven parables

Bk IV *First Product* {14-17 Narrative: forming the Apostles
                        {   "My Ekklesia", Simon = Kepha (Petros)
   K of H   {18   Discourse: norms in His Ekklesia

Bk V *End* { 19-22 Narrative: Conflicts with Officials
   K of H } 23-25 Discourse: Woes; End-time

Climax   26-28 Last Supper; Gethsemane;
                    Passion & Death
                    Resurrection *and Great Commission*

---

19. J. Weingreen, A Practical Grammar for Classical Hebrew, 2nd ed., (New York: Oxford University Press, 1959), pp. 23, 28.

Discourses The specific theme of each book is then distinguished by the overall character of each discourse and by the people who are addressed. The **first** speech (5-7) is the world-famous **Sermon on the Mount.** Because it is so close to the heart of Jesus' evangelical work, it is also called the Evangelical Discourse. It is directed to all Jesus' disciples; it is also noted as the classical place of **didache** (i.e. teaching to those who have already accepted the **kerygma**) in the Gospels. It appears as an **inaugural** address about the things to be believed and done by those who wish to be disciples of Christ. Thus, this discourse gives the first book (I) the character of the beginning or the **Messianic Inauguration** of the reign of God.

The **second** discourse (c.10) is directed to the Apostles. It is known as the **Apostolic Discourse.** In it the Gospel's author has collected a series of instructions which Jesus gave to his future apostles on how to spread the word of God and thus his reign among the Jewish people. At this point in this Gospel, Jesus' disciples have not yet fully perceived that Jesus is the Messiah; consequently, the content of their message can only be fuller "fidelity to the Torah" according to the authoritative teaching of Jesus; they were inspired by the Moses-like teaching and the awesome deeds they experienced from Jesus. This discourse gives this second book the character of the Messiah's **Spreading** of the kingdom of Heaven.

The **third** discourse (c.13) is a collection of parables and is referred to as the **Parabolic Discourse.** It is directed to the crowds. It speaks in figures and symbols of the Kingdom of Heaven and those on earth who people this kingdom. **The Kingdom** is somehow like seeds a farmer sows among rocks or thorns, like little seeds that grow into large tree-like habitats for all kinds of birds, like treasure in a field or a pearl of great price. This **Parabolic Discourse** examines the kingdom from different aspects as one might carefully scrutinize the facets of a diamond to see its secret beauty and value -- its hidden mystery. These parabolic pictures **still** require searching examination to reveal the layers of meaning placed in them by Jesus, - and again later by the Apostles and Evangelists who adapted (redacted) them to solve the changing problems of the growing Jewish/Gentile community of Christ. This discourse characterizes the third book as the **Mystery** of the Kingdom of Heaven.

The **fourth** book (cc.14-18; discourse: c.18) is known as the **Ecclesiastical Book.** Its discourse is again directed to the future

Apostles. It directs them on how to manage the new **ekklesia** (in Latin = ecclesia) by serving Christ's little ones, not by lording it over them. This discourse confronts the question of who is the greatest among them. It notes that scandal given to Christ's little ones calls for terrifying punishment; that one lost sheep should be searched for painstakingly; that fraternal correction should be given to save and heal; that if two or three **pray together**, a new divine dimension is added to that prayer; that forgiveness should be tendered with compassionate generosity, not with penny-pinching meanness. These moral imperatives label this discourse as the **ecclesial discourse** and thus indicate that this whole book highlights the **first product** (= Christ's new kahal or ecclesia) of the Kingdom of Heaven. The term **Church** (ekklesia in Greek) for Christ's new community was already commonplace when Paul wrote I Thessalonians in the year 50, but Matthew is the only Gospel to introduce this term.

The **fifth** and last great discourse (cc.23-25), directed like book one to Jesus' disciples, contains Matthew's adaptation of Mark's **eschatological discourse** [Mt's 24 = Mk's 13] concerned with the prophesy of Jerusalem's destruction and the end (= eschaton in Greek) of the world. Chapter 25 portrays the dynamic, awesome final judgment of everybody by the risen Christ. This discourse characterizes this book as **The End** of the Kingdom of Heaven. Some scholars think that Matthew's chapter 23 is a slightly later insert in which the "woes" against the Jewish leaders are placed in this judgmental context to balance off the "**blesseds**" of the Sermon on the Mount. These scholars see the "woes" as a polemical attitude continuing down until the time that this Gospel was completed. In the town of **Jamnia** Jewish leaders were trying to reconstruct Judaism after the destruction of Jerusalem and the Temple in the year 70; they later wished to exclude Christ-believing Jews from the reconstituted synagogues. The "woes" continued to have meaning for the Christ-believing Jews excluded and thus separated from their families and culture.

On reexamination, **the discourses** complete the story of the **Kingdom's:** 1)beginning, 2)spread, 3)mysterious character, 4)first tangible product, and finally 5)end. Then, the author explicitly makes the point that Jesus has finished **all** his discourses (26:1). Jesus, Messiah and Son in Matthew's account, thereafter enters the climax of his vicarious, self-sacrificing passion, death and glorious resurrection which only then penetratingly illuminates the meaning of all that went before. "The whole Passion narrative is a fulfillment of what is to happen 'according to the Scriptures' (Acts 1:16; 1Cor 15:3)."[20]

Narratives The **narrative section** of each book (3&4; 8&9; 11&12; 14-17; 19-22) appears to have both the horizontal function of carrying the **action** progressively[21] through Mt's Gospel from the infancy account to the climactic death and resurrection, and also the vertical function within each book of serving[22] and eliciting sharper attention to the discourse which follows it. Also, the end of one narrative in some way is connected with the start of the next narrative.[23]

Thus, in **Bk I** Jesus is introduced in relation to John the Baptizer. He overcomes his satanic temptations. He is like, but much greater than, Moses. Then, He gives his inaugural discourse on discipleship to his followers. Here, he goes beyond the Mosaic Torah; he even reverses a Mosaic leniency. He is **Messiah in word.** In **Bk II,** the narrative of his ten miracles demonstrate that Jesus is the Messiah using divine power. Thus, not only in word, but also he is **Messiah in deed.** Then, the Messiah authoritatively initiates his chosen future Apostles in the ministry of **his words and deeds.** In **Bk III** the narrative cites the rejection by the Jewish leadership which builds a barrier between Jesus and his targeted audience. The worsening hostility leads then to a corresponding discourse in mysterious parables which paint distinctions, divisions and rejection in vivid pictures.

In the narrative of **Bk IV** Jesus turns his attention more fully to the instructing of Peter and his other chosen disciples who now firmly believe that **Jesus is the Messiah. Jesus speaks of building his church.** Then, the discourse gives instruction on life in this new ecclesial community. In **Bk V**'s narrative conflicts with the leadership in Jerusalem reveal the intensifying division. True discipleship is distinguished from false discipleship. Those who rent the King's vineyard (Israel) are intent on killing the King's (God's) son. Then, the "woes" are proclaimed on the "blind

20. John Lodge, "Matthew's Passion-Resurrection Narrative", Chicago Studies, Vol 25,1 (April 1986), p.5.
21. W. Harrington, Key to the Bible, #3, (Canfield, Ohio: Alba Books, 1975), p.38
22. Ellis, Matthew, p.16, and passim. The work of Ellis gave the shape to this development.
23. Meier, Matthew, p.80; Vision, p.88.

leaders". The discourse foretells Jerusalem's destruction and the triumphant Messiah's return to judge the living and the dead.

All the teaching-discourses are noted as completed (26:1). Jesus procedes to the **formal covenant act** of offering himself for all at the Last Supper. The covenant act is fulfilled by his climactic Passion and Death. His breath-taking Resurrection terminates the Gospel and illuminates all that led to it.

A few of the many **characteristics** which identify Matthew's Gospel are: concentric relationship of its parts, typology which shows Moses as a fore-type of Jesus, frequent use of parallelism, emphasis on Jesus' starting of "his Church" and the disciple's unity with Jesus. Knowledge of these characteristics enables the exegete or interpreter to see the mind of the inspired author at work, and thus to know as precisely as possible what meaning the author intends to convey. Discovering "precisely what the author intended to say" is the "supreme rule of interpretation."[24] **Exegesis** digs out what the author intends to say for human salvation; this is the content that is inspired. Putting thoughts into his words which the author did not intend is called **eisegesis**; this is erroneous and dangerous.

Concentricity The symmetry of the addressees:1)Disciples, 2)Apostles, 3)crowds, 4)Apostles, 5)Disciples, (formulated: D. A. c. A'.D') appears to reveal the concentric structure that the inspired author had in mind. Further, the fact that Matthew's **later material illuminates the prior material** leads to a discovery that D is illuminated by D' and A is illuminated by A'. For example, in **A** (Apostolic discourse: c.10) Jesus chooses his future apostles, "institutionalizes" them as "the Twelve" and gives them the initial mission (a function which shares his own mission) of proclaiming the Kingdom of Heaven. In concentric **A'** (Ecclesial discourse: c.18) the position of the Twelve is illuminated: their position has now been enlarged; they are the leaders of Christ's new ecclesia. Jesus prepares them for their new function with norms for living in what he called **his Church**. Remembering that the Gospel's author is writing down these instructions after half a century of their being proclaimed and lived, scholars become aware that the inspired author is applying and **adapting** (= redacting) the teachings of Jesus to his community's experienced

---

24. Augustin Bea, The Study of the Synoptic Gospels, ed J.A. Fitzmyer, (New York, Harper & Row, 1965), p.33.

problems. The living doctrine of the risen Christ is vital to this Church. His living doctrine enables his disciples to adapt to the change from Jewish to Greek culture. The risen Christ's command **to teach all nations** means that his doctrine is supra-national. It cannot be limited or confined to any one nation. It is supra-cultural; it is salvific for people of any and every culture. In a word it is **universal** (= **catholicos** in Greek).

In **D** (Jesus' Sermon on the Mount: 5-7) Matthew collects in one place the guiding instructions (being a Christian isn't easy!) that Christ's followers are to learn and do to be Christians. In concentric **D'** (eschatological discourse: 25) Matthew answers the question of "why bother?" He collects the compelling end-time parable-judgments of Christ about what lies ahead eternally for each one: **"Come...Inherit the kingdom prepared for you"** is invitingly addressed to those who follow his guidance with love. On the other hand, the terrifying **"Out of my sight you condemned..."** is levelled at those who rejected him and his teaching. Some scholars see this concentric illumination and reinforcement design of Matthew's Gospel as the key to much of its proper interpretation.[25] Matthew also highlights **Moses** as the great prototype foreshadowing the Messiah. The Messiah would fulfill and go beyond the Mosaic image.

Typology The great Moses, who had said that 'God will send another like me', provides the first Gospel with the image or **type** that forecasts the messiah. As a theme runs through a symphony, this **Moses/Jesus typology** runs through the early part of Matthew's Gospel.

The infancy account (1-2) alludes to some parallels: 1)**as Pharoah sought to kill Moses** as an infant, **so King Herod sought to kill Jesus** as an infant; 2)again, as Moses was an exile in Egypt and came from there, so Jesus was a refugee in Egypt and came from there. One notes that this has special meaning for Jewish Matthew and his predominantly Jewish community[26], but Gentiles coming into this Jewish-Christian community had to learn that these parallels were meaningful. Despite this community's polemic against the Pharisee leaders (ch. 23: the 7 "woes"), it is so steeped in Jewish meaning that it cannot be anti-Semitic. In fact, its

---

25. Peter Ellis, Matthew, (Collegeville:The Liturgical Press, 1974), pp. 19 ff.
26. Ellis, Matthew, p.119.

respect for Moses is so great that it judges the Mosaic episodes to be parallels which worthily foreshadow the Messiah.[27]

The public ministry continues the parallels. **As Moses was in the desert forty years, so Jesus was in the desert forty days.** The people, led by Moses, were tempted in the desert and most disobeyed the divine will there; Jesus, representative of the whole people, overcame the temptations in the desert thus fulfilling the divine plan there. As Moses was a prophet and gave unique signs, so Jesus was a prophet and gave greater signs. For the critical parallel on **The Law**, as Moses from God received **The Torah** on the mountain, so Jesus of himself gave the **Messianic Doctrine** on the mountain. Further, Jesus reversed Moses on divorce and definitively went beyond the Mosaic Torah.

At the climax, **as Moses sealed the Covenant** with the blood of animal sacrifice, **so Jesus, Messiah and Lord, sealed the new covenant**, foretold by Jeremiah, with the blood of his own sacrifice on Calvary. Other striking parallels also exist, but these are sufficient for us to become aware of this important Jewish-oriented theme surfacing throughout Matthew's Gospel.

Parallelism This kind of comparison in **parallel sentences** is very common in the biblical writings. It flourishes in such writings as the Book of Psalms and the Book of Proverbs as well as the first Gospel. Three common types are: synonymous parallelism, antithetical parallelism and progressive parallelism.

1) The Jesus/Moses comparisons above are done in synonymous parallelism which may be formulated: A - B, A'- B'; Mt 10:41 exemplifies this type: He who welcomes a prophet because he bears the name of a prophet receives a prophet's reward; he who welcomes a holy man because he is known to be holy receives a holy man's reward.

2) Antithetical parallelism may be generalized as A - B, B'- A'; Mt 10:39 exemplifies this type. It reads: He who seeks only himself brings himself to ruin, whereas he who brings himself to nought for me discovers who he is. Another one (Mark 2:27) is: The Sabbath was made for man, not man for the Sabbath.

---

27. Ellis, Matthew, p.119.

3) Progressive parallelism fits the form: A - B, B'- C. This type advances the thinking to a new term. Mt 10:40 does this: He who welcomes you [ex. the Apostles] welcomes me, and he who welcomes me welcomes him [the Father] who sent me.

The three foregoing paragraphs themselves form a larger kind of parallelism, the kind in which whole passages and even whole discourses parallel each other; this kind of parallelism, found in Matthew's Gospel, is also an insight which **assists in properly interpreting** Matthew's Gospel. In chapter 6 of the Sermon on the Mount verses 2-4 on almsgiving, 5-7 on prayer and 16-18 on fasting form a parallelism with each other. Close examination shows that the **Our Father** was inserted to complete the passage on prayer without bothering to give it the same paralellism as the almsgiving, prayer and fasting sections.

Further, the whole Evangelical discourse is paralleled and illuminated by the Eschatological discourse, even as the Apostolic discourse is paralleled and illuminated by the Ecclesial discourse. By such structures the inspired author helps the reader to grasp what he intends to say with greater certitude.

His Church   Booklet IV (14-18) has been referred to as Mt's **ecclesial book.** In it, principally in chapters 16 and 18, this Gospel focuses full attention on the decision of Jesus to found his new community, which in the Greek text is termed, **ecclesia** (= church). This is the only Gospel which uses the word **church** (16:18 and 18:17), although it was already in common use when Paul wrote his first letter "to the **church** of the Thessalonians" (1:1) in the year 51. In the overview of this Gospel one notes that preceding material leads to Christ's formation of his community, and his later climactic actions significantly influence its character. In other words, his new community is seen as a product of his whole ministry including his passion, death and resurrection.

In Matthew's Gospel Jesus regarded himself as the Messiah and there is no such thing as a messiah without a community to be a messiah for. As the correlative of shepherd is a flock of sheep, so the correlative of messiah is a messianic community. Further, Jesus' idea and work have in view **only one flock**, only one community which he establishes and claims as his own (= his Father's). He is reconstituting the **The Kingdom** from his own believing followers as his own **community** (Mt calls it **ekklesia**; Lk, in Acts, calls it a **koinonia** as well as an ekklesia). That community's whole being is utterly dependent on the purpose and person of Christ. The new **community** may be compared to the **Kingdom** as the acorn to the oak.

This book IV is one high point of that founding. The choosing of the "the Twelve" prepares a core-base for it; the building of it on the **rock** foundation (= Peter in both Greek and Aramaic forms) sets an authoritative center for it; the pronouncement of the "new covenant" with his Father will formalize it in words, his PD&R will effect it in deeds; - these acts constitute **three significant steps** which Jesus takes to found his new community. The Holy Spirit will vivify and strengthen it in Acts.

1) The Twelve   Jesus chose his special disciples; they did not choose him. They were free to accept or reject his invitation: **Follow me and I will make you fishers of men.** Some rejected it! From those disciples who accepted his invitation (= a vocation) he **instituted "the Twelve"**, with the past and the future their acceptance implied. The institution of "the Twelve" related them to the twelve tribes of their Jewish past; their new function as core of, and witnesses[28] in, the new messianic community projected them into an unknown future. For them the future contained hidden in it the death and resurrection of Jesus, and their own martyrdom for him leading to their eternal union with him.

Flourishing in the Mosaic Scriptures is the concept of "the remnant". This is not the concept of the leftovers, but rather the concept of **the seed** of the divinely planned new beginning. It is the remnant of God's people which gives its whole heart (metanoia) to God for the renewal of his plan. Many are called yet reject Christ (Mt 22:14) but "the Twelve" are the chosen core of the remnant. There is no question of their taking their own initiative while Jesus is with them; he alone leads. Before he goes he will choose one leader for them. Together with that leader thay will teach "the new Torah that has fulfilled the Law and the Prophets"[29]

2) Peter   At **Caesarea Philippi**, speaking for the others as well as for himself, Peter openly acknowledged: **You are**

---

28.   Paul, 1 Cor, 15:4ff.
29.   John Lodge, Op.cit., p.20.

the Messiah, the Son of the Living God. This profession of faith distinguished him and the future apostles as the faithful remnant, — especially in contrast to the unbelieving leaders who would reject the Messiah. Jesus then turned to him and replied:

> "Blest are you, Simon son of Jonah! No mere man has revealed this to you, but my heavenly Father. I for my part declare to you, you are **'Kepha'** (= Petros = Rock), and on this **kepha** I will build **my church**, and the jaws of death shall not prevail against it. I will entrust to you **the keys** of the kingdom of heaven. Whatever you declare **bound** on earth shall be bound in heaven; whatever you declare **loosed** on earth shall be loosed in heaven." (Mt 16:16-19)

Here Jesus chose **Simon alone** and renamed him **Kepha** (signifies foundation) to be his vicar, the one to take his place on his departure, the one on whom Christ will build **his church**. The concepts of the renaming, the name, keys (cf. Isaiah 22:22) and bind & loose are all thoroughly Jewish and firmly anchored in Matthew's Gospel.[30] **Peter alone** is made the "rock" and given the "keys". A bit later Jesus will give all his future apostles a share in the "binding and loosing", but not in the functions signified by "rock" and "keys". In the Gospels of Luke (22:32) and John (21:15-17) too, Peter will be **singled out** to fulfill special functions in Christ's new community. In its treatment of the Last Supper, Matthew's account shows Jesus enacting a third major step in founding **his Church.** He revealed that the sacrifice he is offering to God (his Father) is, in fact, establishing a new covenant. Moses had made the former covenant, the Mosaic covenant, with the blood of sacrificed animals.

3) New Covenant   Since the Reformation, Christians have so concentrated on Jesus' institution of the critically important Eucharistic Mystery (This is my Body for you; This is my Blood which will be shed for you), that the remaining expression **"of the [new] Covenant"** received less than its share of attention. The whole event is, of course, essential for all Christians,[31] but the **covenant concept** (God's self-defined

---

30. Oscar Cullmann, Peter - Disciple, Apostle, Martyr, (London: SCM Press Ltd., 1962), p. 213.
31. Christians believe that eucharistic and covenant realities are for all human beings.

relationship with his people) directly **identifies** the **new community** of Christ as distinguished from the Mosaic covenant-community (Exodus 24:8f) under which the Apostles were, up until that moment, living. When Jesus, in the presence only of his future apostles, made this formal covenant offering of himself, which offering he would complete in the actual total offering of his body and blood on the morrow, he brought the Mosaic covenant to its unforeseen **fulfillment** in the new **Messianic covenant.**

When warning the Jews of the forthcoming destruction of Jerusalem (587 B.C.), Jeremiah (31:31-34) had prophesied: 'Yahweh will make **a new covenant** with you, not like the one you broke'. Jesus' declaration in the presence of his Apostolic witnesses: "This is **the new covenant** in my blood", fulfilled that prophesy. Clearly, the very word covenant constitutes a link with, and a new departure from, the Jewish relationship with the Torah under the developing code of which they had been living for twelve hundred years. The very concept of Covenant provides the link. The fact of a new covenant ratified by the sacrificial blood of Christ on the Cross fulfills and completes the former covenant originally ratified with the sacrificing of animals. The sacrificial self-donation of the Messiah and Son effects a new and unforseen departure for Jesus' **new ecclesia.**

In Matthew's Gospel Christ's acts of: (1)choosing and instituting **the twelve,** (2)making **Peter** the foundation rock and only key-man of his new ecclesia [replacing the sanhedrin's high priest], and (3)his formal and next-day actual sacrificial ratification of a **new covenant,** established Christ as the true Israel. By this fact, Christ's new community, which is mysteriously **one with him,** is the true Israel. **Matthew's** Gospel holds the **proposition** that: **if** God sent his promised Messiah, **then** the leaders who reject him cannot be the true Israel; rather, the faithful remnant which accepts that messiah on God's terms and unites itself with him is to be **the true Israel**

Unity with Jesus This business of "unity with Jesus" surfaces often in the New Testament. The unity revealed transcends the human kinds of unity we experience. It comes primarily from God's side. Matthew's Gospel emphasizes it. In the Infancy account, Matthew identifies the child as **Emmanuel;** this very significant Jewish word he translates immediately. It means "**God is with us**" (1:23). At its very end Matthew's account will illuminate this expression more fully. Christ's identification of the new community as **My Church** (16:18) was already noted.

As the Gospel proceeds, Matthew shows another way in which Jesus is with us. He shows Jesus identifying himself with the apostles he is forming. In pointing out their significance as his representatives beyond their imagining, Jesus informs them: "He who welcomes you **welcomes me**, and who welcomes me **welcomes him who sent me** (10:40).

"Further, in chapter 18, designed to set some norms for living in the new community, Matthew presents Jesus as teaching that he is in union with those who pray in his name. "Where two or three are gathered in my name, **there am I in their midst**" (18:20).

Unity or ?   One can note that these teachings in Matthew's Gospel allow **no middle ground** between arrogance and truth. This unity-assertion appears to be **either** arrogant and utterly unfillable nonsense **or** awe-inspiring and inviting truth. The serious repetitions of the assertion force the hearer to one **or** the other position; no middle ground fits the Gospel data. Jesus' affirmations of unity are beyond the capacity of the merely mortal; what but divine power can effect such unity? The ruling faction of the Sanhedrin said **blasphemy** and tried to get it out of the way; the Apostles identified it as divinely revealed **truth**, proclaimed it and suffered greatly because of it. Paul's witnessing for it led to his beheading; Peter's firm proclaiming of unity with the risen Jesus led to his crucifixion.

At the <u>Last Supper</u> (26:26ff.) Jesus brought this **unity with himself** to a new level of intimacy. In terms oriented to his own total sacrifice on the morrow, he identifies certain bread and wine at the **Passover** celebration as his own body and blood, despite the fact that the outward appearance of the bread and wine did not change. He then invites the apostles to an **unforeseen union with him** by accepting and receiving the gift of himself from him.

Later, in the Matthean preview of the **Last Judgment** (25:31-46), Jesus reveals that all actions done even to the least of his disciples are equivalently done to himself. To the sheep as well as the goats in the preview, the same principle is applied. Both acknowledge their deeds, but back away from the thought that their acts had him in view. To which the Judge of all replies: "I assure you, as often as you did it for one of my least brothers, **you did it for me.**'

Matthew Gospel ends as it began. In the closing passage (28:18-20) in which he collects the major themes of this Gospel, the inspired writer gives Jesus' self-identification with the Emmanuel text:

Emmanuel = **God** is with us;
now, Jesus says = **I AM** with you always
until the end of the world.[32]

The Hebrew name for God is **Yahweh.**[33] Theologians and exegetes recognize that the meaning of the Hebrew name for God,

---

32. Raymond Brown, The Gospel According to John, (Garden City: Doubleday & Company, Inc., 1970). This two volume work in the Anchor Bible Series is paginated continuously. Appendix IV in Vol.I (pp. 533-538), entitled Ego Eimi — "I AM" treats of the name **Yahweh** in both Old and New Testaments. Brown affirms that "The most important use of the OT formula I AM (= YAHWEH) stresses the unicity of God: I AM (= Yahweh) and there is no other." [Parenthesis & = are inserted]. Brown thinks that the Greek translation emphasizes God's existence. But he points out in a footnote that W.F. Albright thought that the Hebrew and the Greek had "exactly the same" meaning. Brown's concentration is on the Johannine rather than the Synoptic texts.
33. John Huesman, "Exodus". Jerome Biblical Commentary, (New Jersey: Prentice-Hall, Inc., 1968), p.50. "In answer to Moses' question regarding his name, God replies with the celebrated "I am who I am" (Exodus 3:14). This statement is certainly the occasion for the divine title **Yahweh.** Of the many suggestions on the meaning of Yahweh, the most satisfactory is Albrights's "He causes to be" (in filling out the Hebrew sense Albright identifies the meaning as "He causes to be what comes into existence"). Huesman continues: "In later times, a deep reverence for the name Yahweh led to the use of the term **Adonai** as its substitute. The LXX uses **Kyrios,** the Vulgate **Dominus...**" and in English **Lord** is used.

Yahweh, = I AM.[34] Thus this concentric set of texts is used by the inspired author to terminate his Gospel's climax with the firm belief that he and his Christian community are celebrating Christ's mysterious transcendent unity with the only God with whom the risen Jesus identifies "**himself**".

Ending   This business of the later passages illuminating the earlier passages rises to a great crescendo at the very end of this Gospel. There, on the mountain in Galilee, **the Risen Jesus** gave his eleven disciples their **great commission** to be his **Apostles.**

> Full authority has been given to me
> both in heaven and on earth;
> go, therefore, and make disciples of
> all the nations.
> Baptize them **in the name** of the Father,
> and of the Son
> and of the Holy Spirit.
> Teach them to carry out everything
> I have commanded you.
> And know that **I AM with you always,**
> until the end of the world.

"All the major themes of Mt's gospel are tied together in this special ending.[35] The risen Jesus with full authority is transferring that authority, not to everybody, but only to his chosen and specially instructed disciples. His words here contain one of the **clearest implications of his divinity**[36] in Matthew's

---

34.   Joseph Ratzinger, Introduction to Christianity, tr. J. Foster (New York: The Seabury Press, 1979), pp. 77-82. "I AM who I AM" appears as the sense in Hebrew; "I AM He that is" appears as the sense adopted in the Greek Septuagint translation done by pre-Christian Jewish scholars. Exodus 3:13-15 is the classical text. Ratzinger says: "It is clearly the aim of the text to establish the name **Yahweh** as the definitive name of God in Israel." Ratzinger points out that the Mosaic covenant is sealed with this sacred name, Israel's nationhood is ratified, and some insight into God's being is given. The text yields "a second attempt at clarification consisting of the statement that **Yahweh** is the God of **(Israel's)** fathers, the God of Abraham, Isaac and Jacob.
35.   John Lodge, op.cit., p.19.
36.   Ellis, Matthew, pp. 109f.

Gospel; note the equality of the Father, Son and Holy Spirit used in this baptismal formula even prior to the time of the writing of this Gospel, (See also 11:25-27). His command is to go to all the nations (goyim in Hebrew); this command is universal; it, of course, includes his own people. An implication of the **Emmanuel** text has already been briefly noted.

Portrait   If you draw or write a portrait of one of your parents, say your father, it will be different from the portrait that your mother would draw of him. Despite the fact that it is the same man, those with whom he works will draw pictures different from yours or your mothers. So it was with the evangelists; Matthew's portrait is different from Mark's. Both have much the same data, many of the same parables, same miracles, same kerygma, but a somewhat **different emphasis** emerges in each.

Mark highlights the action, his Gospel moves; **Matthew** emphasizes the teaching, he shows Jesus modifying and elevating the Jewish Torah. Matthew gathers much of Jesus' authoritative doctrine into five great discourses in which the Master teaches Apostles, disciples and crowds. For faithful Jews **Moses** was the teacher of teachers; Jesus solemnly and majestically interpreted and superceded the Mosaic Torah. Never had they heard a teacher like this. Their Rabbis quoted other Rabbis (some say this, some say that), Jesus directly modified the **Word of God**; You have heard it said to them of old, **But I say to you....** In Matthew's **Sermon on the Mount** Jesus didn't hedge on questions: not only dont kill, dont hate! Love your enemies; not only dont commit adultery, dont contemplate it, dont will it! Finally with majestic and transcendent solemnity the risen Jesus proclaimed : "Full authority has been given to me both in heaven and on earth;" then he commanded his chosen Apostles to make disciples of all nations, baptize them and:"**teach them.**to carry out everything I have commanded you...I **AM** with you **always.**"

Questions

1. What **prior literature** provided the Gospel-writers with their most fruitful source of concepts and images?
2. **Which Gospel** is held to be the most Jewish? Four **reasons**? Does the name of the Gospel **ordinarily** stand for the author or the book? [**Mt** = **abbreviation** for this Gospel.]

3. What do **first century writers** say about Matthew's Gospel? Papias? Irenaeus? What **reasons** militate against Matthew's being alive at the completion of the first Gospel? **Place & Date** of Mt?
4. Name two elements of **greater concern in Mt** than in Mark?

5. What was the "**Birkath ha Minim**"? What was it designed to do? What text-series indicates the **opposition** of Matthew's Jewish-Christian community **to the Pharises**?
6. By chapters what appears to be the **overall structure** of Matthew's Gospel? On what **basis** are the chapters divided?

7. For Matthew's Jewish-Christian community what might a **structure of five books** of the Messiah's teaching **suggest**?
8. Does Mt give a **relationship** between the Old Law (Torah) and the New? For Mt what did Jesus do to the Torah?

9. For Jewish people **Moses** was their greatest legislator of the divine law; what **Jesus/Moses** comparison does Mt make??
10. What **theme** is **common** to Mt's five books? Why does Mt express this theme differently than Mark (cf. Mk 1:15)?

11. What is the **Hebrew name for God,** ____? **In reverence** what substitute is used? What is the substituted word's translation in Greek, Latin, English?
12. What is the **overall focus** of each of the five great discourses? **To whom** is each discourse directed?
    a)What name & content identify the first discourse?
    b)The second? c)The third?

13. The fourth discourse is **especially characteristic** of Mt; What is its name? What is its content?

14. The fifth discourse contains Mt's apocalyptic and the famous **last judgment** description; what are they about?

15. What is the **specific theme** of each book?
16. What function do the **narrative** sections of Mt's Gospel fulfill?

17. Regarding **Jesus' messiahship** how may books 1 and 2 be compared? In book 3 how does the Jewish leadership respond?
18. Why is book 4 called the **ecclesial book**? What word does Mt use for the **community** Christ is forming? **On whom** will Christ build his community? **How many** communities is Christ building?

19. In book 5 who seem to be the **chief opponents** of both the Messiah and Mt's community? How will God's way be vindicated if the vineyard tenants kill the King's Son?
20. **How** does Mt's hearer or reader **know** that all of Jesus' teaching-discourses are finished (cf 26:1)?

21. Explain the concentric-symmetry contained in **Mt's arrangement** of his addressees. What is the purpose of this most careful design? Give two of Mt's examples of this illumination-device.
22. How does **Matthew answer** the disciple who asks why bother to live according to Christ's principles?

23. Mt uses the kinds of **parallelism** common in the old Testament; explain and exemplify the kinds called synonymous, antithetical, progressive.
24. Was Mt's use of the word **ekklesia** for Christ's new community the only &/or earliest use of this term? What overall moves or steps did Jesus take in founding **his ekklesia**?

25. **Who initiated** the Apostles' connection with Jesus? **Why 12?**
26. Did Jesus establish **one man** to be a foundation for this newly established group? What **foundation symbols** did Jesus use? Do other N.T. books **support** Mt's data?

27. What is a (divine-human) **covenant**? How does this new covenant relate to the former covenant? Was it foretold? How is the **Last supper profoundly related to Calvary**?
28. Name four ways in which Mt focuses on **unity with Jesus.**

29. Exemplify the **Moses/Jesus typology** in Matthew?.
30. Why does the **end of Mt** warrant close attention? What Christian beliefs are quite clear in Mt's closing verses?

31. Does Mt's **Portrait** reveal messianic lines?

Chapter IX: The Gospel According to Luke

Before starting the third Gospel it is useful to recall the time spent in the **three stages** of the gospel development.[1] We have taken the year 30 as the year in which the public ministry of Christ (the **first stage**) ended with his Passion, Death and Resurrection. The time-frame of <u>Acts</u> (30 to 62) almost coincides with the **second stage**; the addition of seven or eight years to the year 62 brings us to the <u>generally accepted</u> (but not conclusively proven) date for the publication of Mark's Gospel. This publication of Mark's account starts the **third stage** in the genesis or production of the Gospels. This last stage ends with the publication of the last Gospel which is <u>generally thought</u> to be John's Gospel.

Steps in understanding It must be recognized that all the Gospels contain expressions and impressions about Jesus **from all three stages.** The evangelists (the Gospel authors) are manifesting the steps in understanding that Jesus' chosen Apostles went through. <u>At first</u> Peter and the others perceived and followed Jesus only as an **extraordinary man.** On the basis of Jesus' powerful teaching in word and sign, many began to realize that Jesus was comparable to their great prophets; he was a **Prophet.** About nine months <u>before</u> his death and resurrection, the chosen disciples <u>advanced</u> to the firm conviction that he was, in fact, **THE promised MESSIAH,** (= Christos in Greek). <u>Finally,</u> Christ's establishment of the new covenant by his own sacrificial death, his resurrection and **Pentecost** brought them to the full belief that he is also the **very Son of God.**

The Apostles after Pentecost proclaimed their extraordinary experiences. The Apostles proclaimed experiences, not theories or speculation.[2] Undoubtedly, they spoke about the **different levels of their understanding,** "but always in such a fashion that they

---

1. Pontifical Biblical Commission, <u>Instruction on the Historicity of the Gospels,</u> April 21, 1964
2. The Apostles did not theorize as if they were speculative theologians; they spoke of what they experienced. They already believed in <u>the one God.</u> The experienced the risen Jesus! They experienced the Holy Spirit at Pentecost! They had to fit all the experiences together with the words and ideas Jesus and the Holy Spirit gave them.

have told us the honest truth about Jesus."[3] Concerning Easter Sunday resurrection, John (20:9) could reveal "they did **not yet understand** the scripture that he had to rise from the dead"; and Luke (Acts 1:6) could note their **pre-Pentecost** lack of comprehension, "Lord at this time are you going to restore the kingdom to Israel?"

The **post-Pentecost** high point of understanding who and what Christ is, may sometimes be referred to as "**high Christology.**" Exegetes examine the titles and expressions about Jesus in the New Testament to determine which level of understanding the sacred author intends at that point in his writing.

Today we might say Christ is **ontologically** the Son of God in order to communicate to others that his divine sonship is **reality** and not merely a matter of saying nice high-sounding things about him. This belief transcends everything the Jewish people had expected. All the Gospels profess this transcendent belief. Each evangelist expressed this belief in a way that fit his own purpose and style. Recall that Matthew, beside the Emmanuel text (1:23) and Peter's "you are . . . the Son of the living God" text (16:16) had said:

> All things have been handed over to me by my Father. No one knows the Son except the Father, and no one knows the Father except the Son and anyone to whom the Son wishes to reveal him.(Mt 11:27)

As widely-recognized, scripture-scholar Pere Benoit O.P. said of the synoptics: "There is no doubt that the first three evangelists believe in the **divinity of Christ.**"[4] A younger exegete, Bruce Vawter C.M., similarly said:

> "The Synoptic gospels . . . share together with Paul, John, Hebrews and others a belief in the **divine sonship** that was **unique to Christ**, that made it right for him

---

3. Dei Verbum, a. 19.
4. Pierre Benoit, Jesus and the Gospel, tr B. Weatherhead, (New York: Herder and Herder, 1973), p.47.

alone among men to be accorded even **divine titles** (Mark 12:35-37, etc.)."[5]

During the period of transmitting the Gospel **orally** in Acts the Apostles (= commissioned witnesses) had to find the words to tell listeners, of different capacity to understand, who the risen Jesus is and all the steps that they themselves had gone through to come to the conviction which the Apostles, like Peter and Paul, witnessed to by their martyrdoms. In grappling for words adequate to proclaim **who Jesus is**, they were **shaping** the narratives and discourses in which the Gospel would be told when Mark and the others later came to write it. Students of the Gospels must be **mindful of these developments** when they search for the meaning of specific passages. It is particularly important to keep Mark's structuring of the oral (some parts probably in writing already) tradition when reading the Gospel according to Luke. Many exegetes are convinced that Mark's Gospel was available to Luke[6] when Luke, a Gentile-Christian, started to write his own Gospel account to Theophilus, and through him to other Gentile-Christians.

This **third Gospel** has an **initial feature clearly different** from all the other gospels. It was written by someone who came to Christ, not from Judaism, but from paganism. **Luke** was a **gentile** convert. "He is the one New Testament writer whom we can identify with almost utter certainty as a non-Jew . . ."[7] In writing to the Colossians (4:11), Paul identifies his companions who are the only circumcized ones (i.e. Jews) working for the Kingdom and afterwards mentions Luke along with others (i.e. non-Jews). Luke's interest in **all** human beings (i.e. Gentiles as well as Jews) and his fluent Greek corroborate his non-Jewish up-bringing. Paul adds another quality to the portrait when he refers to Luke as "our dear **physician**"(Col 4:14). **Eusebius**, in his Historia Ecclesiastica[8], says:

---

5.   Bruce Vawter, This Man Jesus, (New York: Doubleday & Company, Inc.,1973), p. 141. Vawter points out that the Synoptics do not have the notions of Christ's pre-existence, or of his incarnation in the same sense as Paul or John.
6.   Fitzmyer, Luke
7.   B. Vawter, The Four Gospels, (New York: Doubleday & Company, Inc., 1967), p.23.
8.   Eusebius, HE, 4.6.4. p.109.

Luke, by birth an **Antiochene** and by profession a physician, was for long periods a **companion of Paul** and was closely associated with the other apostles as well. So he has left us examples of the art of healing souls which he learnt from them in two divinely inspired books, the Gospel and the Acts of the Apostles. The former, he declares, he wrote in accordance with the information he received from those who from the first had been eye-witnesses and ministers of the word, information which, he adds he had followed in its entirety from the first. The other he composed not this time from hearsay but from the evidence of his own eyes.

An updated scholarly work, The Oxford Dictionary of the Christian Church[9], citing St. Paul, Eusebius and others, accepts Luke's background as Gentile and physician. It adds the note of Luke's "being one of the **first members** of the Christian community at **Antioch**". This fits in very well with Luke's information in Acts about the the missionary journeys which started and ended there, and about first being **called Christians** there.

Who wrote it? The early Christian tradition accepts Luke's authorship of the Third Gospel. Irenaeus, Tertullian, Eusebius and others affirm this Gospel as **Luke's work.** In the post-apostolic period, the urge was to identify as much of the Christian writings as possible with an Apostle. Thus, the community's attribution of a gospel's authorship to one who was not an apostle and not a Jew, but on the contrary a later convert and even a Gentile is very **strong attestation.** So today's scholars accept Luke as the author. As we today argue identity from fingerprints, and now even from voice-prints, so scholars find that the mind-set (as if a mind-print) [words, sentences, ideas, and style] of **Acts** is the same as that of his **Gospel**; so, they conclude, **Luke** is the author of both. This internal evidence corroborates the external evidence of the ancient Christian authors.[10]

When? Some scholars **dated** Luke's work as early as the year 62 or before, **because** Acts ends with Paul

---

9. The Oxford Dictionary of the Christian Church, eds. F. Cross & E. Livingston, rev. 1983 (London: Oxford University Press, 1985), p. 844.
10. W. Harrington, Key to the Bible #3, p.48.

under house arrest in Rome in that year. It was thought that Luke surely would have told of the heroic martyrdom of Peter and Paul if he had written after they died. Both had been martyred for the faith by 67. However, Luke had fulfilled his stated program for Acts (1:8) when he showed that the Gospel had reached Rome.

Samuel Sandmel, a Jewish commentator, dates Luke's Gospel as late as 150 and thinks Rome is its place of origin.[11] This very late dating fails to note that Luke shows no knowledge of Matthew's Greek Gospel which was in existence in the 80's. Further, Luke, obviously interested in heroic Paul, shows no knowledge of Paul's letters (including his letter to the Romans in 57 A.D.) which were already being collected around the year 100. Luke seems to know of the Destruction of Jerusalem in 70, but his knowledge of ecclesial developments doesn't appear to reach into the 90's. Thus "**most critics** nowadays would date the Gospel of Luke **around 80** or so."[12] Some say between 80 and 90.[13] The mood of Luke's account is peaceful and some suggest the work was done in northern Greece.

Luke addresses both books (they really are two fairly large parts of one book) to a certain **Theophilus** (= lover of God in Greek). Some authors thought this was a general title for any pious Gentile. But today it is recognized as the name of a particular man with the title of honor: **Your Excellency.** Luke is addressing Theophilus as a convert who wishes to find out more about the faith to which he has committed himself. In what has been termed "excellent Greek" Luke indicates in his prologue to this third Gospel the answer to the question of **why** he decided to write it:

> Many have undertaken to compile a narrative of the events which have been fulfilled in our midst, precisely as those events were transmitted to us by the original **eyewitnesses and ministers of tne word.** I too have carefully traced the whole sequence of events from the beginning, and have decided to set it in writing for you, Theophilus, so that Your Excellency may see how reliable the instruction was that you received.

---

11.   Samuel Sandmel, A Jewish Understanding of the New Testament, (New York: University Publishers Inc., 1956) p.191.
12.   Vawter, The Four Gospels, p.24.
13.   E. LaVerdiere, Luke, (Wilmington: Michael Glazier, Inc.,1980), p.xi.

This prologue indicates that Luke in writing to Theophilus is addressing the "gentile mind". The other gospel writers did not do this so pointedly. Thus, Luke omitted some dispensable Jewish data as might be expected. Luke indicated that others have written before him. Close examination of his account reveals that he follows parts of Mark so closely that scholars feel sure that he must have had Mark's Gospel available to him[14]. But Luke softens Mark's blunt statements about the disciples' slowness to grasp Jesus' predictions of his passion, death and resurrection. Luke also skips passages in Mark, such as: Jewish defilement, contrasts of Jesus' teaching with the Torah (You have heard it said to them of old...,But I say to you..., etc.), which Gentiles, ignorant of Moses and the Torah, generally could not appreciate.

Thus, an overall summary of who, what, when, where and why could include convert Luke's authorship of his Gospel account first, then Acts, completed between 80 and 90, somewhere in northern Greece for the sake of strengthening gentile Theophilus in the Christian faith to which he had recently converted. A majority opinion would include Luke's judicious use of Mark's Gospel and the non-availability to him of the Gospel according to Matthew which you read (if it yet existed when Luke wrote).

Lukan Inserts The content of Luke's Gospel, when compared to Mark's, enables one to see that Luke has three significant sections of material which are **absent from Mark's account**. They are the beginning (consisting of the **Prologue** and the **Infancy Account**) up to 3:1, the little section 6:20-8:3 (called the **little Lukan Insert**), and the very large section 9:51-18:14 (called the **big Lukan Insert**). Although many of the ideas contained in these three sections are present in Mark and the overall framework in Luke seems to be from Mark, not a single paragraph of this inserted material can be found in Mark. Luke, a later convert, had to get the inserted data from another source or sources.

Before looking at the inserted data, it is useful to examine some of the material that Luke apparently took from Mark's account. Its use by Luke confirms its validity and usefulness as

---

14. J. Fitzmyer, To Advance the Gospel, (New York: Crossroad Publishing Company, 1981), pp. 1-40; (hereafter, Fitzmyer, To Advance and page.)

Structure of Luke's Gospel

{ 1:1-4 **Prologue**

{ 1:5-80 Diptych of the Annunciations: John/**Jesus**
{ 2:1-52   "   of the Births: John/**Jesus**

Galilean

3:1-4:13 Opening triptych (genealogy insert)
4:14 Galilee/Nazareth Manifesto
5:1 Call of first disciples
5:17 Galilean conflicts (**D-E-F-G-H**)
6:13 Institutes "the 12"

4:14
to
9:50
Ministry

Little { 6:20 Sermon on the plain
Insert } to   Centurian's servant
       { 8:3 Widow of Nain, Baptst's Q

8:4 Sower & seed, Lamp
8:22 Storm/Geresene man/Jairus' D./hemorrhagic W.
9:1 Missions "the 12"/Antipas/5000
9:18 Peter says: **You are the Messiah of God**
Prediction # **1**; Prediction # **2.**

9:51   **Big**
to   **Insert**
18:14 *Journey to Jerusalem*

9:51 Journey to Jerusalem (to Jesus'PD&R)
10 Good Samaritan
11 Our Father
12 $ Greedy barn-builder
13 Few saved; Herod/that fox
14 Dinners:Sabbath;lowest pl;excuses
15 Lost things: sheep; coin; son
16 $; adultery; Lazarus & the rich man;
17 Ten lepers;
18 Persistent widow; Pharisee & Publican

Jerusalem
Ministry

18:14 [rejoins Mark's acct: Let the children come
18:15 to 19:27 Prediction # **3** & Markan content
19:28 Entry into Jerusalem/Clearing Temple
20 Authority? Jerusalem conflicts (**V-I-R ? O**)
21 Luke's Apocalyptic

{ 22 Judas/Passover/Eucharist/denials foretold
{ 23 Pilate/Herod//Pilate/via crucis/**Crucifixion**

{ 24 After **Resurrection:**Women/Emmaus 2/Simon/The 11

-123-

source material valuable for leading the gentile mind toward faith in Christ. With some adaptation Luke used Mark's opening triptych: John the Baptist, the baptism of Jesus, and the temptations in the desert. Between panels two and three Luke added a **genealogy**. Matthew has a **genealogy** too, but his originates with **Abraham**, the father of the whole Jewish nation whereas Luke's originates with **Adam**, the biblical father of the whole human race. In this way Luke manifests that the Gospel is for Gentiles as well as Jews; in a word Luke's account is for all, it is **universal**. Matthew waits until the very end of his Gospel for the great commission (28:18-20) to show that the risen Christ identified his salvation as universal, "Go teach **all nations.**".

Mk/Lk correspondence In the Galilean ministry Luke presents the **five Galilean conflicts** (D-E-F-G-H)[15] in exactly the same order and almost exactly the same words as Mark. This very close Mk/Lk correspondence continues down to the little Lukan Insert (6:20-8:3). It picks up again at 8:4 and leads through episodes familiar from a reading of Mark until Peter's acknowledgement of the **Messiahship of Jesus at 9:20.** It is the familiar lead-in: 'who do the crowds say that I AM?' but Luke did not mention Caesarea Philippi where it happened. Further, he somewhat varies Peter's response to Jesus' question,: "But you - who do you say that I AM?' Peter replies: "**The Messiah of God**".

The title "messiah" by itself would say nothing to a gentile mind ignorant of Judaism. **Luke felt he had to add "of God"** to help non-Jews reading or hearing it for the first time to recognize that if some one comes from God, and the one and only God, then he must be very important and should be listened to. Luke doesn't stop to say all this, he just goes on with the episode. Jesus, after strictly forbidding them to tell this to anyone, continues:

> The Son of Man must **first** endure many sufferings, be rejected by the elders, the high priests and the scribes, [= the composition of the Sanhedrin] and be put to death, and then be raised up on the third day.

Notice that Luke added the word **first** into Mark's 8:31 which lets the gentile reader know that something else had to happen

---

15. Descent through the roof, Eating at Levi's, Fasting question, Grain on the Sabbath, Healing of hand.

before the disciples could reveal their new exciting conviction that **Jesus** is in fact **THE MESSIAH of God.** Mark had so bluntly told of the apostles' clinging to the earthy idea of political and even military messiahship, that Mark's readers know that the disciples' obtuseness makes them too ready to talk about the **wrong idea** of Jesus' status and kingdom. By Luke's time, the martyred Apostles had become inspiring and beloved Christian heros; Luke is much more gentle in telling about the Apostles' original obtuseness; he mutes it but he doesn't omit it.

Passion predictions Recalling that Mark had three predictions of the PD&R in an orderly row (8:31ff: Prediction/ Obtuseness/ Discipleship/ Insight;[16] 9:30ff: **PODI**; 10:32ff: **PODI**), the reader is not surprised to meet Luke's account of the second prediction (9:44) 22 verses after the first (9:22). But soon one meets the **Great Lukan Insert** extending from 9:51 to 18:14 which is filled with words and deeds of Christ unknown from Mark's Gospel. Finally, in 18:15 Luke again returns to the familiar order of Mark's account and in 18:32 there appears the third prediction of the PD&R. Thus it appears that, **between Mark's 2nd and 3rd predictions of the PD&R**, Luke inserted much of the extra traditional information he had learned in his "careful tracing the sequence of events" under the heading of Jesus' final journey to Jerusalem (= the journey to his PD&R). Mark in his long Galilean section (1:14-8:30) had highlighted the **mystery** of Jesus' identity; Luke appears to compress some of Mark's data into into a shorter, more pointed **identity sequence** of his own.

Identity Sequence Continuing the assumption that Luke had a copy of Mark before him as he composed his own Gospel account for Theophilus, it is fascinating to see how Luke omitted parts of Mark in order to concentrate attention

---

16. Reducing this somewhat extensive data to an acronym helps to grasp the parallelism and relationships of the whole units. Further, acting as a symbol for a part, it helps in grasping the development of the Gospel as a whole.

on the answer to the **identity** question[17]: **Who is this Jesus?**

Mark (6:14) pictures Herod Antipas, ruler of Galilee, hearing the opinions about Jesus, [John the Baptist raised back to life, or Elijah returned to earth, or (at least) a risen prophet]. Mark quotes fearful Herod Antipas anxiously guessing about Jesus: "It is John whom I beheaded. He has been raised up." Then Mark digresses into a flashback to tell of the dance of Salome, the hatred of Herodias and the beheading of John.

Following this, Mark narrates **a panel of events**: the miraculous feeding of the 5000 [in Jewish teritory], Jesus' trip across the Sea of Galilee, disputing with the Pharisees about defilement, taking his chosen disciples to Tyre and Sidon and the cure of the deaf & dumb man in the Decapolis. Mark's **next panel of episodes** partially parallels the preceding panel of events. Jesus feed 4000 [in Gentile territory], again goes across the sea of Galilee, confronts the Pharisees who demand another sign, warns his disciples about the insidious pharisaic teaching and heals the blind man at Bethsaida.

As an inclusion, Mark, **at last returns** explicitly to the **identity question**: who do the crowds say that I am? The disciples reply: John the Baptizer, Elijah, one of the prophets. Mark then asks the **climax question** of the first half of his Gospel: "**Who do YOU say that I am?** Peter responds: "You are the **Messiah.**"

Luke here makes his **geat omission** of all the materials between the identity questions except for the feeding of the five thousand which focuses on Jesus as a **Miracle-worker** exercizing divine power. With Mark's account in from of him, Luke skips the Herodias/Salome flashback to give a powerful answer to Herod's question: **Who then is this. . .?** The **answer** to Herod's question **dominates** Luke's text from 9:9 until 9:50 after which Luke makes his great insert (9:51 - 18:14) into the Gospel frame-work he adapted from Mark.

---

17.   New Testament of the New Amerian Bible, revised edition 1987, (New York: Catholic Book Publishing Co. p. 115. footnote 9:7-56), "This section in which Luke gathers together incidents that focus on **the identity of Jesus** is introduced by a question that Herod is made to ask in this gospel: '**Who then is this about whom I hear such things?**' **In subsequent episodes, Luke reveals to the reader various answers** to Herod's question"

To Herod's "**Who then is this?**", Luke answers He is **the one using divine power** to feed 5000 at once. Luke skips Mark's nine intervening episodes to continue with Peter's answer (9:18): He is **the Messiah of God!** Luke immediately adds Jesus' own self-identification: He is **The Son of Man** about to complete the mission of his passion, death and resurrection (9:22). In this decision he is **the one leading his disciples to [divine] glory** (9:23-27).

In awe at the transfiguration, Peter, James and John recognize Jesus is **the one identified by 'The Law and the Prophets'**. As the disciples' life-time guides, Moses and Elijah, recede from view a cloud overshadowed them; they then heard the most profound answer to: "**who then is this?**" "**This is my chosen Son; listen to him**" (9:35). The special disciples pondered their secret revelation. Next day, descending from the mountain where they learned such transcendent things, the chosen disciples with Jesus encountered a demonically distressed boy; Luke again discloses Jesus' identity through his use of transcendent power to cure the striken youngster. **Who is this?**. Luke emphasizes the palpable awe by affirming "all were astonished by the majesty of God." Luke then goes beyond his redaction of Mark; near the beginning of his great insert (9:51-18:14) Luke quotes Jesus himself responding in a revealing climax to Herod's question, "**Who then is this?**":

All things have been handed over, to me by my Father. **No one knows who the Son is except the Father**, and who the Father is except the Son and anyone to whom the Son wishes to reveal him. (10:22)

Jerusalem Conflicts   The close Mk/Lk correspondence which picked up again at 18:14 leads through familiar items toward Jesus' triumphal entry into Jerusalem and the ejecting of the money-changers from the temple area. This precipitates the Jerusalem conflicts. Mark's account (12:1-37) had narrated these conflicts: **Vinedressers**, **Image** of **Caesar**, **Resurrection** question, **Great** commandment, and **Origin** of the Messiah which may be symbolized by the acronym, **V-I-R-G-O**. Interestingly, **Luke**, in the sequence which corresponds with Mark's, just uses four of the episodes, the **V-I-R-O** conflicts, but omits the **G**. Did Luke wish to avoid the 'Greatest Commandment in the Torah' question[18] for his Gentile readers? Or did Luke already narrate this episode, thus indicating that he avoided cluttering

---

18. This involves the "SHEMA" prayer (Dt 6:4-7) with its focus on **monotheism** and worship which, for centuries, characterized the Jewish people, as the unique monotheists of the world.

his limited scroll with repetitions? Reading his Good Samaritan narrative (10:25ff) answers this question.

Close examination reveals that Luke, beside avoiding unnecessary repititions, also retouched some Markan episodes, omitted others, transposed a few items and added from his other sources many of the findings (but not all, scrolls were that limited in size!).[19] For example, Luke omitted the Jewish defilement question of Mark 7:1ff. He retouched the first PD&R episode. He transposed Jesus' choosing of his first disciples until after Jesus had publicly performed some works. If Mark had written for Christians he knew to be suffering in Nero's persecution, he had not paused to refine the direct order of the traditional material.

These activities of Luke convinced exegetes that the inspired authors were more free in handling the traditional data than was at first realized. For example, **Mark** (8:34) writing for Christians suffering severe persecution has: "If a man wishes to come after me, he must deny his very self, take up his cross, and follow in my steps." **Luke**, apparently writing in much less threatening circumstances, has in the same sequence of texts (9:23): "Whoever wishes to be my follower, must deny his very self, take up his cross **each day**, and follow in my steps." Luke's addition retains Mark's sense, but widens it to embrace also the crosses in the humdrum struggles of daily life.

One notes, too, how the sacred author can add the sufferings for the faith that the community may have experienced, such as arrests, beatings, jailings, etc.[20] as explicit completions of **Christ's principle** to "take up your cross **daily** and follow me," even though Jesus might not have explicitly said them in those exact words during his public ministry. The inspired author was not an academic researcher looking for documented quotations; such documents and methods did not exist then. He was rather a "careful tracer" of the Risen, Living Christ's deeds, teachings and principles "precisely **as those events were transmitted** to us **by the original eyewitnesses** and **ministers of the word.**" For Luke, the whole Gospel tradition is presently thriving and moving forward in his lifetime; Luke's inquiry wants to give assurance to Theophilus that it is on track **"from the beginning".** Luke's concern about "events and witnesses" distinguishes Luke's "infancy account" when it is compared to

---

19. W. Harrington, Luke, (Wilmington: Glazier, 1967), p. 9-11
20. Mt 10:17-18

Matthew's "infancy account". Matthew's more Jewish mind-set lends itself to using his "infancy introduction" as a sort of "fore-flash"[21] or miniature projection of his whole sharply-designed Gospel.

Infancy Accounts Matthew's infancy account has the somber and foreboding shadow of the cross over it to introduce his judgment of Jesus' rejection by so many of his own people. Oppositely, Luke, the gentle Gentile, lets the joy of the Heaven's rejoicing characterize the infancy introduction to his Gospel which happily emphasizes God's gracious salvation for the Gentiles, including Theophilus and himself. Mark had no infancy narrative. Scholars are convinced that Luke never saw Matthew's account, nor Matthew Luke's. Matthew's came from a Palestinian or Syrian provenance, some think **Antioch** itself. On the other hand, Luke's Gospel is thought by some to come from the region of **Greece**. Both are dated about 85 +/- 5.

Common data Both Infancy accounts **affirm** that Mary was a **virgin**, that her son was named **Jesus** (= Yahweh saves), that he was born in **Bethlehem** (of David's family), that he was raised in **Nazareth** by Mary and the carpenter Joseph, his putative father. Aside from these high-points and a few more items of common data, the accounts are as different as the gloom of the cross and the sunrise joy of the resurrection.[22]

Differences Matthew presents the clandestine visit by Magi (gentile star-interpreters), the malevolent intent of King Herod to slaughter the the Child Jesus, the sign of the star, and the Holy Family's anxious flight into Egypt. Luke's **atmosphere**, on the other hand, displays the excited joy of the poor shepherds, the angelic song on the mysterious night, the presentation in the Temple and the happy fulfillment for Simeon who sees the Child (2:32) as "a revealing **light to the Gentiles** [and] the **glory of your people Israel.**"

---

21. A "fore-flash" can be thought of as being in the opposite direction to a "flash-back"; Jewish **midrash** frequently implies this prophetic or even proleptic approach; this latter brings the prophetic future into the present as happening as Mt's raising of many deceased at Jesus' resurrection.
22. J. Fitzmyer, Luke, Infancy narratives, pp. 303-448; Common elements, pp. 307-312.

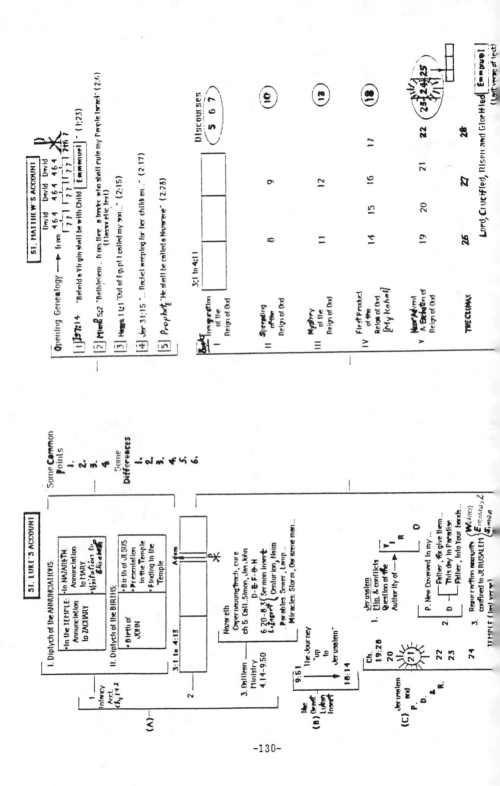

Once the common points of the infancy accounts are identified, the remaining **contents** of these two accounts are so different that exegetes have been unable to compose a single account from them. Their differences convince scholars that that neither author saw the other's Gospel. Matthew seems to **structure** his account on a frame of five Old Testament prophecies whose fulfillment is accomplished by the Messiah's birth with its accompanying events. Luke structures his narrative into a double diptych filled with song. His song are laced with allusive theology rich in Israel's history and prophecy.

For the more Jewish Gospel (Mt), the man, Joseph, is the leading **secondary character**; for Luke, Mary is the important personage next to her Son who is identified as <u>Savior</u> for Gentiles unfamiliar with the concept of "messiah". Matthew conveys God's message to Joseph by means of a dream, Luke by means of a divinely sent messenger, the angel Gabriel. Matthew focuses his attention on **Bethlehem**, the city of David, Luke highlights **Jerusalem** as the place where Jesus' real Father will approve his work with the glory of resurrection and from which the Good News will be sent out to the Gentiles.

The difficulty of reconciling the differences in the two infancy accounts has led some exegetes to identify both narratives as a Jewish kind of writing called **midrash**. This type of writing brings the relevant Old Testament texts into the description of the main event as attending circumstances. In midrash, the O.T. texts illuminate the meaning of the main event. Sometimes in midrash it is not clear that the O.T. details actually happened in the N.T. event. Thus, Matthew's infancy account would be like a miniature introductory picture of his whole Gospel. It says that the Messiah came to his own people, the leaders (Herod and his advisors) rejected him and sought his death, but the Gentiles (Magi) accepted him and by means of their gifts acknowledged who he was.

W. Harrington, in his book-length commentary on <u>Luke</u>, thinks that possibly the account in Matthew is midrashic, but he rejects this category as proper for Luke. a) Luke was not Jewish. Further, b) Theophilus would have read his account as basically conforming to his prologue where he talked about "events being fulfilled" and "eyewitnesses". Again, c) Luke may be giving Theophilus a clue to his source when he writes (2:19 and 2:51) that Jesus' "mother meanwhile kept all these things in her memory." Harrington says of **Luke's Infancy chapters**: "These chapters are **not midrash** and it is not helpful to characterize them as such."[23]

Resurrection   Luke's resurrection account differs from those already seen in the Gospels of Mark and Matthew. All three had available to them the common tradition of the resurrection appearances cited by Paul:

> For I handed on to you as of first importance what I also received: that Christ died for our sins . . .; that he was buried; that he was raised on the third day . . .; that he appeared to Kephas, then to the Twelve. After that he appeared to more than five hundred brothers at once, most of whom are still living, . . . he appeared to James, then to all the apostles. Last of all . . . he appeared to me. (1 Cor 15:3-8)

Luke chose not to quote this traditional list but rather to tell the appearances that best suited his purpose of assisting Theophilus to sense how God led the Apostles to belief. The Jewish-flavored list above mentions only men, no women, and Peter's name is the Aramaic name "Rock" given to him by Christ. Luke wanted to mention women who participated in the exciting events and he used the given name, Simon, instead of Kephas. Further, Luke wanted to show Theophilus the stages of uncertainty which unsettled the Apostles before they arrived at belief.[24]

The women discovered the empty tomb! They were puzzled, then terrified. God's message confronted them: "Why do you seek the living among the dead? He is not here, but he has been raised." Remember what he told you. The women believed. Breathlessly, they hurried to tell the Apostles. The Apostles did not believe them.

Peter ran to the tomb; he was amazed! Luke does not mention John, nor does he say that Peter yet believed that Jesus had risen.

---

23.   W. Harrington, The Gospel According to St. Luke, (Westminster: Newman Press, 1967), p.73.
24. Joseph Plevnik, "The Eyewitnesses of the Risen Jesus in Luke 24", The Catholic Biblical Quarterly, v.49, n.1, January 1987, pp. 90-103. My brief presentation of Luke's resurrection account is dependent on the development in Plevnik's article. [hereafter: Plevnik, "Eyewitnesses", CBQ, and page.]

Meanwhile, **two disciples,** presumably giving up, left the group and headed for the town of **Emmaus.** Jesus, unrecognized, joined them as they were "conversing and debating" about these events. Luke says: "but their eyes were prevented from recognizing him." With eyes and spirits downcast, they complained that they had hoped Jesus would redeem Israel, but our authorities had him crucified.

Slowly, Jesus opened the Scriptures to them; don't you recall that the prophets had said, it was necessary "that the Messiah should suffer these things and enter into his glory." Their hearts burned with excitement as they recognized the scriptures. As darkness closed in, they stopped for supper. At table, when he blessed and broke the bread, they recognized him; then he vanished from their sight. They rushed back to Jerusalem to tell "the Eleven" they had seen him with their own eyes!

When they got back, "the Eleven" were buzzing with excitement. Jesus had appeared to **Peter!** Peter himself had seen him. Notice what Luke is doing. He is telling Theophilus that different ones came to belief in Jesus' resurrection because the risen Jesus gave them eye-witness evidence.

Next, approaching the climax, Jesus appeared to "**The Eleven**".[25] While they were still buzzing, Jesus "stood in their midst and said to them, Peace be with you." They were amazed! He ate in their presence! He opened the Scriptures to them! He told them the prophecies had to be fulfilled. "You are **witnesses** of these things." Go, tell "**all the nations**".[26]

Luke had taken Theophilus through the steps that led the first Christians to belief in Jesus' resurrection as evidence of his

---

25. This appearance to the Apostles is narrated in all the accounts; it has a sort of official character for the first Christian community since the Apostles with Peter will be establishing Christ's Church wherever they go.
26. Recall Luke in 1:2 had said his Gospel account depended on "those who were eyewitnesses from the beginning." Thus, Luke started his Gospel with the eyewitness claim and he ended with the eyewitness fact.

Messiahship and more.[27] Luke used his **last sentence** (24:52-53) to affirm the Apostles' conviction of the risen Jesus' divinity.[28] It is the climax of his Gospel. He invites Theophilus to do as the Apostles have done; the invitation was to join in the worship of the risen Lord.

Lord Luke had used the title, **Lord**, for Jesus throughout his Gospel account.[29] If this title had been about Jesus during his public ministry (i.e. in stage one of the formation of the Gospel), it would generally have been used with secular overtones. Those convinced that Jesus was the Messiah would have invested the title, **Lord**, with new meaning but scarcely yet with the sense that Jesus was equal to Yahweh before his death, resurrection and Pentecost. But in the light of the risen Jesus' multiple appearances (cf. 1 Cor 15: 3-7) and the Holy Spirit's profound influence, the use of the Aramaic **Adonai** (Kyrios in Greek; Lord in English) applied to **Yahweh** in the Septuagint, was now applied to Jesus with the sense of awe belonging properly to God. Luke, a later convert to **Jesus, the Lord**, manifests his profound belief by his use of this title, **Lord**, for Jesus throughout his Gospel. Luke uses it frequently to imply Jesus' **transcendence** in the material special to himself, such as: the infancy account, the little Lukan insert (6:20-8:3) and the big Lukan insert (9:51-18:14).

The infancy account:
1:43 How is it "the mother of **my Lord** should come to me?";
[1:46 Mary's "my soul magnifies the Lord" refers to Yahweh.]
2:11 "Savior . . . born for you who is Messiah and **Lord**.";

---

27. Plevnik, "Eyewitnesses", CBQ, p. 102 "The disciples' worshiping Jesus is thus their acknowledgement of his divinity." p.103 "When the disciples give worship to the ascending Jesus, this is indeed, an act of faith. It is, however, not faith in Jesus' resurrection, for this occurred earlier, but their acknowledgement of Jesus divinity." For Luke it is the deepest meaning of faith; thus it is the mountain peak and end of his Gospel.
28. Recall Luke's "Father/Son" revelation passage 10:22: "All things have been handed over to me by my Father. No one knows who the Son is except the Father, and who the Father is except the Son and anyone to whom the Son wishes to reveal him"
29. W. Harrington, The Gospel According to Luke, (New York: Newman Press, 1967), pp.28f; (hereafter, Harrington, Luke and page.

The little Lukan insert:
7:13 "When **the Lord** saw her" (Widow of Nain);
7:19 The Baptist "sent them to **the Lord**".

The big Lukan insert:
10:1 "After this **the Lord** appointed . . . others";
10:39 "Mary sat beside **the Lord** at his feet";
10:40 Martha: "**Lord**, do you not care . . .";
10:41 "**The Lord** said to her . . .";
11:1 "**Lord**, teach us to pray . . .";
11:39 "**The Lord** said to him [Pharisee at table]";
12:41 Peter, "**Lord**, is this parable for us?
12:42 "And **the Lord** replied . . .";
13:15 "The **Lord** said to him in reply, . . .";
17:5 "Apostles said to **the Lord**, 'Increase our faith.'"

The title is inserted in other material as well:
22:61 "**The Lord** turned and looked at Peter;"
24:3 "They did not find the body of **the Lord Jesus**";
24:34 They said: "**The Lord** has truly been raised. . ."

Luke also uses this title elsewhere in his Gospel and in <u>Acts</u>
as well. Luke's passages remind us of Paul's affirmation: "that
Jesus is Lord . . ." (Rom 10:9) and "every tongue should confess
that **Jesus is Lord**" (Phil 2:11) of which exegete, W. Harrington,
says: "in both cases **the divinity of Christ** is professed."[30]

Exegetes   see   this   use   of   the   title   as   the   post
resurrection/Pentecost conviction retrojected by Luke into Jesus'
historical public ministry (referred to as the first of the three
stages   in   the   genesis   of   the   Gospel).[31]   One   scholar,   Joseph
Fitzmyer, estimates that "Luke is simply using the title that had
become current in his own day. . ."; in applying this same title
to both Yahweh and Jesus there had to be some profound sense
in which the early Christian community "regarded Jesus as on a
level with Yahweh."[32]

At Jesus' ascension, the gathered Apostles and disciples "**did
him homage.**" As Jesus ascended to glory, they worshipped him.

---

30. Harrington, <u>Luke</u>, p. 29.
31. Joseph Fitzmyer, <u>The Gospel According To Luke I-IX</u>, (Garden
City: Doubleday & Company, Inc. 1981; Anchor Bible vol 28) pp.
200-204; (hereafter, Fitzmyer, <u>Luke I-IX</u> and page.
32. Fitzmyer, <u>Luke I-IX</u>, p.203

Scriptural scholar, G. Lohfink thinks, "It is the christological highpoint of the Gospel. Faith in Jesus is here faith in the divinity of Jesus."[33]

Portrait St. Luke is deeply attracted to the compasssion and sensitivity which Jesus manifested to people.[34] Luke, a **gentle Gentile** himself, softens the stark edges of Mark's Gospel and mutes some of the obtuseness of the Apostles who by the time Luke wrote his Gospel (c. 85 A.D.) are the martyred heroes of the growing Christian community. Luke notes the disciples' slowness in understanding Jesus, but highlights more the compassion, and prayer of Jesus. Luke's Gospel alone identifies Jesus with the title, **Savior** (2:11)! When the Jewish saintly man Simeon received Jesus, he proclaimed that the child was "for **all the peoples** to see: a revealing light to the **Gentiles...**"; thus, Gentile Luke's vision was focused on Jesus as the universal compassionate savior. Where Matthew in his **Sermon on the Mount** used traditional material to highlight the plan of Christian perfection for following Christ, Luke emphasized that **self-sacrificing love** was at the heart of this perfection in his **Sermon on the Plain** (6:20-49).

A bit later Jesus showed his loving concern for the poor **widow of Nain.** Luke alone preserved this beautiful and touching episode for the reflection of post-apostolic readers. More than the other evangelists, Luke's **Gospel-portrait of Jesus** embraced the concern that Jesus manifested to women, and to the poor. In Luke's Gospel Jesus (expressed simply as "Luke's Jesus") **challenges** his disciples: "**Be compassionate** as your Father [in heaven] is compassionate, (6:36)" The narratives of the good Samaritan, the Prodigal son, the good Shepherd **highlighted compassion.** Jesus' statement when being crucified, "Father, forgive them, they know not what they do", demonstrated Jesus' **forgiveness** at an astounding moment of severe suffering; this deeply influenced Luke's portrait of Jesus. The dying Jesus' profound compassion for the repentant thief on the cross touched a responsive chord in Luke's heart, "This day you will be with me in Paradise". Luke attributes this deeply compassionate judgment to **crucified Jesus** he has so frequently identified as **"the Lord".**

---

33. Plevnik, "Eyewitnesses", CBQ, p. 90, footnote: For G.Lohfink the longer readings of Luke 24, "now supported by **P**[75]," go beyond acknowledgement of Jesus' resurrection; the disciples' worship looks to his divinity.
34.   Warren Dicharry, C.M., To live the Word Inspired and Incarnate, (New York: Alba House, 1985), p.51.

Questions

1. What is the **position** of the Gospel according to Luke in the order of the four Gospels?
2. What **steps** did Jesus' Apostles have to go through to gain a full understanding of who and what Jesus is? [Failure to see the development here leads to misinterpretation of the N.T.]

3. After Pentecost, as each apostle separately told of his personal experiences, his narratives would come from different moments of awareness in his growing understanding of Jesus;
4. What is the **highpoint** of the Apostles' understanding (of who and what Jesus is) sometimes called?

5. What is the **name for** "scriptural determination of the level of understanding the Evangelist intends in a given episode"?
6. Was **Jesus the Messiah** in se: a)below, b)equal to, or c)beyond the O.T.'s understanding of "the Messiah"?

7. Is Jesus' **divine sonship**, in the belief of the Catholic Church, a)metaphorical, or b)ontological reality?
8. What **level of belief about Jesus** do the Synoptics manifest, according to: a) Pere Benoit O.P.; b)Rev. Bruce Vawter C.M.?

9. Why according to exegetes is an understanding of **Mark important when studying** the Gospel according to **Luke**?
10. To whom **explicitly** is Luke writing? What kind of **mind-set** is Luke addressing? What consequences flow from this?

11. How does Paul (Col 4:14) refer to Luke? Others: a)Eusebius; b)The Oxford Dictionary of the Christian Church?
12. Name **three** post-apostolic **witnesses** who identify the third Gospel and Acts as Luke's work.

13. What is significant about the ancient affirmation of **Luke as the author** of a Gospel account? Is this attestation of much value for modern scholars? On what **basis** can the knowledge of Luke's authorship of the gospel be applied to Acts?
14. Why did some scholars **date** Acts as early as 62 A.D.? Why was 62 not generally accepted?

15. Why is Sandmel's **late dating** of Luke's Gospel account not accepted by scholars who date the works at 85 +/-5?
16. Who is the **addressee** of Luke-Acts? What evidence seems to identify the addressee as a real person

17. What **reason** does Luke have for so much work? What **mind-set** is Luke addressing?
18. Does Luke's account contain **evidence of sources** used by him?

19. What **3 sections** of Luke's account are not found in Mark? In what way is Luke's **overall gospel-framework** like Mark's?
20. What does **Luke's use** of Markan material indicate? Name some **Markan sequences** which Luke seems to have used?

21. Why does Luke start his **genealogy** differently from Matthew's?

22. What would the title **Messiah** say to a Gentile mind ignorant of Judaism? How does Luke modify Peter's expression (9:20) at Caesarea Philippi? How does Luke modify Mark's presentation of the Apostles' obtuseness?

23. **Where** in Mark's order of the 3 predictions of the **PD&R** does Luke make his great (9:51-18:14) insertion?
24. Does Luke correspond with Mark in presenting the **Jerusalem conflicts**? Why does Luke omit there Mark's presentation of the greatest commandment (shema)?

25. Why did Luke omit Mark's **defilement** conflict (Mk 7:1-23)?
26. **Did Luke feel free** to add words to the statements made by Peter or Paul, - even a statement by Christ? Did 1st century authors use quotation marks around quoted statements? Whom did Luke cite and suggest as his **sources**? [Cf. Lk 1:1-4]

27. Contrast the **infancy accounts** of Lk and Mt as to the **atmosphere** or mood of each. As to either evangelist copying from the other, what is the conviction of scholars?
28. What data are **common** to Lk's and Mt's infancy accounts?

29. Name five elements in which they **differ.**
30. What is **midrash**? Scholars differ as to the **genre** of the infancy accounts? How does Harrington assess the 2 accts?

31. Name the **resurrection appearances** which Luke cites. Does he know more? What plan seems to govern his selection?
32. Discuss Luke's use of the title, **Lord**, for Jesus.

33. What elements highlight the gentle Luke's **portrait of Jesus**?

Chapter X: The Gospel According to John

"In the beginning was THE WORD (Logos), THE WORD was with God, and THE WORD was God." Thus, in the rarefied air of Divine transcendence begins the Gospel according to John. Immediately we recognize that John has ushered us into the presence of Divine mystery more than light years beyond the more mundane preaching of John the Baptist which started Jesus' public ministry. Even this Gospel's opening words (en arche = in the beginning), are the very words with which **Genesis** starts the creation narrative; the Gospel according to John thus implies that a **new creation** is about to take place.

This evangelist writes as if the people addressed already know a lot about Jesus , but not deeply enough. The author's attention is focused on the divine, transcendent Jesus throughout his Gospel. As **Eusebius** says: John begins "with the proclamation of His [Jesus'] **divinity**, since the Holy Spirit had reserved this for him, as the greatest of the four [Evangelists]."[1] Unlike the synoptics, this Gospel doesn't delay to let the reader first appreciate Jesus' **humanity**, then the awesome belief in His **messiahship**, before making the quantum leap to his **divinity**. But the fourth Gospel still proclaims Jesus' humanity, and Messiahship along with the towering reality of his divinity. "Through him all things came into being, and apart from him nothing came to be."(1:3)

Before entering into the Gospel itself, however, the ordinary questions, asked of the the other New Testament books, must be asked of this Gospel too. **Who** wrote it? **When? Where? To whom?** And **Why?** For this fourth Gospel some of these questions appear to be more difficult to answer than for the other Gospels. Some reasons for this difficulty are: **1.**five N.T. 'books' with different writing styles (John's Gospel, the Apocalypse, and three Epistles), are attributed to the teaching of John; **2.**early Christian writers spoke of more than one man named John; and **3.**an assumption has been held for many years that John's Gospel is so elevated that many decades had to pass before Christians could speak in such transcendent terms about Jesus of Nazareth.

---

1. Eusebius, Historia Ecclesiastica, p. 133, or 24.15; hereafter, Eusebius, H.E. and page.

When written? Interestingly, this assumption of so late a date (150 or later) has rather recently been overturned by the finding of a small 7-verses bit of John's Gospel (18:31-33,37-38) on a piece of papyrus located in the John Rylands Library in Manchester, England. It is labeled **Rylands Papyrus 52**[2] [**P52**].[3] It was found in Egypt. All the methods of dating (nature of: the papyrus, the uncial writing, the ink used, carbon dating, etc.) concluded that it existed about 125-130. Its Egyptian location (no scholar thinks it was written there) meant its prior existence elsewhere at a time sufficient for prior spread of its influence and recognition of its value, so that it was worthwhile for distant places to request it and pay for scribes to makes copies and transport the copies to the requesters' locations. These steps and others take time! More recent scholarship [ca. 1982] has suggested that **P52** should be dated closer to the year 100 A.D. Thus, scholars now date John's Gospel no later than **95 +/- 5**, and perhaps earlier.

A scholarly exegete, Frederick Grant, dated John's Gospel as late as 120 A.D.; his equally scholarly son, Robert Grant, at last writing, was dating John's Gospel not much later than 70 A.D. (the destruction of Jerusalem),[4] because it shows no suggestion of the post-destruction changes in the Roman/Jewish relationships! J.A.T. Robinson, who enjoys goading other scholars,[5] dates this Gospel before 70, but the before-70 argument has not convinced most scholars.

Eusebius wrote that John was exiled to the island of Patmos in the reign of Emperor Hadrian (81-96), that he returned to Ephesus during the reign of Emperor Nerva (96-98), and **died in Trajan's time** (98-117).[6] This would probably mean that John died

---

2. A.Wikenhauser, New Testament Introduction, p.320.
3. Aland, Text of the New Testament, cf. Index.
4. A. Hunter, Introducing The New Testament, (Philadelphia: The Westminster Press, 1972), p.63 ftnt 2; Hunter himself places the date at 80 or earlier.
5. J.A.T. Robinson, Redating the New Testament, (Philadelphia: Westminster Press, 1976), p. 310f; (hereafter, Robinson, Redating, and page.
6. Eusebius, Historia Ecclesiastica, tr G.A. Williamson (Baltimore:Penguin Books,1965), p.127f quoting Irenaeus and Clement of Alexandria; p. 141 quoting Polycrates, Bishop of Ephesus: "John...who became a sacrificing priest wearing the mitre, a martyr and a teacher; he too sleeps in Ephesus." 31.5.

about the year 100. If he had been about eighteen in the year of Christ's Passion, death and Resurrection, then he would have been about 88 by the turn of the century.

An **ancient tradition** exists that John took Jesus' mother, Mary, with him to **Ephesus** (modern Efes), where she stayed until her assumption. The remnants of an ancient house there have been rebuilt as a shrine cared for by the Daughters of Charity of St. Vincent de Paul. A counter tradition locates Mary's death and assumption in Jerusalem. Sufficient evidence is not available to resolve the dilemma. It may be noted that the third Ecumenical Council, [which identified Mary as the Mother of the Divine Christ, thus the **"Theotokos"** (= Mother of God)], took place at **Ephesus.** Many scholars accept the ancient tradition that the central source of the Johannine teaching was **Ephesus.**

In the ancient world the **person who was the source** of teachings was identified as the **authority** behind, or the author of, the teachings regardless of who committed them to writing. The fact that significantly different styles are present in the Johannine corpus of writings, even within the Gospel itself, convinces modern critics that different disciples of John committed his profound teachings to the scrolls. It is even thought that if John directly dictated anything to a scribe, it would have been the Apocalypse, because more Aramaic expressions surface in this book. In any event, it is now held that as Jesus gathered "THE Twelve" and formed them, so His Apostles, following His example, gathered, taught and formed believing disciples around themselves.

Redaction   A biblical scholar, Raymond Brown, from the characteristics of the various passages within the Gospel, theorizes that the Apostle John was the primary oral **source** of the traditional apostolic data with which he inpired and formed his (= Christ's primarily) community of disciples. **Secondly,** John's insights and way of saying the primary data, **shaped it,** and gave it characteristics, such as: double expressions, and proceding from monologue to dialogue, which become noticeable when studying the Gospel. **Thirdly,** a disciple wrote it; he is called the "disciple-evangelist". Somewhat later, in a **fourth** step, the original writing was edited and added to, perhaps by the same disciple-evangelist. **Finally,** one who may be called the "disciple-redactor" added some more material from the oral tradition, probably added chapter 21 and thus finished the final edition.

This is a much-simplified version of Brown's theory which W. Harrington[7] and other exegetes work from, while other scholars modify it from different interpretations of the same kinds of evidence. A good example of evidence which indicates that different hands were involved in producing the fourth Gospel is present in 20:30f and 21:24f. The first passage is clearly **an ending** to the Gospel. But some time after that ending and with writing which uses **different personal pronouns**, the book starts up again to focus attention on the "shepherd-function of Peter" as primary among the Apostles, and an implication that John will not live until Christ's second coming, then it **ends again** in 21:24f.

Why written?   That first end gives the clearest answer as to **Why** this Gospel, but also the whole New Testatment, was written (20:30f):

> Jesus performed many other signs as well - signs not recorded here - in the presence of his disciples. but these have been recorded to help you believe that **Jesus is** the **Messiah**, the **Son of God**, so that through this faith you may have life in his name.

This original last line of the scroll forms a very clear **inclusion** with the Gospel's first line in which the divinity of Christ is so clearly affirmed. In fact, the inclusion is so pointed that some exegetes think the highlighted expression should preferably read: **Jesus**, the Messiah, **is** the **Son of God**. The Greek sustains both translations equally well, but the relationship with the opening line calls for the choice of this translation in which we place the "**is**" after the title "Messiah" rather than before it.

To Whom? This Gospel was not written to get disbelieving Gentiles or unbelieving Jews to join the faith. It was "intended for **believing Christians** (regardless of origin), to lay a solid foundation for their conviction and faith."[8] Its design is to help the believers, whether Jew or Gentile in origin, to so preserve and deepen their faith that they might possess the **Life** which the Son of God had come to give. Nevertheless, the Gospel is clearly dealing with things Jewish; it speaks of Abraham, Moses

---

7. W. Harrington, Key to the Bible #3, "The New Testament, (Canfield, Ohio: Alba Books, 1966) pp.154f.
8. A. Wikenhauser, New Testament Introduction, tr J Cunningham, (New York: Herder & Herder, 1958) p. 307.

and the Temple. John's term Jew is used by him to contrast the Jewish leaders with the believing Jews and Gentiles; the term is "practically synonymous with 'unbelieving Jew.'"[9] It must be remembered: that John himself, the source of the Gospel's tradition, was a Jew, that the Jesus he is proclaiming is the very one spoken of in "the Law and the Prophets", that he refers with praise to Abraham and Moses, so this Gospels's term Jew, far from being applied to all Jews, is restricted to the unbelieving opponents of Jesus, and later of John's community.

A general **summary** of the who, what, when, where and why questions, may hold the position that John is the authoritative teaching source of the fourth Gospel's account, that the writing of it dates from about 95 +/- 5 A.D., that it's place of origin is Ephesus and that its purpose is to support and confirm belief in Jesus as Messiah and Son of God so that believers may receive and live "the life" Jesus came to give.

Overall Structure   Many scholars agree that the overall
structure of John's Gospel consists of:
1. Prologue, 1:1-18
2. The Book of Signs, 1:19-12:50[10]
3. The Book of Glory, 13:1-20:31
4. An Appendix, 21 (sometimes called an epilogue).[11]

Prologue   Exegetes think that the **Prologue** consists of a hymn
into which has been inserted data about John the
Baptist as the one who prepared the way for Jesus, the unique Messiah.[12] John's Prologue sets the tone of the whole Gospel. Unlike the Synoptics, this Gospel, along with some of Paul's letters

---

9.   Ibid, p.307.
10.   The **Book of Signs** is analyzed differently by various scholars. C. H. Dodd focused on the signs in a Narrative + Discourse structure.
11.   Aland, Text of the New Testament, "It is only in this form...[i.e., in the sequence as we now have chapters 1 through 21] that the book is found throughout the manuscript tradition".
12.   Conzelmann, Early Christian History, pp. 168f. Governor Pliny's letter to Emperor Trajan had indicated that Christians sang a song to Christ as God. This hymn perhaps originated from the teaching of John or Paul in Asia Minor; it introduces one immediately to the Divine Person who came to save and give new life to all who believe in him.

and the Epistle to the Hebrew's, contemplates and affirms the
Son's pre-existence, - i.e. his existence with the Father before
creation: "Through him all things came into being,..."(1:3). John
speaks of his **incarnation** (i.e. his "enfleshment", or his coming
among us in flesh and blood human nature[13]) with the words: "The
Word (Logos) **became flesh** and made his dwelling among us" (1:14).
John uses this special term "**Logos**" to identify God's eternal **Son.**
When he came among men in human flesh, the Son entered into
mankind's history in a specific time and place, and of Jewish flesh.

In his account John continues to remind the reader of the
Son's existence prior to the creation of time and place. In 8:58
when opponents contested his reference to Abraham (c.1850 B.C.),
Jesus replied: "I solemnly declare it: before Abraham came to be,
I AM." And again in 17:5 in Jesus' prayer to **His Father** at the
last supper, he says: "Do you now, Father, give me glory at your
side, a glory I had with you **before the world began.**" Thus, the
prologue's transcendent point of view pervades the whole fourth
Gospel. The Gospel as a whole is like a great letter **| |.** The Son
starts off in Eternity, then descends to assume a human nature
and goes (as it were horizontally) through many human experiences
until by means of his Passion, Death and Resurrection he ascends
to the Glory that was his from the beginning.

Witnesses John's Gospel frequently has two (sometimes more)
levels of meaning. In 1:19-51 the level of giving witness
to Jesus catches immediate attention. John the Baptist identifies
Jesus as the **Lamb** (talya in Hebrew) **of God. Talya** illudes to both
a "lamb" and a "servant". Jesus' sacrifice as "**the Lamb**" will
replace those sacrificed in the Temple; and in its meaning as **THE
Servant of God** the talya-expression refers to the suffering servant
proclaimed by the prophet in the "servant songs" (cf. especially
Is.53). Andrew, as a witness tells his brother Simon: "We have
found the **Messiah!**"(1:41). When Simon comes to the person pointed
out, Jesus tells him: "Simon bar Jonah, your name shall be **Cephas**
(which is rendered Peter)." It looks like the evangelist is giving
a quick summary of the persons in his account and their respective
insights and significant title-names in order to be very clear at
the start of his Gospel.

---

13. Jewish anthropology considered man to be composed of flesh,
blood and spirit, unlike Greek anthropology which conceived of
man as consisting of body and soul.

Prologue 1:1-18

Book of Signs
   1:19-51 Witnesses: Baptist, Andrew, Philip,
   [Simon], Nathanael, Jesus.

I *New Life*	2	Cana	N	
		Clearing the Temple	N	
	3	Nicodemus discourse		D
	4	Samaritan woman		D

II *His Word gives Life*	5	Nobleman's son (Cana)	N	
		Sheep gate pool	N	
		Discourse: Word of Life		D

III *Bread of Life*	6	5000 fed on loaves & fishes	N	
		Walking on the Sea	N	
		Discourse: Bread of life		D

| IV *Light of The World* | 7 | Tabernacles Feast | N | |
| | 8 | [Adultress]; Conflict-dialogue | | D |

| V *Light > Dark* | 9 | Man born blind | N | |
| | 10 | Discourse: Good Shepherd | | D |

| VI *Life > Death* | 11 | Lazarus raised | N & D |

| VII *Glory through Death* | 12 | Triumphal entry | N | |
| | | Disc:Glory thru His death | | D |

Book of Glory

Last Supper	13	Washing of the Apostles' feet
	14	Dialogue: Departure & return
		If you love me...
		Holy Spirit
	15	Discourse: Vine & Branches
	16	Abiding love/World's hate

	17	Prayer of Jesus: work completed
		for Apostles
		for those who believe them
	18	Arrest/before Annas/before Pilate

	19	Crucifixion: Mary.John/I Thirst/Finished.
	20	**Risen Lord:** Magdalen/Apostles/Thomas
		first end

Appendix: 21 Risen Lord: Peter/John/second end

Philip is next and he identifies Jesus to Nathanael as the one spoken of "**in the Torah (Law) and the Prophets**"(1:45). Nathanael in his turn adds the fullest belief expression: "Rabbi, you are the **Son of God**; you are the **King of Israel**,"(1:49). Jesus uses the self-identification **Son of Man** which carries the implication (Dan 7:13) of the special one sent from God. This Gospel will tell us after Jesus' death and burial, when Peter and John ran to the empty tomb: "Remember as yet they did not understand the Scripture that Jesus had to rise from the dead" (20:9), so this tomb-statement makes it clear that John is letting the believing reader know the end of the Gospel right in the beginning so that the reader can appreciate the pre-eminence of the one who came to share their lives in order to make them **sharers in his life**; and at what a cost!

Signs   The fourth Gospel doesn't delay to give the overview triptych with which the Synoptics started the public ministry. Rather, taking the reader's knowledge of that for granted, it gently moves into the Galilean ministry with the marriage feast at **Cana** and the miracle there. "Jesus performed this **first of his signs** at Cana in Galilee. Thus did he reveal his glory, and his disciples believed in him" (2:11). John, subordinating historical data to theological significance, next narrates Jesus' revealing act of clearing the money-changers out of the Temple area, (the Synoptics tell it near the end of his ministry). "Stop turning **my Father's house** into a market-place!"(2:16). The stunned Jews (= the authorities in John's Gospel) challenge: "**What sign** can you show us authorizing you to do these things?" Jesus identifies **himself** as God's **New Temple** when he says: destroy it, and "in three days I will raise it up." John shows Jesus implying here that Jesus' resurrection will be the "sign of signs" even while he is indicating to his believing hearers that the Temple in Jerusalem will no longer be the center of divine worship; Jesus will be the center and sign of his Father's worship. In 2:23, John continues with the sign language: "many believed in his name, for they could see **the signs** he was performing."

"For his part, Jesus would not trust himself to them (recall the reason for the messianic secret in Mark's Gospel) because he knew them all. He needed no one to give him testimony about human nature. He was well aware of what was in man's heart." From the use of "sign" (= semeia in Greek) above it is clear that "sign" primarily signifies miracle; so that every miracle Jesus performs is a sign.[14] C.H.Dodd's outline unites the two Discourses [Nicodemus and the Samaritan woman] with the first two Narratives. [It forms a complex like this: **N N D D**; C.H. Dodd refers to such groupings of narratives and discourses as "an episode".] In the first D (= Discourse) to Nicodemus' question about being born again (anothen in Greek), Jesus specifies that this **new birth** comes from above (anothen). "No one can enter God's kingdom without being begotten of water and Spirit (= **baptism**). Flesh begets flesh, Spirit begets spirit"(3:5-6). [John deliberately used the one word (anothen) with the two meanings: the material one: again born from flesh, and above from the Holy Spirit; he does this here and elsewhere[15] in order to cancel the material meaning and give exclusive emphasis to the spiritual meaning.]

In the second D with the Samaritan woman Jesus, a Jewish stranger to her, speaks of giving her **living water** (= Baptism in John's Gospel), startles her with his knowledge of her adulterous life and apparently encourages her to a **new life** of repentence. Dodd reads this N N D D combination as a unit [called an episode] in which John is saying that Jesus came **to give New Life.**

Episode 2 After the cure of the Nobleman's son (4:50) in which the word **sign** was again used, and the cure by the Sheepgate Pool (5:8), Jesus' two acts and following discourse (the discourses give **the meaning** of the acts) convey the realization for John that Jesus' **very word gives life.**

Episode 3 The feeding of the 5000 (6:1ff) and the walking on the water constitute the N, N which lead to the D (= discourse) of Jesus on: faith in him, and the life-giving bread. Jesus' statement; **I AM the Bread of Life** indicate the evangelist's intention in this episode. Here, as at Caesarea-Philippi in the Synoptics, Peter expresses the firm belief of "THE 12". Many in the crowd rejected Jesus' "Bread of Life" revelation. At this moment of crisis, Jesus challenged the Twelve: "Do you want to leave me too?" Peter spoke for them: "Lord to whom shall we

---

14. But even some things which are not seen as miracles are signs. The non-miraculous clearing of the Temple appears to be a sign as well, although John does not identify it with the word, sign.
15. John uses this kind of intentional double-meaning here, and also with the word "temple" as well as with "living water", "lifting up" and "hour".

go? You have the **words of eternal life. We** have come to **believe;** we are convinced that **you are God's holy one (= Messiah)."**

Episodes 4   The feast of Tabernacles (Booths or Tents), a feast of lights and water, provides the occasion on which Jesus reveals **I AM the Light of the world.** Exegetes think that the adulterous-woman narrative is an insert (perhaps from Luke's Gospel) into John's narrative. Jesus' stance now leads to a series of dialogue-conflicts with the authorities and others in which Jesus is **shedding light** on Jewish priority questions touching Moses, Abraham and the Torah. Those beginning to believe in him ask the identity question: "Can the Messiah when he comes be expected to perform more **signs** than this man?" (7:31). At the climax of the conflicts, to the taunt that he cannot have known Abraham because he has not even reached the age of fifty, he replied: **Before Abraham was, I AM** (8:58). The arguments in these conflicts carried more force in a Jewish or Jewish-Christian milieu than in a predominantly gentile community.

Episode 5   In this episode John shows the blind man cured by Jesus deepening in faith while the Sanhedrin rejected this widely known and obvious miracle to continue on the path of blindness to the signs God gave them. The blind man sees the Messiah; the seeing Sanhedrin yields to blindness regarding him. John is showing that their **final judgment** (eschatological judgment) is "being realized" or taking place then and there. The accompanying discourse to complete the N + D of Episode 5 has Jesus identifying himself as **The Good Shepherd** (a function of Yahweh for Israel) for those who can see. His **light overcomes the darkness** which is the realm of the diabolical.

Episode 6 The N & D are intertwined in this episode. C.H Dodd's overall perception does not fully fit this section of John's "Book of Signs". It involves the raising (not resurrection) of Lazarus, the brother of Martha and Mary. Jesus demonstrates that his relationship to his Father so transcends the observers' vision that in his hands **Life overcomes death.** So many of the people are coming to believe in him, that the infuriated Sanhedrin (= the Jews in John's Gospel) decide to do away with him!

Episode 7 The N of this closing episode of the Book of signs is the public and triumphal entry of Jesus into Jerusalem, the capital of Israel. The D which illuminates the event reveals that his triumph is not the political one which disbelievers perceive, but the faithful fulfillment of his Father's will which in his facing

-148-

death for its truth will lead to eternal glory. **Divine Glory will come through His death and resurrection.**

Book of Glory   The term "Glory" is a technical term signifying God's own life and the manifestation of that divine life. This "book" is divided into two main parts: The **Last Supper** section (13-17); and the **Passion, Death and Resurrection** section (18-20). The **Narrative/Discourse** structure of the episodes in the Book of Signs is here reversed into one major Discourse followed by one major Narrative unit.

Last Supper   Unlike the Synoptics which focused attention on the eucharistic body/blood significance of the next day's sacrifice, John gives his attention to Jesus' relationships to His Father, the Paraclete (the Holy Spirit) who will be sent to them and his relationship with them and those who will believe through them. To his future Apostles' utter amazement, he, whom they now keenly believed to be the promised Messiah, washed their feet! They were abashed at his act of humility, especially Peter. The lesson was vivid! In their future work it was not for them to "lord" it **over** others. 'You do, as I have done', he told them. In sequences of dialogue which yield to his instructive monologue (a Johannine characteristic), Jesus tells them that, to their sorrow, he will depart from them, but he will return. He will send another (The Holy Spirit) to them who will bring to mind the things he has taught them. John does **not** relate the **institution account** (of the Eucharist) during the Last Supper as the Synoptics had done; John had already strongly underscored its reality, meaning, and necessity for union with him in chapter 6; John alludes to it again at Jesus' death on the cross.[16]

Love's measure   "If you love me, you will keep my word," he says to his followers five times."This is my commandment [its measure goes beyond the golden Rule]: love one another **as I have loved you.**" Jesus pictures for them (and all who believe in him) the branch on the vine thriving and the branch

---

16.   St. John Chrysostom "Good Friday" (p.474 in the lenten breviary) notes John's **symbolism** in reflections on the crucifixion: the O.T.'s blood of the lamb was "a sign of the Lord's blood... [which] flowed from the master's side." "The water was a symbol of baptism, and the blood of the eucharist." "From these two sacraments the Church is born...."

cut from the vine dying. In the light of this everyday image, he says (15:1):

"**I AM the true vine** and **my Father** is the vinegrower...Live on in me as I do in you....apart from me you can do nothing. A man who does not live in me is like a withered, rejected branch, picked up to be thrown in the fire and burnt....As the Father has loved me, so **I have loved you**....All this I tell you (15:11) that my joy may be yours and **your joy may be complete.**"

Having thus spoken of the supreme measure of self-giving love, Jesus leads his Apostles to Gethsemane where the agonizing test of fidelity and love will begin.

Suffering In the garden it began with a betrayal by **Judas.** Arrested, Jesus was questioned by Annas. Annas sent him bound to the high priest, Caiaphas, his son-in-law. The evangelist leaves unsaid the blasphemy charge which was well known from the oral tradition and the Synoptics. Meanwhile elsewhere, **Peter** denied he knew Jesus. At daybreak the high priest, Caiaphas, had him taken to the Roman praetorium. Later, Pilate could find no charge against him. Pilate felt pressured to yield to the demands of the chief priests and the shouts of the temple guards: "Crucify him! Crucify him!" Pilate gave them a choice; they chose Barabbas. He had Jesus scourged to evoke their pity. The crowd pressed their demand (19:7): "We have our law... and according to that law he must die because he made himself **God's son.** When Pilate heard this kind of talk he was more afraid than ever." In John's account Jesus is returning through his suffering and death to the **Glory from which he had come.** At his death the water from his pierced side, for John, was the water which made baptism effective; the blood from his side was the blood of the Eucharist.

Resurrection John confined himself to three appearances of the risen Christ in chapter 20, to: Mary Magdalen, the Apostles without Thomas, and Thomas with the

Apostles; (recall 1 Cor 15:3-8)[17]. The risen Jesus chides "<u>doubting</u> <u>Thomas</u>" for his failure to believe the others without seeing him in his risen state. After his planned appearances others would have to believe on the testimony of the **intended witnesses!** Aware that others in his own time struggled with doubt as Thomas did, the inspired author terminates his brief but sufficient record of Jesus' signs by giving **the reason** for this Gospel:[18]

> Jesus performed **many other signs** as well - **signs** not recorded here - in the presence of his disciples. But these have been recorded to help you believe that Jesus is the **Messiah, the Son of God**, so that through this faith you may have **life** in his name."

Appendix Text scholars identify chapter 21 as a P.S. added to the Gospel rather quickly after the ending just quoted. It was apparently added before the Gospel was copied because this appendix is present in all the ancient manuscripts we have. The reason for the addition seems to be twofold: 1)to identify the primacy of Peter among the Apostles and in the Church; and 2)it appears to be separating the death of the Beloved disciple from the time of the second coming (parousia) of Christ at the end-time (eschaton). This second point seems to imply that John had recently died, which event, according to Eusebius, occurred in the reign of Trajan (98-117).

---

17. This passage in 1st Corinthians is the earliest written record of Jesus' resurrection appearances. It does not claim to be exhaustive; its omission of women as witnesses and the use o f the Aramaic name, Kephas, indicate that it was formulated by Jewish-Christians. The passage reads: "For I handed on to you as of **first importance** what I also received: that Christ died for our sins in accordance with the scriptures; that he was buried; that he was raised on the third day in accordance with the scriptures; that he appeared **to Kephas,** then to **the Twelve.** After that, he appeared to more than **five hundred brothers at once,** most of whom are still living, though some have fallen asleep. After that he appeared **to James,** then to **all the apostles.** Last of all, as to one born abnormally, he appeared **to me."**
18. The purpose for John's Gospel given here turns out to be fundamentally the same purpose for all the other New Testament books as well.

The second conclusion seems to be an effort to fend off constant requests from the community to put more of the signs, episodes and instructions into writing. Interestingly, the "he", "we" and "I" gives us the very strong evidence that different disciples were involved in the redaction of "John's" Gospel. Nevertheless, it is John, the apostle, the one intimately connected to Christ, who proclaimed the transcendent Jesus to his disciples.

It is this same disciple who is the **witness** to these things; it is he who wrote them down and his testimony, we know, is true. There are still many other things that Jesus did, yet if they were written about in detail, I doubt there would be room enough in the entire world to hold the books to record them.

Brown's Outline   After analyzing Dodd's masterful work on John's Gospel, Rev. Raymond E. Brown,[19] thought that the evidence in the Gospel pointed to a structural intent different from Dodd's. Brown acknowledged the validity (or intentionality) of the N/D i.e. "sign-Narrative/interpretative Discourse" relationship. However, he thought that the equating of chapter 11 with chapters 2-3-4 as merely equal episodes regarding their value in Dodd's **sequence of seven episodes** to be out of line with the inspired author's intention.

Although there are **seven signs** (= miracles), the Gospel's Book of Signs definitely does not have the neat, logical distribution of one sign for each one episode. Had that been the case, Dodd's Interpretation would have been hard to argue with. Brown suspects that Dodd, as other commentators before him, was overly facinated by the acknowledged Jewish concern with the number **seven**. Brown asks: "Has not Dodd too been hypnotized by a desire to find a pattern of **seven** in the Gospel?"[20]

Brown estimates that the Gospel's author gave us an intentional unit in C's 2-3-4 by enclosing the contents within the **Cana to Cana inclusion**. With this start he thinks that the Book of Signs

---

19. Raymond E. Brown, The Gospel According To John, vv 29 & 29a in The Anchor Bible, (New York: Doubleday & Company, Inc.,1966), p. cxlii; (hereafter, quoted as Brown, John and page); the text of vol 29a which is paginated continuously with vol 29, starts on p. 539.
20. Brown, John, p.cxlii.

appears to fall into **four parts** rather than seven. The following summary adapts Brown's analysis and highlights some key points.[21]

Part **1.** The theme of John the Baptist and his disciples who become **Jesus' disciples** seems to hold 1:19 to 2:11 together as a unit. This part may also be alluding to the seven days of the new creation.

Part **2.** The **Cana-to-Cana** inclusion is a unit that is clearly implied. The author's text (4:46) says: "He [Jesus] went to Cana in Galilee **once more**, where he had made the water wine." Replacement of Jewish customs by the Messiah's new way. Water to wine appears to be the thrust of John's Gospel here; similarly, replacement of the shekinah in the Temple by the divine presence (in Jesus) takes place in this part. **Reaction to Jesus** (no belief to partial belief to full belief) is also a theme in this part.

Part **3.** "The **emphasis on feasts** as the occasion and indeed subject matter of Jesus' discourses is underlined by the evangelist"; this gives a unity of focus to chs 5 through 10. What only God can do, Jesus does on the Sabbath; on the Feast of Lights, Jesus proclaims **I AM the Light** of the world.

Part **4.** The **focus on Lazarus** and also "certain stylistic peculiarities bind together" the remainder of the book of signs, namely chs 11 & 12 and thus make them a unit. In the raising of Lazarus Jesus (The Life-giver) overcomes death. Then, the life of **Glory** will come through his death.

Brown proposes this structural division with some hesitancy born of the recognition that it is all too easy to divide the text in a way the author never intended it. Yet Brown senses that the relationship of **these four parts** and the flow of the Gospel's thought are close to the inspired author's purpose.

For the **Book of Glory** (13-20) Brown's overall outline is as follows:[22]
Part **1.** The Last Supper (13-17)
Part **2.** The Passion Narrative (18-19)
Part **3.** The Risen Jesus (20:1-29)
Conclusion (20:30-31)

---

21. Brown, John, p.cxliii.
22. Raymond E. Brown, The Gospel According To John, v.29a Anchor Bible, (New York: Doubleday & Company, Inc.,1970), p. 542.

Brown does not include c. 21, which he calls an **epilogue**, with the outline of the primary edition of John's Gospel. Practically all scholars recognize that c. 21 is a **later addition** or a postscript to the Gospel. However, it seems to have been added at a time very close to the writing of the Gospel because it is present in every ancient extant manuscript. Brown points out that the Gospel never circulated without c.21.[23]

This **epilogue**, which adds symmetry to the Gospel that started with such a beautiful prologue, contains five points: **1)** another confirming appearance of the risen **Lord**, this was "the third time . . . to his disciples"; **2)**the great catch of 153 fish after Jesus' instruction is followed; **3)**Peter's triple affirmation of his love tied to the triple confirmation of his unique, authoritative responsibility for the risen Savior's flock; **4)**an intimation as to Peter's martyrdom and John's different end; and **5)**a second ending to the Gospel.

When we ask **why** this epilogue was **added** to the apparently finished (20:30-31 = a very definite ending) Gospel, each of the items contained in the chapter seems to supply part of the answer. As an example, the Gospel tradition had been definite about Peter's denials during the Passion, so it appeared **useful** to include in the Gospel the episode of Peter's humble and repentent love. **Perhaps**, this addition even seemed **necessary** if some of the new Christian communities were resisting the leadership of the Apostles and especially Peter because of his denials during Jesus' trial. It is interesting that the episode came to light in John's Gospel rather than Mark's.

Also, Matthew's Gospel affirmed that Jesus had (during the public ministry) given Simon a new name, **Kepha (= Petros = Rock)**, and had indicated (Mt 16:18ff) that He would give Peter new responsibility (foundation, keys, binding & loosing). This epilogue fulfills that promise in a way nowhere else so clearly spelled out in the New Testament, although Luke's account cites Peter's confirming function (22:32), and Peter's position is implied in Paul's letter to the Galatians. If scholars are right in dating John's Gospel at about 95, then this testimony to Peter is especially significant in that it is being affirmed nearly 30 years after Peter's martyrdom.

_____

23. Brown, John, p.1077.

The passage seems to hint that John has died. Further, those who thought that the **Parousia** would occur before John's death had to be given the right meaning of what Jesus had said to both Peter and John.

Finally, the last two lines suggest that the community of the Beloved Disciple wanted the final redactor of the Gospel to add more of the **many other signs** (20:30) that Jesus had performed, but that the writer thought that what was already written was enough. Maybe, he didn't want to have to buy another piece of expensive papyrus, write other episodes on it and try to attach it permanently to the original, so he agreed that there are many other things but declined to add any more. The **disciple-redactor** who wrote these lines seemed, gently but firmly, to be saying **enough is enough!** In any event, he ended with:

> There are still many other things that Jesus did, yet
> if they were written about in detail, I doubt there
> would be room enough in the entire world to hold the
> books to record them.

Here we are, centuries later, and millions of books later, still trying to probe and capture the transcendent and breathtaking mystery of **Jesus Christ, the Son of God** who loves us beyond telling and told us that his love should be the measure of ours.

Portrait   John is so at home with the transcendent reality of the **divine Son of God** that the divinity of Jesus illuminates this whole Gospel. This account pictures the Eternal Son, the Logos, in his **preexistence** with God the Father from all eternity with its very first line. Jesus, the Son <u>is one with</u> his Father.

John paints his picture with simple and uncomplicated strokes colored a tone of reverent dignity. Somehow, this Gospel manages to combine the awesome **mystery** of 'who Christ is' with warm **familiarity.** The Son who mysteriously lives beyond created time and beyond the deserts of this world came to live among us, – to pitch his tent (taberna in Greek) familiarly among us.(1:14).

John portrays Jesus' easy familiarity with those close to him, "do you want to leave me too?" he asked his chosen disciples simply when many deserted him (6:67); "**Do you love me?**" he gently asked Peter three times after his resurrection (21:15ff). John does not neglect to display Jesus' same directness when it rankles those opposing his miracles, - "your sin remains"(9:41) he publicly responded to the Pharisees who rejected his cure of the man born blind. John's Jesus is decisive and **in command.** When Jesus identified himself in **Gethsemane** his opponents, confronted with his sovereign dignity, "retreated a little and fell to the ground" (18:6).

John pictures Jesus decisively affirming that his divine work be continued through at least three identifying activities, namely: the reception of baptism (3:5), the eucharist (6:53) and penance (20:23).[24] Through these activities Jesus definitively unites his followers to himself. In the eucharistic passage, Jesus says: "Whoever eats my flesh and drinks my blood has eternal life, and I will raise him on the last day. . . . Whoever eats my flesh and drinks my blood remains in me and I in him."

This fourth Gospel portrays the transcendent Son coming down to earth for us; it next depicts him spending his brief sojourn identifying his own person as decisive (especially with his mysterious Yahweh statements) for our gaining eternal life:

"**I AM** [= **Yahweh**] the way, the truth and the life; no one comes to the Father except through me, (14:6);

- then, through his salvific death, resurrection and ascension, the sovereign Jesus goes back to the eternal glory **from which he came.**

---

24. The New Testament indicates the belief that Jesus' Passion, death and resurrection effectively produced **salvation.** More slowly, Christians came to realize that their salvation was mediated through the identifying acts [later called by the name **Sacraments**, indicating their mysterious divine nature].

Questions

1. Mark started his Gospel with an assertion and the triptych; Matthew and Luke began with infancy accounts; **how does** the Gospel according to **John start?**
2. **What connection** does John's Gospel have **with Genesis.**

3. On what does John's Gospel immediately **focus** its attention? How does **Eusebius** note the 4th Gospel's special character?
4. Why do **questions** of: who wrote it? when? where? etc.,seem **more difficult** to answer for this Gospel than for others?

5. What **discovery** overturned all late 2nd century datings of John's Gospel? Explain.
6. Scholar Fred Grant dated John's Gospel before papyrus **P52** was known and understood; what is his scholarly son Robert's dating? Basis? Consensus position?

7. What does the traditional data suggest about **John's age** at death? Jesus, dying, committed his mother to John's care; what does **traditional data** say about John's care of Mary?
8. In the ancient world **how widely** was authorship viewed? What method of teaching did John probably use?

9. According to Brown what **5 steps** were taken to complete John's Gospel? Name two **characteristics** (probably) from John's teaching?
10. What is the **evidence** that the original text was added to?

11. **Why** was John's Gospel written? What is the **key word** in John's stated reason for writing?
12. What **inclusion** sandwiches the contents of John's Gospel?

13. **For whom** was John's Gospel written?
14. What data discloses a **Jewish** background in John? Name **3 things** which challenge **Jewish** rather than Gentile **thinking?**

15. Briefly stated what is the **overall structure** of John's Gospel?
16. According to exegetes what was used to compose the 4th Gospel's **Prologue?** In what **theological point** does John's prologue **go beyond** the Synoptics? Do other of the 27 books thus go beyond the Synoptics? What **term** is unique to the Johannine tradition in identifying the divine Son?

17. Indicate some other places in the Gospel according to John where the son's **preexistence** is brought out. What letter of the alphabet suggests the **overall shape** of John's Gospel?
18. What meanings are alluded to by the expression, **Lamb of God**?

19. In chapter one **which persons** give witness to the identity of Jesus? What **identification title** does each witness make?
20. What is given as **the first** of Jesus' signs? What does the sign reveal? What does the term, **sign**, primarily signify for John? What is the **sign of signs**?

21. [Dodd calls orderly **combinations** of narrative(s) & discourse(s) an episode.] What **episodes** compose the **Book of Signs**?
22. What **double-meaning expressions** are found in this Gospel? Why use them? In this "Gospel of the Sacraments", what **sacrament** is declared necessary to Nicodemus?

23. Where in John is Peter shown coming to the **realization** somewhat **implicitly** that Jesus is the Messiah? [The Synoptics' Caesarea-Philippi event was **explicitly** a bit later.]
24. In episode 5 does the Sanhedrin judge the miraculously-healed blind man, or does he make **final judgement** on them?

25. In Dood's analysis each episode has a dominant theme; what **themes** dominate each of the 7 episodes of the **Book of Signs**?
26. What chapters constitute the **Book of Glory**? What is **Glory**?

27. Contrast the **Last Supper** accounts in John and the synoptics? What **new reality** does Jesus reveal in John? How does Jesus' measure of love go beyond the "Golden Rule"?
28. What **sacraments** are alluded to at Jesus' death? What sacrament originates in the risen **Jesus' commission to the 12**?

29. Was **chapter 21** added **later** to this Gospel? Evidence? Was it **soon** after chapter 20 was finished? Evidence?
30. Why does Brown disagree with Dodd's **outline** for the Book of Signs? **How** does Brown **divide** the **Book of Signs**? Into what 3 parts does Brown divide the **Book of Glory**?

31. What does the **appendix** contain? Why was it added?
32. What portrait of Christ emerges from John"s Gospel? Of what Hebrew word is each special **"I AM"** the translation?

Appendices

Appendix 1: Theology

The term, **theology**, is composed of two Greek words: **Theos** = God, **logos** = word and all its developed senses, such as words about, study of, science of, etc. Thus the <u>nominal</u> definition of Theology = study about God.

The names for the "study about God" are distinguished in the light of the <u>sources</u> used to do the "study about God". To signify that the **human mind alone** produced the knowledge, philosopher Leibniz coined the hybrid term: **Theodicy** (**Theos** from the Greek and **Dicere** = Latin: to say or talk about); the unaided human mind, he knew, could only produce a philosophy, not theology in the strict sense, but only in a loose or broad sense.

On the other hand if the **Divine self-revelation** was the springboard of the knowledge, then the reflection seeking to understand God and His actions was termed **Theology** in its strict sense. Thus **Theodicy** = the study of God in himself and all his relationships from the light of reason only. Whereas, in its strict sense, **Theology** = the study of God in Himself and all his (and consequently our) relationships **in the light of his self-revelation.** Since philosophers like Plato (347 B.C.) and Aristotle (322 B.C.) knew of no special self-revelation by God, they termed their differing conclusions about the ultimate cause of all reality - theology.

One of the shortest definitions for theology ever formulated was given by **Anselm** (+ 1109 A.D.). He was convinced that a person, who said "yes" to the special divine revelation that came through Christ, was making an act of **faith**. If such a believing-thinker reflected on the significance of that faith for himself and for others, Anselm concluded that such a person seeking to penetrate that divine revelation was **theologizing**. Thus, he concluded that **Theology = faith seeking understanding.**[1] Anselm implies in his definition that the believer had made his initial act of **faith** on the **basis** of the evidence such as the miracles and

---

1. Yves Congar, <u>A History Of Theology</u>, tr. & ed. H. Guthrie (Garden City, Doubleday & Co., Inc., 1968), p.133. (Anselm's **T = FSU** is a handy formula or norm for testing other definitions of theology.)

prophecies found in the public ministry of **Christ**.[2] It takes God's **gift** of grace for anyone to make an act of faith in Christ; reason alone cannot achieve this. It is the healthy inquiring appetite of this faith which begets theology.[3]

One might pause for a while here to **reflect** that some kind of a self-revelation is even necessary for us to get to know the unknown mysteries of each other as far as purposes (and much more) are concerned. For example: why are you here at the university? - for learning (the proper purpose of the university)? - for money? - for marriage? - as an agent checking on local activities? etc. etc. Thus, if this be true of us, then a fortiori, the mystery of God's being requires God's own self-revelation to us.

The mystery of God, as a **Trinity** of persons, is the highest and most awesome mystery of the Christian revelation. The human mind could simply never have arrived at the fact of it without God's self-revelation. Many things far more simple than this are nevertheless still beyond the cognitive grasp of most human beings.[4]

A symposium of theologians (chaired by J. Murphy) concluded after critical discussion that **Theology** = "a wisdom acquired by human effort considering, in the light of divine revelation, all the truths that God revealed." A close analysis shows that the parts of this definition correspond to the concepts compressed into Anselm's: "Theology = Faith Seeking Understanding" [T = FSU].[5] Thus, this symposium's definition consists essentially of an expansion of Anselm's with a view to acknowledging the scholastic four causes of any reality. The final cause is wisdom, the fullness of understanding; the efficient cause is human effort probing and

---

2. Anselm's three terms constitute a unity; they focus on a person who believes in the divine revelation from Christ and seeks to understand the meaning this has in all his or her relationships. Anselm's thought, of course, also embraces God's self-revelation to Moses and the Prophets as contained in the Old Testament.
3. M.D. Chenu, Is Theology a Science?, tr. A Green-Armytage, (New York: Hawthorn Books, 1959) p. 35.
4. Some things, even about ourselves, are still beyond the grasp of all human beings; one thinks of the intimate connection between the body and soul!
5. F=in the light of divine revelation, all the truths that God revealed; **S** = human effort considering; **U** = wisdom.

seeking; the "material cause" all the reality God has given to human beings; and the formal cause is the light of revelation itself.

The SUPREME SOURCE of Christian theology is **Christ**. Thus, to do Christian theology one must search the living oral (Sacred Tradition) and written (Sacred Scripture) intertwined source which came from Christ through the Apostles and the one Apostolic koinonia[6] to us.

Moreover, this one koinonia, (or ecclesia[7] = Church) invoking the Holy Spirit as instructed by Christ (John 14:26, 15:26, 16:13),[8] decided on the orthodox and necessary understanding of its faith in meetings such as the ones at Jerusalem (Acts 15) and Nicaea (325), Constantinople (381), Ephesus (431), etc. to Vatican II (1962-1965). These two different paths (i.e. oral and written sources) of getting at the teaching of Christ must be taken into account if one wishes to theologize as a Christian.

Further, as Peter led the Apostolic community (koinonia was Luke's word), his properly selected successors led the continuing community and constituted the **living teaching authority** (= Magisterium) without which what Christ called **"My Church"** cannot continue to exist as His ONE intended community. [For the Scripture/Tradition relationship, cf. **Dei Verbum** (II, a.10)].

Questions

Test the following definitions using Anselm's as **a norm**:

1)Theology = "the methodical attempt to secure an explicit understanding of what has been heard and accepted as the Word of God".[9]
2)Theology = "the rational construction of Christian Doctrine".[10]

---

6. Acts 4:32
7. Thes 1:1
8. John 14:26 "The Advocate, the holy Spirit that the Father will send in my name - he will teach you everything and remind you of all that [I] told you"
9. Karl Rahner, On the Theology of Death 2nd English ed., (New York: Herder and Herder, 1965, p. 7.
10. Congar, Op.cit., p.92.

Notes:

a)If no Divine revelation, then no true divine faith
b)   "   "   "   , then no FSU (no theology)
c)Faith does not = theology; thus one may get
        90% in faith and only 59% (= **F**) in theology!
d)**Faith** = the yes-response of the WHOLE PERSON to God revealing Himself, not merely an assent of mind alone to the truths revealed by God.[11] Faith is not merely intellectual alone, it embraces the will; it involves everything one does.

---

11. Karl Rahner, Theology of Death, p.7.

Appendix 2

Instruction On The Historical Truth of the Gospels[1]
(Pontifical Biblical Commission April 21, 1964)
[Condensed, paraphrased, excerpted and highlighted][2]

1. "The Church, 'the pillar and bulwark of truth,' (1 Tim 3:15) has always used Sacred Scripture in her task of imparting heavenly salvation to men."

2. Examine "with the greatest charity the very difficult work of the faithful exegetes,[3] since even illustrious Jerome himself, tried at times to explain the more difficult questions with no great success" The **impression should in no way be given** "that truths of revelation and divine tradition are being called in question."

3. "Today . . . the **work of exegetes** is **needed**, because [there are] many writings [which question] the truth of the deeds and words . . . contained in the Gospels." Thus, the **Pontifical Biblical Commission** [P.B.C.] insists on these guidelines.

4. "**1.**[4] **Let the Catholic exegete, following the guidance of the Church . . . accurately adhere to** the norms **of rational and Catholic hermeneutics.**" The interpreter will " . . . examine what contribution the manner of expression or the literary **genre** used by the sacred writer makes to a true and genuine interpretation. And let him be convinced that this part of his

---

1. This is a translated version of the Instruction put out by the Pontifical Biblical Commission (P.B.C.) on April ?1, 1964; (highlighting has been added.)
2. Translations of this significant document (in Latin) have been published by the Paulist Press (11/27/64), The BIBLE Today (Oct/64), The Catholic Biblical Quarterly, (July/64), The American Ecclesiastical Review (July/64) and others. Joseph A. Fitzmyer S.J. did the Paulist Press translation which is here quoted with permission. The booklet entitled The Historical Truth of the Gospels, was first published in 1964.
3. This is from the Encyclical, Divino afflante Spiritu, article 46 promulgated by Pope Pius XII on Sept. 30, 1943 (hereafter DaS + the appropriate article number)
4. Numbers in bold-face type are the numbers of the original document.

task cannot be neglected without serious detriment to Catholic exegesis"(DaS 38).

5 ". . .The interpreter may examine **what reasonable elements** are contained in the "**Form-Critical method**" that can be used for a fuller understanding of the Gospels. But let him be wary, because quite inadmissable philosophical and theological principles have often come to be mixed with this method, which not uncommonly have vitiated the method itself as well as the conclusions in the literary area. For some opponents of this method have been led astray by the prejudiced views of rationalism. [1] They refuse to admit the existence of a **supernatural** order and the intevention of a personal God in the world through strict revelation, and the possibility and existence of miracles and prophecies. [2] Others begin with a false idea [or **notion**] of faith as if it had nothing to do with historical truth - or rather were incompatible with it. [3] Others DENY THE HISTORICAL VALUE and nature of the documents of revelation almost **a priori.** [4] Finally, others make light of the authority of the apostles as witnesses to Christ, and of their task and influence on the primitive community, [**giving**] rather the **creative** power [to] that community. All such views are not only [a] opposed to Catholic doctrine, but are also [b] devoid of scientific basis and [c] alien to the correct princples of historical method."

6. "**2.** To judge properly concerning the reliability of what is transmitted in the Gospels, the interpreter should pay diligent attention to the **three stages of tradition** by which the doctrine and the life of Jesus have come down to us."

7. [**Stage one**] "CHRIST OUR LORD joined to Himself chosen disciples, (Mk 3:14) who followed Him from the beginning, saw His deeds, heard His words, and in this way were equipped to be witnesses of His life and doctrine (Lk 24:28; Jn 15:27; Acts 1:8). When the Lord was orally explaining His doctrine, He followed the modes of reasoning and of exposition which were in vogue at the time. He accommodated Himself to the mentality of His listeners and saw to it that what He taught was firmly impressed on the mind and easily remembered by the disciples. These men understood the miracles and other events of the life of Jesus correctly, as deeds performed or designed **that men might believe in Christ** through them and embrace with faith the doctrine of salvation."

8. [**Stage two**] "The apostles proclaimed above all the death and resurrection of the Lord, as they bore witness to Jesus. (Lk

24:44-48; Acts 2:32) They faithfully explained His life and words, (Acts 10:36-41) while taking into account in their method of preaching the circumstances in which their listeners found themselves. (Compare Acts 13:16-41 with 17:22-31.) **After Jesus rose from the dead and His divinity was clearly perceived**, (Acts 2:36; Jn 20:28.) faith, far from destroying the memory of what had transpired, rather confirmed it, because **their faith rested on** the things which Jesus did and taught. (Acts 2:22; 10:37-39.) Nor was He changed into a 'mythical' person and His teaching deformed in consequence of the worship which the disciples from that time on paid Jesus as the Lord and the Son of God. On the other hand, there is **no reason to deny** that the apostles passed on to their listeners what was really said and done by the Lord with that **fuller understanding** which they enjoyed, (Jn 2:22; 12:16; 11:51-52) having been instructed by the glorious events of the Christ and taught by the light of the Spirit of Truth. So, just as Jesus Himself after His resurrection 'interpreted to them' (Lk 24:27.) the words of the Old Testament as well as His own, (Lk 24:44-45; Acts 1:3) they too interpreted His words and deeds according to the needs of their listeners. 'Devoting themselves to the ministry of the word,' (Acts 6:4.) they preached and made use of **various modes** of speaking which were **suited to** [a] their own purpose and [b] the mentality of their listeners . . . But these modes of speaking with which the preachers proclaimed Christ must be distinguished and (properly) assessed: catecheses, stories, testimonia, hymns, doxologies, prayers . . . in Sacred Scripture and . . . [as] used by men of that time."

9. **[Stage three]** "This primitive instruction, which was at first passed on by word of mouth and **then in writing** - for it soon happened that many tried 'to compile a narrative of the things' (Lk 1:1) which concerned the Lord Jesus - was committed to writing by the **sacred authors** in four Gospels for the benefit of the churches, with a method suited to the **special purpose** which each (author) set for himself. From the many things handed down they selected some things, reduced others to a synthesis, (still) others they explicated as they kept in mind the situation of the churches. With every (possible) means they sought that their readers might become aware of the reliability (Lk 1:4.) of those words by which they had been instructed. Indeed, from what they had received the sacred writers above all selected the things which were **suited to** the various situations of the faithful and to the **purpose** which they had in mind, and adapted their narration of them to the same situations and purpose. Since the meaning of a statement also depends on the sequence, the Evangelists, in

passing on the words and deeds of our Saviour, explained these now in one context, now in another, depending on (their) usefulness to the readers. Consequently, let the exegete **seek out the meaning intended by the evangelist** in narrating a saying or a deed in a certain way or . . . context. For the truth of the story is not at all affected by the fact that **the Evangelists** relate the words and deeds of the Lord in a **different order**, (Cf. John Chrysostom, Hom.:Mt. 1,3) and express His sayings . . . differently while preserving (their) sense; (Augustine, De Consensu Evangelistarum 2, 12, 28.)." For, as **St. Augustine** (+ 431) says,

> "It is quite probable that **each Evangelist** believed it to have been his duty to recount what he had to in that order in which it pleased God to suggest it to his memory - in those things at least in which the order, whether it be this or that, detracts in nothing from the truth and authority of the Gospel. But why the Holy Spirit, who apportions individually to each one as He wills, (1 Cor 12:11) and who therefore undoubtedly also governed and ruled the minds of the holy (writers) in recalling what they were to write because of the pre-eminent authority which the books were to enjoy, permitted **one** to compile his narrative **in this way, and another in that**, anyone with pious diligence may seek the reason and with divine aid will be able to find it" (Augustine, Ibid. 2, 21, 51-52).

10. "Unless **the exegete** pays attention to all these things . . . he will not fulfill his task of probing into **what the sacred writers intended and what they really said.** From the results of the new investigations it is apparent that the doctrine and the life of Jesus were not simply reported for the sole purpose of being remembered, but were 'preached' **so as to offer** the Church **a basis** of faith and of morals. . . ."

11. Let each exegete "contribute his part to the advantage of all . . . [to the] support of the judgment to be exercised by the ecclesiastical magisterium, and to the defense and honor of the Church. (DaS 47) . . ."

> "Now we have not learned of the plan of our salvation from any others than those through whom the Gospel has come to us. Indeed, what they **once preached** they **later** passed on to us **in the Scriptures** by the will of God, as the ground and pillar of our faith. It is not right to say that they preached before they had acquired perfect

knowledge, as some would venture to say who boast of being correctors of the apostles. In fact, after our Lord rose from the dead and they were invested with power from on high, as the Holy Spirit came down upon them, they were filled with all (His gifts) and had perfect knowledge. they went forth to the ends of the earth, one and all with God's Gospel, announcing the news of God's bounty to us and proclaiming heavenly peace to men" (**Irenaeus**, Adversus Haereses).

12.   **3. Teachers** . . . "should have it as their 'prime concern' that...Holy Scripture be so taught as both the dignity of the discipline and the needs of the times require" (Apostolic Letter: Quoniam In Re Biblica). "When they practice the art of criticism, especially so-called **literary criticism**, let them . . . perceive **the sense intended by God through the sacred writer**. . . . Let them . . . show how these things really contribute to the clearer understanding of revealed doctrine, or to the refutation of errors. . . . Find in Sacred Scripture that which can 'raise the minds to God, nourish the soul, and further the interior life'" (DaS 25).

13.   **4.** In sacred **sermons** above all pass on doctrine, mindful of St.Paul's warning: "Look to yourself and your teaching; hold on to that . . . ."

14. Exhortation to **publishers.**

15. Request for vigilance by diocesan **Bishops**

16.   "**5.** Those who are in charge of **biblical associations** are to comply faithfully with the norms laid down by the Pontifical Biblical Commission."

17. The second Epistle to Timothy says: "The Sacred Writings 'can instruct (us) **for salvation** through faith in Christ Jesus. All Scripture is divinely inspired and profitable for teaching, for reproof, for correction, and for training in uprightness, so that the man of God may be perfect, equipped for every good work.'"(2 Tim 3: 15-17)

18. In Rome, the Holy Father, "Pope Paul VI . . . on April 21, **1964**, approved" [the original full] **instruction** and ordered the publication of it."

Appendix 3: Outline and Excerpts: Dei Verbum[1]
(Vatican II/Nov. 18, 1965)

Chapt I   Revelation itself.
"   II Handing on Divine Revelation
"   III Its Inspiration and Interpretation
"   IV O.T.
"   V   N.T.
"   VI S.Scripture in the Church's life

Chapters

I. Revelation Itself

a.1 (= article 1) is The document's preface: "Hearing the word of God with reverence and proclaiming it with faith, the sacred synod takes its direction from these words of St. John: 'We announce to you the eternal life. . . '(1 Jn 1, 2-3)"

a.2 says: "**God chose to reveal Himself.** . .through Christ [that] man might come to share in the Divine Nature. . ." Christ = the **fullness** of all revelation[2].

a.3 God revealed Himself in created realities; further, He taught mankind through the Patriarchs, Moses and the Prophets (i.e. the O.T.).

a.4 Then He sent **His Son**; the Son perfected revelation by his 'speaking and doing' presence, & esp. by His P.D. & R and [with the Father] sending the **Holy Spirit**; this is the **final** covenant until His last coming [the Parousia].

a.5 Persons respond by the obedience of faith, – committing one's whole self to God's love, – the H. Spirit moves & assists us.

a.6 God chose to reveal & share with us treasures **totally transcending** human understanding. God can be known by reason, but **better** by faith. Thus far Chapter I.

---

1. The 26 articles of (Dei Verbum) "The Dogmatic Constitution on Divine Revelation" are contained in the New Testament of the New American Bible, pages [11] to [18]. This is merely a skeleton outline and some brief excerpts.
2. Heb 1:1

II. Handing on Divine Revelation

a.7 God arranged that 'what He revealed for the salvation of all would abide in integrity and be handed on.' Therefore Christ commissioned his **apostles** to do this work and they **handed on** (= Tradition) this commission to their successors, bishops.

a.8 The Apostles warned them: "hold fast to the tradition learned"; thus, the Church hands on what **she herself is and believes**. This tradition develops; insight grows toward the fullness of Divine truth. It is only through this divinely protected **tradition** that the full canon of Sacred Scripture is known.

a.9 [**Both S. & T.**]   Both Scripture and Tradition are
from the same divine wellspring,
are intimately intertwined and tend toward the same end. Both are to be accepted and venerated. Thus, the Church does **not** draw her certainty about revelation **from scriptura sola.**

a.10 [**Interrelation**]   Scripture and Tradition form **one**
sacred deposit of the Word of God committed to the Church; the task of authentic interpretation of this deposit was **entrusted to** the living office of the Church exercised in the name of Jesus Christ.[3] This office is not above the Word of God but serves it by teaching, listening, guarding and explaining it by divine commission and the guidance of the Holy Spirit. **These three**, Scripture, Tradition and the living teaching authority [called the Magisterium] are **so linked** that one cannot stand without the others.[4]

III. Inspiration & Interpretation

a.11 [**Inspiration**]   The divinely revealed realities. .
. written down under the **inspiration**
of the H.Spirit. The Church accepts as sacred & canonical O.T & N.T. on the ground that written under the **inspiration** of the H. Spirit[5] "they have **God as their author**. . ." God chose certain men who made full use of their powers, - as **true authors** to write

---

3. This living, teaching office of the Church is referred to as **the Magisterium.**
4. A triangle might be a good image to show the necessary linkage between Scripture, Tradition & Magisterium.
5. cf.Jn,____ 2Tim____, 2Peter____

what God wanted and no more. Thus the books of S. Scripture ".
. .without error, teach **that truth** which God, **for the sake of our
salvation, wished** to see confided to the Sacred Scriptures."

a.12 [**Interpretation**]   The interpreter should search out
the meaning the sacred writer had
in mind. . . .must be read and interpreted   with its divine
authorship in mind. . . .attend to the content & unity of the
[1]whole of Scripture, the [2]tradition of the entire Church and
[3]the analogy of faith. **Ultimately, the Church** must exercise the
divinely conferred commission of **interpreting** the Word of God.

a.13 ". . .without prejudice to God's truth and holiness . . ."
and ineffable love we should note [the proportion] that 'the words
of God/are in the words of men **as** the Logos of the Father/is in
the flesh [of Christ] like ours.'

IV.   The Old Testament

a.14 God, in prep. for the salvation of all, **chose a people** .
. .through Abraham & Moses. God revealed himself as the one,
true, living God that Israel might experience the ways of God
with men.

...a.15 The economy of the O.T. . . . to prepare for the coming
of Christ and the messianic kingdom. The O.T. books, even though
containing **"matters imperfect and provisional"** yet show us
"authentic divine teaching". Accept with veneration these writings
which express many valuable things.

a.16 O.T. & N.T. are deeply & at times hiddenly interrelated;
the books of the O.T. "show forth their full meaning in the New
Testament."

V. The New Testament

a.17 "The **Word of God,** which is **the power of God for salvation**
to everyone who has faith"(Rom 1:16), is . . . in the writings of
the N.T. The Logos himself became flesh & lived among us. He
established the Kingdom of God, died and rose and sent the H.
Spirit to complete the work. Christ alone had the words of eternal
life. This mystery was revealed to the Apostles to: preach, awaken
faith in Christ, & bring together the church.

a.18 **[The Gospels]**   Among all the inspired writings, even of the N.T., the Gospels have a **special place** because they are our principal source for the life & teaching of our Savior [1st stage]. The Church has always maintained the **apostolic origin** of the four Gospels. The Apostles preached [2nd stage] as Christ commissioned them to do and then they and others of the Apostolic age handed on to us in writing [3rd stage] the same message, the foundation of our faith: the four-fold Gospel according to Matthew, Mark, Luke and John.

a.19 The Church maintains that the 4 Gospels (whose historicity she unhesitatingly affirms) faithfully hand on what Jesus, the Son of God, really did and taught for our eternal salvation. The Apostles, after the Resurrection, Ascension and Pentecost, proclaimed these data. The sacred authors, in writing the 4 gospels, selected, synthesized, explained these data in such a way that **they told us the honest truth about Jesus.**[6]

a.20 The N.T. also contains the 23 other epistles and apostolic writings composed under the inspiration of the Holy Spirit to establish, proclaim, formulate the data concerning Christ and foretell its glorious consummation.

VI: S.Scripture in the Ch.

a.21 The Church venerates the divine Scriptures. She regards the **Scriptures taken together with Sacred Tradition** as the **supreme rule of her faith.** . . .in an unalterable form . . .nourishment & rule. In S.Scripture the Father gives us strength, food and fountain of spiritual life.

a.22 Should be open access to S. Scripture; thus, translate into various languages; translations with separated brethren.[7]

a.23 The Church strives to reach a more profound understanding of the Sacred Scripture. Thus, fosters study of the Fathers, Sac. liturgies, etc. according to the mind of the Church.

------

6. Article 18 and 19 reflect the April 21, 1964 Pontifical Biblical Commission: Instruction on the Historicity of the Gospels. The PBC "Instruction" was promulgated over a year and a half before Dei Verbum.

7. 'Translations with separated brethren' reflects the Decree on Ecumenism (Unitatis Redintegratio) of Vatican II.

a.24 **Sacred Theology** depends on the Word of God & Sacred Tradition; The study of the "sacred page" should be the very **soul of Theology.** Preaching, catechetics & instruction thrive in holiness through Sacred Scripture.

a.25 Priest, deacons, catechists should immerse themselves in sacred scripture. All the faithful, esp religious, should frequently read the divine Scripture. **"Ignorance of the Scriptures is ignorance of Christ."** Prayer should accompany the reading; in prayer we speak to God; in scripture we listen as He speaks to us.

a.26 Concluding article: "So may it come that, by the reading and study of the sacred books, 'the word of God may speed on and triumph'"(2 thes 3:1). . . .

Appendix 4: "God As Author"

Vatican II, in proclaiming the Holy Spirit's **inspiration** of Sacred Scripture, reaffirms the centuries-old Christian belief that the books of Sacred Scripture **"have God as their author**, and have been handed on as such to the Church herself."[1]; hence, this **God = Author** doctrine applies to the four Gospels. And to particularize these reflections further, God is somehow to be explained as the author of Mark's Gospel. But Mark is also said to be the author of that Gospel.

To give **a beginning explanation** of this believed but mysterious reality, one must be careful to safeguard the following: the twofold authorship, the truth of God's influence, and the true human input of the earthly author. A theory of inspiration which envisions Mark as an instrumental agent of God (which can be called an **Instrumental Theory of Inspiration**) might be expressed as follows.

Instrumental theory of Inspiration

God is the author of Mark's Gospel and Mark is also the author of Mark's Gospel. **God is the primary and ultimate author** and Mark is the secondary and immediate (or proximate) author. **Both are authors**, but the primacy of God's authorship makes it His book ultimately. He inspired Mark as a human **instrument or agent** to write what He (God) wanted "for the sake of man's salvation". Without God's inspiration it would never have been written; without God's supervisory authorship the Gospel could not have presented 'the divinely revealed realities contained in its text'(art.11.).

But **Mark** is not a mechanical or electronic instrument like a typewriter or a dictaphone; he is a **fully human instrument or agent.** Mark did the work **freely**; he could have refused and God may have chosen another. Mark also used his own **intellect and memory**; he chose, he ordered, he emphasized as he judged fit

---

1.   Vatican Council II, "Dogmatic Constitution on Divine Revelation" ed. A Flannery (Collegeville: The Liturgical Press, 1975), art. 11, p.756; (hereafter quoted as Dei Verbum).

among the things he had heard from Peter[2] and his other oral (and written?) sources. In a word, he did the ordinary things that authors do to write a book. Further, Mark did not have to advert to the fact, **or even know**, that he was being inspired by God. His driving urge may well have been to help his Christian community which was suffering persecution for its belief in Jesus Christ. This Gospel, traditionally identified and listed as the second Gospel[3], is in Mark's own picturesque, yet direct, **style** which differs noticeably from the styles of the other evangelists.

The theory and social dimensions

This **theory of instrumental causality**, which seeks to explain God's and Mark's dual but unequal authorship, may also carry a **social dimension** since Mark is a particular person living within all the social specifics of: time, location, informal education (knowledge of Aramaic and Greek), and Jewish cultural and religious experiences. If it is Mark's mother (with a home in Jerusalem) who is referred to in Acts (c.12), then Mark's family went through the conversion experience of those who came to believe that Jesus is the Messiah and more. Briefly, Mark's community and family contributed something to the mind-set which he brought to the work of writing his gospel account.

This **instrumental explanation** of God's and Mark's dual but unequal authorship is relatively easy to apply to some of the books of the New Testament (however, not all!), but it is **much harder to apply** to most of the books of the Old Testament. The Pentateuch, for example, as a finished collection of books "probably dates from the 5th century B.C."[4] The five books of which it consists (Genesis, Exodus, Leviticus, Numbers, and Deuteronomy) were in the process of **oral formation** with ongoing contemporary

---

2.   Eusebius, The History of the Church (Baltimore: Penguin Classics, 1967) p.152 quotes Papias identifying "...Mark who had been Peter's interpreter..."; further, Eusebius quotes Papias saying "...Mark who followed Peter's instruction in writing it [Mark's Gospel] p.265; (hereafter quoted as Eusebius, History, and page).
3.   Papias says that **Matthew** wrote first in Aramaic, but this writing is no longer extant. Of the extant Gospels many exegetes think that Mark's is first.
4.   Joseph Jensen, God's Word to Israel, (Wilmington, Delaware, Michael Glazier, Inc., 1986), "Appendix I", p.266; hereafter, [Jensen, God's Word and page.]

insights and additions for the twelve or more **centuries** from the time of the patriarchs (Abraham, Isaac, Jacob) about 1850 B.C.; the period of Moses about 1250 B.C. contributed heavily to the Pentateuch's content, as did the Davidic period about 1000 B.C.; **anonymous scribes** conceivably wrote, and contributed to, some parts of the Pentateuch during and after the Davidic period; but the books were probably **not fixed in writing** until about the 5th century B.C. The overall, long-term, **community character** of the Old Testament tradition seems to overwhelm our vision of **individual scribes** as the instruments or agents of God's inspiration.

The "theory of instrumental causality" becomes very vague when dealing with centuries of community oral transmission while trying to focus on the many, mostly unknown, writers of the books believed by both Jews and Christians to be inspired. Yet **Joseph Jensen**, referring to the "theory of instrumental causality", writes: **"no** systematic and comprehensive **explanation** has been provided **to take its place."**[5] **"Karl Rahner**...proposed to understand **inspiration** in the NT as a grace which resides primarily in the primitive Church itself rather than in the individual authors...; these authors wrote simply as representatives of the Church."[6] This theory of "inspiration in the **Church instead** of the individual **writer"** appears to enhance God's primacy of authorship and the position of the Church determining its canonical books, but at the same time it appears to diminish the significance of Mark's notable contribution as well as the work of the other authors of the Sacred Scriptures.

Related Question: Error in Scripture?

Since God is the primary author of the Gospel, a **related question** arises: God's teaching, because it is God's, must be true; Did God assist Mark in avoiding **error**? Vatican II responds to this question by referring to "truth" rather than to individual words; further, the Council limits its attention to **"truth for salvation"** in the Sacred Scripture, rather than address the various kinds and levels of truth contained in the Bible. Mark and the other New Testament authors were attending not to truths of science, economics and geography, but to the Gospel-truth of what was done for us by Jesus Christ. The Church in the Vatican II document on Divine Revelation entitled, **Dei Verbum**, says that God so

---

5. Jensen, God's Word, p.265.
6. Jensen, God's Word, p.266.

preserved the books of Scripture that they "...**without error**, teach that **truth** which God, **for the sake of our salvation** wished to see confided to the Sacred Scriptures..."[7] The Vatican document here focuses on the salvation-begetting-truth in the sacred books rather than on any non-salvation data that Mark may incidentally have used or the process by which God influenced Mark.

But, of course, this 'truth for the sake of our salvation' is contained in Mark's words. It is the word of God in the words of particular authors. Gospel-truth is this kind of truth. Mark's major concern was about Christ and his reader's relation to Christ. In his Gospel Mark was not overly interested in geography or dates or emperors, etc. If they entered the narrative incidentally, he told it incidentally. He wasn't writing a technical history book; he was writing a book **for the sake of salvation.**

Thus, God's Scriptural 'truth for the sake of our salvation' comes to us in the words of men,-- "the Word of God" in the words of Mark, John, Paul, etc. In writing to the Thessalonians, Paul says:

> "...we thank God constantly that in receiving his message from us you took it, **not** as the **word of men**, but as it truly is, **the word of God**"[8]

In the process of inspiring Mark, as well as Paul, **God did not dictate** words into Mark's ear. An expression such as "**God dictating words**" corresponds rather to a fundamentalist mechanical-dictaphone theory. Mark, like Paul, had to use all his powers and possible human sources to write what God wanted written **for the sake of our salvation.** In the instrumental explanation, the finished product is both God's book and Mark's book; each in a different way is author of the book bearing Mark's name; but primarily it is God's Gospel. And Mark, chosen by God despite his human limitations, did not fail to publish the '**truth God wanted known for the sake of our salvation**'.

The expression **without error**, applied to the Sacred Scripture, is tied to the expression: '**truths needed for our salvation**'; it is not to be tied to every single word that Mark used! Mark's

---

7. Dei Verbum, a.11, p.757.
8. I Thes 2:13.

grammatical competence was not in question, neither was his knowledge of things like science, geography, economics, etc. that had nothing to do with **what we needed** for our eternal salvation with God.[9]

Mark does not <u>explicitly</u> state **why** he wrote his Gospel. Many scholars think <u>he</u> wrote it to help fellow Christians who were undergoing suffering and even martyrdom for being Christian. Mark wanted to help them preserve and deepen **their saving-faith** against a persecuting Roman power bent on destroying Christians and even Christianity. Vatican II indicates[10] that God inspired Mark to write the Gospel to fulfill that encouraging purpose. Mark need not have been even vaguely aware that Divine inspiration was helping him to fulfill God's purpose. One of the most explicit statements of this **awareness of purpose** is found in John's Gospel. Its penetrating statement may well be affirmed of the whole New Testament canon. This fourth Gospel clearly states as its purpose:

"These things are written that you may believe that Jesus is the Christ, the Son of God, and that **believing this** you may have **life** in his name"[11]

This belief of the Church, that Mark's Gospel is error-free in the truth proposed for our salvation, is a centuries-old belief. But it is not an explicit statement contained in each book of Sacred Scripture. Fr. Raymond Collins states as a matter of fact that "in no passage of the Old or New Testament is the claim made that the biblical books are free from error".[12] He further points out that the Hebrew word, <u>'emeth,</u> which[13] English translates as truth emphasizes <u>fidelity,</u> <u>reliability</u> and <u>trustworthiness</u> [of God] **rather than** the Greek emphasis on

---

9. Raymond Collins, <u>Introduction to the New Testament</u>, (Garden City: Doubleday & Co. Inc, 1983) p.319, (hereafter quoted as Collins, <u>Introduction</u>, and page).
10. The documents of Vatican II are <u>authentic teaching</u> of the Catholic Church.
11. <u>John</u> 20:25f.; the Greek equally well sustains the translation "...that Jesus Christ <u>is the Son of God</u>",...
12. Collins, <u>Introduction</u> p.350.
13. Greek translates <u>'emeth</u> as <u>aletheia.</u>

correspondence, or equality, between words and things.[14] The scriptural term, 'emeth, keeps its emphasis on **God's** transcendent **goodness and fidelity** in His words **to us.** The Scriptures focus primary and overall attention on the complete and utter **reliability of God.**

Men so easily say the word "God", that they sometimes fool themselves into thinking that they are His equal; this common human error is called anthropomorphism. It tends to blind us to the enormous gulf that exists between the Infinite Creator and His finite human creatures whom He preserves in existence. God is the one who bridges the gulf; man's most ambitious "**Tower of Babel**" cannot reach Him, let alone fully comprehend Him. God designed the communication signals to us.

God's reliable **free self-communication** (in the limited human words of the sacred writers) is itself a **gift** (or charism) given to us. As His Son is a gift to us in human flesh, so His Gospel word (by, to and for members of the Church) is a gift to us in human words. **Inspiration** is the **added gift** by which God safeguards his self-communication, whether the gift be given to the human author or to the Church.

This gift which characterizes the Sacred Scriptures as a whole is **for something**; it is **for** the Church (i.e. for the salvation of its members). It is not a private gift given to Mark. The letter to Timothy (2 Tim 3:16) expands on what the gifted Scriptures are **for**: they are "for teaching, for reproof, for correction, and for training in righteousness." The gift should not be thought of as making it any easier for Mark to do his work than for us to do ours. His finished **work**, even if others put their hands and heads to it[15], is what is believed to be endowed with error-free **salvation-truth.** Thus Collins can say: "The scriptures themselves are the primary and proper object of biblical inspiration.[16]

---

14. Ibid. pp. 350-351; This Greek correspondence concept implies a sort of "human check" to see if the **Word of God** is in accord with our experience.
15. Exegetes think that the so-called "Markan ending" (16: 9-20) is the work of someone other than Mark.
16. Collins, Introduction, p.347.

Similar considerations may in general apply to other N.T. books, with allowances made to explain each book's special circumstances.[17]

---

17. The Gospel is the Church's own self-reflection on the Father's transcendent **gift** of His Son to us. The Church and her Gospel-reflections on this gift are so intertwined as to be not-fully separable. Collins observes that, "the scriptures and the Church so belong to one another that they are partially constitutive of one another." Thus, the character of inspiration, which the Scriptures enjoy, shares in trustworthiness of God as regards all His gifts. **Inspiration is the gift of the "written communication of the word of God as a constitutive element of the Church"** Collins, p.345. [To the Q: Does inspiration = (a)the Divine communication itself or does inspiration = (b)its preservation of the salvific truth? The expression "Word of God" points to = (a).] [Collins' definition needs to address the Q: how can the not-yet-written N.T. be essentially **constitutive** of the already constituted Church which produced that N.T.?]

-181-

Appendix 5: Servant of Yahweh[1]

Isaiah 52:13

See, my servant will prosper,
he shall be lifted up, exalted, rise to great heights,

14 As the crowds were appalled on seeing him
-so disfigured did he look
that he seemed no longer human-
15 so will the crowds be astonished at him,.
and kings stand speechless before him;
for they shall see somnething never told
and witness something never heard before;

53:1 'Who could believe what we have heard,
and to whom has the power of Yahweh been revealed?'
2 Like a sapling he grew up in front of us,
like a root in arid ground.
Without beauty, without majesty (we saw him),
no looks to attract our eyes;
3 a thing despised and rejected by men,
a man of sorrows and familiar with suffering,
a man to make people screen their faces;
he was dispised and we took no account of him,
4 And yet **ours** were the sufferings he bore,
ours the sorrows he carried.
But we, we thought of him as someone punished,
struck by God, and brought low.
5 Yet he was pierced through **for our faults**,
crushed **for our sins.**
On him lies a punishment that brings us peace,
and **through his wounds we are healed.**

6 We had all gone astray like sheep,
each taking his own way,
and **Yahweh** burdened him
with the sins of all of us.
7 Harshly dealt with, he bore it humbly,
he never opened his mouth,
like a lamb that is led to the slaughter-house.

---

1. The Jerusalem Bible (New York: Doubleday & Company, Inc., 1966), p.1228.

like a sheep that is dumb before its shearers
never opening its mouth.

8. By force and by law he was taken;
would anyone plead his cause?
Yes, he was torn away from the land of the living;
for our faults struck down in death.
9 They gave him a grave with the wicked,
a tomb with the rich, though he had done no wrong
and there was no perjury in his mouth.

10 Yahweh has been pleased to crush him with suffering;
if he offers his life in atonement,
he shall see his heirs, he shall have a long life
and **through him what Yahweh wishes will be done.**
11 His soul's anguish over
he shall see the light and be content.
**By his sufferings shall my servant justify many,
taking their faults on himself.**

This is one of the famous **Servant of Yahweh** songs
in the section of **Isaiah** known as **2nd Isaiah.** The
others are: 42:1-7; 49:1-9; and 50:4-9.

They depict a perfect disciple of **Yahweh**; he proclaims
the true faith and suffers to atone for the sins of his
people, but God exalts him in the end. In all of this,
the Christian tradition sees a foreshadowing of the true
Servant of God, of the life and redeeming death of **Jesus.**[2]

The first part of Isaiah, largely from Isaiah himself (765 to
perhaps 690 =/- 5) and confronting problems of his own time,
consists of Chapters 1 through 39. It is called **Proto-Isaiah**
The second part, which confronts problems of the Jewish exile
in Babylon (587-538 B.C.) and appears to be from a devout group
of Jewish men who carried on as an "Isaian school of prophecy",
is known as second- or **Deutero-Isaiah.**
The last part of the book, labeled Isaiah, is composite; it
goes from 55-66 and is referred to as third- or **Trito-Isaiah.**

---

2. The Jerusalem Bible, "The Prophets", p.1124.

-184-

Appendix 6: Celebrated Textual Problem
Luke 22:14-20

If you have seen a newspaper clipping which had been kept
for a long time, you know how the paper itself turns brown and
gets brittle. It gets so brittle after twenty or thirty years that,
unless specially preserved, its edges break off even with careful
handling. How long could the constantly used **autographs** (= the
original handwritten copies) of the Gospels of Matthew, Mark,
Luke and John have lasted?

Very soon after the **autographs** were completed, other
handwritten copies (literally manuscripts) had to be made for the
preservation of the Gospel's content. As the word of each Gospel's
existence spread from its source location to nearby Christian
communities, each neighboring community would want a copy for
its own use, especially in the liturgy but also to have an
authoritative source for teaching and the resolution of
misunderstandings. Within twenty-five years of Christ's
resurrection, Christian communities (= local churches) had spread
over the 2000 miles of the foot-journey **from Jerusalem to Rome**
and to many of the towns off on the side roads.

In a word, obtaining manuscript copies, especially of the
Gospels had to be a serious preoccupation of each church's leader.
Thus, **many** papyrus, and some more expensive parchment, **scriptural
manuscripts** were in existence by the year 100; in the second
century the number of copies had to multiply as the Church
continued to spread despite the ten Roman persecutions (from
Nero to Diocletian) which martyred Christians and tried to destroy
their sacred books.

In the last century and continuing into the present, information
about, and the contents of, all the New Testament's **ancient
papyrus manuscripts** (some in bits and pieces) have been collected
and catalogued. Some of the discoveries are whole fragile
manuscripts that somehow remained despite destructive moisture
and temperature changes. They are constantly sought in the
interests of getting a **Greek New Testament text** as close as
humanly posssible to the original.[1]

---

1. K. Aland and B. Aland, The Text of the New Testament, tr
E.F.Rhodes, (Grand Rapids: William B.E. Erdmans, 1987), p. 305;
[hereafter this book will be cited as Aland, Text of NT and page.]

As of the late 1980s over 90 papyri (**pieces** of papyrus **and sometimes clusters** of fragile papyrus pages containing gospels and epistles) have been discovered and photographed. Further, well over 200 codeses[2]., some of which contain some or all of the books of the New Testament, are also available and under study.

The earlier a papyrus or codex is, the closer it is to the inspired writer's original manuscript (= **the autograph**); and thus, the more it can tell us about the accuracy of the later documents that were copied from it. The earliest is P^{52} (papyrus[52]) which is a small, but now famous, piece of John's Gospel dated at or before the year 125 A.D.! This papyrus gets us very close to the date, 95 +/- 5, commonly accepted as the date of John's Gospel. Another discovery was papyrus P^{75} which contains most of John's Gospel and also Luke's and is now dated at or before the year 200. Famous codeses come later: **Codex Vaticanus** and **Codex Sinaiticus** in the fourth century; these documents contain most of the New Testament. From the fifth century come Codex **Alexandrinus** and Codex **Ephraemensis** which also contain much of the New Testament. A bit later came **Codex Bezae** Cantabrigiensis. These few documents can illustrate how knowledge of such **early** New Testament copies helped to solve a **difficult text problem.**

Probably the most celebrated texual problem in Luke's Gospel is the omission of **Luke 22:19b–20** from the copy of Luke's Gospel contained in **Codex Bezae**. A Century ago text scholars did not have the knowledge of all the texts already cited above. In the absence of such knowledge Protestant text scholars, B.F. **Westcott** and John **Hort** of Cambridge, gave far too much credit to the relativly late Codex **Bezae** and its **omission** of **22:19b–20** from Luke's account of the Last Supper. Their scholarly opinion more or less influenced a century of Protestant scholarship; Catholic scholars were less influenced by the omission of the Bezae text. Luke's account of the Last Supper which contains the bold-faced, bracketed text in question follows:

Luke 22:14-20
[14]When the hour came, he took his place at table with the apostles. [15]He said to them, "I have eagerly desired to eat this **Passover** with you before I suffer, [16]for, I tell you, I shall not eat it [again] until there is fulfillment in the kingdom of God." [17]Then he took **a cup,** gave

---

2. A codex is a manuscript preserved in its original **book form**

thanks, and said, "Take this and share it among yourselves; [18]for I tell you [that] from this time on I shall not drink of the fruit of the vine until the kingdom of God comes." [19]Then he took **the bread**, said the blessing, broke it, and gave it to them, saying, "This is my Body,⟦**which will be given for you; do this in memory of me.**" [20]**And likewise the cup after they had eaten, saying, "This cup is the new covenant in my blood, which will be shed for you.⟧**"

This whole passage (Lk22:14-20) with the bracketed **19b-20** is called the longer account; when the highlighted verses are missing it is referred to as the shorter account.

A very early **papyrus** of the Greek New Testament is **P75** (papyrus **75**) **which contains** major portions of the Gospel according to Luke and the Gospel according to John. **P75** dates from the early third century, possibly as early as the year 200 A.D.[3] This very early papyrus contains **all** of the above-quoted part of Luke's gospel, namely Luke 22: 19b-20, which had been missing from the centuries-later Codex Bezae.

Next, the famous **Codex Vaticanus** (symbol = **B**) which dates from the fourth century, (thus earlier than Codex Bezae); this outstanding Codex which contains most of the Greek New Testament, seemsrelated so closely to **P75** that a leading text-scholar suggests: **P75** may even be part of the **exemplar-source** of Codex Vaticanus.[4]

A third **Codex** (earlier than C.Bezae), the famous **Codex Sinaiticus** (symbol = the Hebrew letter **aleph**) was discovered by Constantin von Tischendorf in the library of St. Catherine's monastery at the foot of Mount Sinai (hence its name). Codex Sinaiticus contains almost all of the Greek New Testament (incl. Lk 22:19b-20) and dates from the fourth century; all three of these sources contain Luke 22:19b-20, the highlighted text within the brackets. There are also other early uncial manuscripts which contain the verses missing from Codex Bezae.

Sometime in the fifth century an unknown copyist brought into existence a text called **Codex Bezae Cantabrigiensis** which

---

3. Aland, Text of NT p.101
4. Aland, Text of NT, p. 57.

omitted the highlighted verses in question. This codex was in the personal library of Theodore Beza[5] (hence its name). Theodore Beza, "(the friend and successor of John Calvin as leader of the [reformed] church in Geneva, . . .was responsible for no fewer than nine editions of the Greek New Testament between 1565 and 1604)".[6]

> "Under the influence of [nineteenth-century scholars] Westcott-Hort's theory [which relied **very heavily** on the accuracy of Codex Bezae]. . .,the whole of verses 19b-20,. . .was printed in double brackets[7], even as recently as **GNT**[2] [Greek New Testament/2nd revision]. However, most (though not yet all) [scripture scholars] have yielded to the **overwhelming evidence** attesting to originality of **Luke 22:19b-20** in the Gospel text, recognizing that . . .[it is] the **"longer" account** of the Last Supper that is **authentic.**"[8]

In his book, The Gospel According to Luke, W. Harrington thinks that Luke's text so closely corresponds with Paul's (1 Cor 11:23b-25a) "that both Paul and Luke have echoed the liturgical text with which they were familiar, doubtless the one in vogue in **Antioch** and then in the Pauline churches."[9]

---

5. Aland, Text of NT, p.4
6. Ibid.
7. Double brackets signified maximum doubt as to the authenticity of the bracketed material.
8. Aland, Text of NT, p.306.
9. Wilfrid Harrington, The Gospel According to Luke, (Westminster, Md., Newman Press, 1967), pp. 246-249.

Luke 22:[10]	1 Cor 11:
19 Then he took the bread	[He] took bread, and,
said the blessing,	after he had given thanks,
broke it,	broke (it)
and gave it to them,	
saying °	and said,
"This is my body	**"This is my body**
which will be given for you	that is for you.
Do this in memory of me"	Do this in remembrance
	of me."
20 And likewise the cup	In the same way also the
	cup,
after they had eaten, saying,	after supper, saying,
"This cup is	**"This cup is**
the new covenant in my blood	**the new covenant in my**
	blood:
which will be shed for you."	
	Do this, as often as you
	drink it, in remembrance
	of me."

Harrington concludes that "Literary dependence. . .on the liturgical tradition ...is undeniable"; Harrington further surmises that Luke's "literary construction is dominated by a theological idea: the Eucharist is the **Christian Passover**"; perhaps, the copyist of the Bezae Codex, being unfamiliar with the Jewish Passover liturgy, may have wished to avoid the mention of two different passover cups in the Last Supper account, which might confuse the hearers. Harrington further suspects that the copyist may have been familiar with the **shorter** eucharistic form.

Another modern commentator, Joseph A. Fitzmyer in the second volume of his extensive work, The Gospel According to Luke,[11] also addresses the problem of the **Codex Bezae omission.** Fitzmyer wonders **why**, in view of the length of the papyri witnessing to the longer account, any scholars are still resting

---

10. Quotes are from The New Testament (of the New American Bible). revised edition (New York: Catholic, Book Publishing, Co.,1987)
11. Joseph A. Fitzmyer, The Gospel According to Luke, (Garden City, N.Y., Doubleday & Company, Inc. 1985) pp. 1386-1403

antiquated and vitiates the rest of his analysis of the Lucan passage..."[12]

The text scholars who published the third (and latest) edition of the Greek New Testament (identified thus **GNT**[3]) have devised a **graded evaluation** of each variation in the text. The Committee doing the work on the Greek text "sought to indicate the **relative degree of certainty** of the text adopted and of the variants in the footnotes.They formulated a scale from A to D whose **official definitions** are given in **GNT**[3].

"The letter **A** signifies that the text is **virtually certain**, while **B** indicates that there is **some degree** of doubt. The letter **C** means that there is a a **considerable degree** of doubt whether the text or the apparatus contains the superior reading, while **D** shows that there is a **very high degree** of doubt concerning the reading selected for the text."[13]

Fitzmyer objects to the rating of **C** which the textual scholars have given to the longer text the evidence for which far surpasses the Codex Bezae and lesser bits of evidence for the shorter text. Fitzmyer in his 1987 commentary says: "The rating of "C" given [to the longer text]...is decidedly too low; it should be a "B" at least...."

With regard to the celebrated Lukan text-problem, front line scholars are practically convinced that the highlighted verses in question are **authentically Luke's** and that the Bezae copyist for some reason (???) overlooked or omitted it. Thus the original text of Luke 22:19-20 should be read as follows: [14]

19Then he took **the bread**, said the blessing, broke it, and gave it to them, saying, "This is my Body, **which will be given for you; do this in memory of me."** [20]**And likewise the cup after they had eaten, saying, "This cup is the new covenant in my blood, which will be shed for you."**

---

12. Fitzmyer, Luke, p.1387.
13. Aland, The Text of the NT p. 44.
14. Fitzmyer, Luke, p.1388.

Appendix 7

Inerrancy in "Salvation Truth"

Fundamentalism in the reading of Sacred Scripture insists on a belief (which it labels Christian) that God **so inspired** the writings of the Bible that, as a consequence, the Scriptural books, for example Mark's Gospel, must be without any kind of an error. **Inspiration**[1] can be described as God's giving Mark the **special grace** Mark needed to write what God wanted in the Gospel account which Mark wrote. The special grace Mark received didn't have to make Mark a genius in writing Greek or anything else, but it did have to preserve the divine message of salvation to mankind in a substantive way. Fundamentalism rejects any kind of an error even in non-substantive data in the Gospel account; it's belief demands **absolute inerrancy.**

The Second Vatican Council (1962-1965) spelled out the Catholic position on **Divine Revelation** in its constitution entitled **Dei Verbum** on Nov. 18, 1965.[2] Article 11 of Dei Verbum is focused on the question of **the kind of inerrancy** to be expected in Sacred Scripture. The position is different from that of Biblical Fundamentalism's absolute inerrancy; it may perhaps be termed **qualified inerrancy.**

Art. 11 reads: "The books of Scripture must be acknowledged as teaching solidly, faithfully and **without error that truth** which God wanted put into the sacred writings **for the sake of our salvation.**" "That truth . . . for the sake of our salvation" is what is meant by this article's title Salvation Truth.

Thus, in Mark's Gospel[3] the material believed by the Church to be **without error** is **that truth** which God wanted in the book **for the sake of our salvation.** Dei Verbum says nothing about non-

---

1. Inspiration is not the same as infallibility.
2. The English translation of the official Latin title is: The Dogmatic Constitution on Divine Revelation; the Latin document begins with the words: Dei Verbum. The document Dei Verbum consists of 24 articles each of which is 1-4 paragraphs in length.
3. Mark's Gospel is chosen as exemplary because it is easier to cite one book than all the books together; the considerations can be applied to the other books of Scripture with proper adaptations made for each.

salvational, incidental material of dates, places, or relationships which the inspired author(s) used in presenting the divinely-safeguarded data.

An example of an incidental point may be the identification of the husband of Herodias before she entered into the incestuous relationship with Herod Antipas. Mark, including this in his narrative on the martyrdom of John the Baptist, says "Herodias, the wife of his brother Philip"[4]; whereas the Jewish historian, Josephus, says that Herodias had been the wife of his brother Herod Boethus. The question here is one of historical fact: had Herodias been the wife of Philip or of Boethus before entering her new incestuous relationship with Herod Antipas? Mark's concern was to show that John the Baptist had been martyred because he had been proclaiming God's Law to the Jews in Palestine; Mark was not really concerned about the identity of those other uncles with whom Herodias had previously elsewhere lived in sin. Yet, when considering scriptural matters, it is not improper to inquire into the incidental historical facts which are present in the inspired books. Josephus, as a secular Jewish historian, was more interested,than Mark, in the political marital-relationships of the dynastic rulers.

On balance, it appears that Josephus, because of his political interests, was more apt to be correct. Actually our reflections are resting only on the statements of Mark and Josephus, - i.e. the word of one man against the other. The translator's footnote on this matter in the revised edition of the New American Bible (p.34) sides with Josephus. This, of course, does not close the case, but it does lead us into the consideration of how we may respond to the possibility of an error in Sacred Scripture. The incidental nature of the fact that Herodias was incestuous whether she had lived with either Philip or Boethus helps one to see that the Dei Verbum statement is in no way undermined by this slip of Mark's - if, indeed, it was a slip![5] Another discrepancy: Mark 2:26 names Abiathar instead of his father, Ahimelech, (1 Sam 21:2-7) as the high priest who gave the famished David and his

---

4. Mark 6:17
5. Better cases can be made for Luke's precisioning of Mark's time between Peter's "You are the Messiah" at Caesarea Philippi and Jesus' later transfiguration; also Paul's change of his expectation of the Parousia between his writing of 1,2 Thessalonians and Romans.

men the bread which Scripture allowed only the priests to eat. The Jerome Biblical Commentary (J.B.C.) here cites Mark's "faulty memory".[6]

Fundamentalists in the interpretation of Sacred Scripture, or more briefly **Biblical Fundamentalists**, would insist that Mark was correct and Josephus was wrong. Fundamentalism implies that God **somehow dictated** every word of Mark's Gospel and the other books of Scripture too. Thus, for Biblical Fundamentalists, an admission that there is **any kind of an error** in Sacred Scripture is tantamount to an admission that God has erred. And, of course, to say that God has made the mistake is equivalent to denying God's nature as omniscient or denying his existence altogether.

Catholics do not find themselves in such a difficult position. They believe that the books of Sacred Scripture were written **by** believers in Christ, **to** believers in Christ, **for** the sake of their Christian community's belief and life in Christ. To say it in another way, the inspired books were written **by, to and for** the Christian community's belief and life in Christ. The Apostles, and especially Peter, were given the commission **by Christ Himself** to teach what Jesus said and did for everyone's salvation. This commission contains the obligation to safeguard Christ's teaching, which, of necessity, means in its **proper interpretation.** This command was not given to anybody else. But all human beings have the normal obligation of seeking and saying the truth, especially the successsor of Peter, the Pope. Christ told Peter that he would build **his church** on Peter and that what he (Peter) bound on earth would be bound in Heaven (Mt 16:16ff).

Thus Catholics recognize that **article 11** of Dei Verbum saves them from the difficulty encountered by Biblical Fundamentalism. Catholics realize that an item in the Sacred Scripture which is **not essential for salvation** does not have the same protection from error with which the truth necessary for salvation is protected.

Biblical Fundamentalism rests on the position that sacred **Scripture alone** is the only source of human knowledge about God and what God wants of us. Admittedly, Scripture is a very important source of such knowledge. But nowhere does Scripture

---

6. Jerome Biblical Commentary, eds R. Brown, J. Fitzmyer, R. Murphy, (Englewood Cliffs, N.J.: Prentice-Hall, 1968) p. 28.

itself make such a claim to being man's **only source** of knowledge about God and his will for us.

When absolute inerrancy is added to the "only source" concept, the combination has led some people to look for all their knowledge even of science, history and geography from scripture. They have tended to make Sacred Scripture **inclusive** of all other human knowledge. Again Scripture itself makes no such claim. Further, Biblical Fundamentalism tends to make the Sacred Scripture time-predictive of the end of the world (eschaton) and the second coming of Christ (parousia) and to cause undue anxiety among its adherents.[7]

A "**Scripture only**" position thus **excludes** the actual ways in which people first learned about Christ. Jesus did not tell his Apostles to write Scripture to the world; He told them to teach all nations, which they did **orally** for years. The **first generation of Christians** lived and many of them died without ever seeing a single one of the New Testament's 27 "books". Those Christians lived and died within the community started by Christ and led by the Apostles and those they appointed or ordained.

The first century Christians called their community: the **Church.** This "handing on" of what Christ taught (and intended his community to believe and live) is called **Tradition.** This living tradition was preserved by the **living teaching authority of the Apostles** and those they appointed or ordained. It appears that the living "handing on" (Tradition) from Christ came simultaneously with the living teaching authority of the Apostles commissioned by the risen Jesus. This living teaching authority divinely set up by Jesus is called the **Magisterium.**

Hence it appears that many early Christians lived their whole lives with Christ's gifts of His Tradition and His commissioned Magisterium without ever seeing a book of the New Testament. How then can "**Scripture alone**" have helped the early Christians to solve problems or reach Heaven? The "**Scripture only**" position clearly excludes both the **Living Tradition** and the Magisterium set up by Christ as the new faith's safeguarding sources. Before any New Tesament book was written it was the living, Apostolic

---

7. Scripture does speak of these events but day or hour predictions are disclaimed and very careful, even ecclesial, interpretation is needed for the passages.

Church which preserved the Christian knowledge of who and what Jesus is, what he did and what He wants of us.

Actually, **many more Christians** than merely the first generation of Christians are involved. The passion, death and resurrection of Christ took place in or very close to the year 30 A.D. The first piece of writing presently in our New Testament appears to be 1st Thessalonians written in the year 50/51.[8] Rather substantial scholarly opinion holds that **Mark's Gospel** was not written as we have it until about the **year 70** A.D. i.e. forty years after Christ's resurrection. The written Gospels of **Matthew and Luke** probably came into existence about 10 to 15 years after Mark's account. **John's Gospel** appears to have been finished as we have it about the year 95 A.D. Further, each Gospel was written in a different country. Time was needed for the widely separated Christian communities to learn of each Gospel's existence, have it copied (perfectly?), transported and collected as "**the four Gospels**". Was this possibly done **before the year 125 A.D?** Did every Christian community immediately call for the hand-copying of each gospel for its own collection? How then could "**Scripture alone**" have been the source of Christian living and salvation?

It took **about** 65 years after Christ's resurrection to finish the Greek Gospels our texts are dependent on. The time gap becomes greater still when considering the writing, separation of recipient communities and unequal desire to collect the many **epistles**[9] contained in the New Testament. Finally, it wasn't till about the year 367 (as far as scholarship has presently determined) that the 27 books of our New Testament are identified as **all and only** the books to be used in the one, universal Christian Church's sacred liturgy. Countless numbers of Christians had lived, died and even been martyred without having all, most, or frequently even any, of the books of the New Testament available to them. **Scripture** can **not** possibly have been their **only source** of Christian knowledge and life. **Fundamentalism's "Scripture alone"** doesn't square with either the historical data or even the teaching of Scripture itself.

---

8. This date is a solidly-founded scholarly consensus; still some leeway may be allowed.
9. Epistles were written before and after the Gospels, but the desire to collect them could hardly have matched the desire to have the Gospel accounts about Christ himself.

As it turns out, the **Living Teaching Authority** (Magisterium) of the Church was itself the determining body that **decided** which of the many Christian books were **inspired and canonical.** Also, the many widely-separated Christian communities, extending the 2300 miles of the Mediterranean and hundreds of miles on either side of it, were living their Christian lives on the basis of the oral handing on (Tradition) of Christian believing and living. The focus of Christian life was the local Church shepherded by the appointed and ordained successsors of the Apostles.

It appears then that Biblical Fundamentalism mistakenly rests on: 1)Scripture alone; 2)no acknowledgement of Christ's Church (with its Apostolic baptism, eucharist, penance, and orders) persevering into the present; 3)absolute literal inerrancy of Scripture; and 4)and an exaggerated, even predictive, sense of the parousia.[10]

In 1987 a committee of the National Conference of Catholic Bishops (**NCCB**) drafted a brief instruction[11] entitled A Pastoral Statement for Catholics on Biblical Fundamentalism.

---

10.   +John F. Whealon, "Answering the Challenges of Biblical Fundamentalism", Catholic Evangelization, vol I /no. 4, July/August 1988), pp.10-13.
11.   The National Conference of Catholic Bishops through its Administrative Committee set up An Ad Hoc Committee on Biblical Fundamentalism which drafted "A Pastoral Statement for Catholics on Biblical Fundamentalism"; this publication was authorized on March 31, 1987; Most Rev. John F. Whealon, Archbishop of Hartford, Conn. was the directing authority of the drafting committee.

Appendix 8: Synoptic Problem

In the last century, the Gospels according to **Matthew, Mark and Luke** were labeled the **Synoptic Gospels** because each of them presented the public ministry of Christ from the **same overall point of view,** (syn = together, optic = eyed or viewed). In each the 4 topics of Christ's public ministry, which provide the common framework, are: 1)John the Baptist, 2)Jesus' Galilean ministry, 3)Jesus' journey to Jerusalem and his Jerusalem ministry, 4)the climax of Jesus' passion, death and resurrection. The **Gospel according to John** goes its own independent way. It touches some of the same topics, especially the passion, death and resurrection, but John's Gospel features a strikingly different overall design and perspective. Placing the contents of the synoptic Gospels in **three parallel columns** reveals the overall similarity of structure and order shared by Matthew, Mark and Luke;[1] this column arrangement reveals differences in detail too. A fourth column for John doesn't help much until Christ's passion, death and resurrection is reached.

As one might expect, the similar structures of the synoptic Gospels contain many similar episodes and even sentences. As we become familiar with the Gospels according to Mark and Luke (hereafter referred to only as Mark and Luke) we become aware of these **samenesses.** Similar sentences are sometimes in the same words and even the same word-order. Yet, close examination reveals striking **differences** both in events narrated and also within the same event. This **combination of samenesses and differences** within the Gospels of Matthew, Mark and Luke is **a fact.** It has been named **the synoptic fact.**

Samenesses

When reading the synoptic Gospels in sequence one soon senses that the material is familiar. In fact, if Luke is read after Mark, the sense of "deja vu" occurs repeatedly when reading the so-called **Galilean conflicts. Mark** chapter 2 verse 1 to chapter 3 verse 6 [ordinarily written Mark 2:1-3:6] narrates a sequence of five conflicts (or disputes) starting with the Descent (or lowering)

---

1. In scriptural studies, the names Matthew, Mark and Luke usually signify **the Gospels** rather than the persons to whom they are attributed; the context generally indicates if the persons who did the writing are intended.

of the cripple through the roof, then the **E**ating at the house of Levi (a tax-collector), the question of **F**asting, picking **G**rain on the Sabbath and ending with Christ **H**ealing a man's hand on the Sabbath. The highlighted capital letters are useful in symbolizing each conflict and also the sequence of the disputes, thus: **D-E-F-G-H**. In reading **Luke** (5:18-6:11) one meets the very **same five conflicts** in the **same order**, thus **D-E-F-G-H!** When turning to **Matthew** 9:2-9:17 the first three conflicts are read in the same order, thus: **D-E-F** but in a somewhat different context. Matthew retains the **G-H** in 12:1-12:14 in the same order but also in a different context. Within some of the episodes the three synoptic Gospels have whole sentences written in exactly the same words in the same order. These **samenesses** argue strongly to a process of copying from a common source or from the original Gospel writer.

The **Jerusalem conflicts** (Mark 12:1-37 with the parallels in Luke and Matthew listed in the New Testament) provide another sequence with the **same** characteristics. In examining the synoptic Gospels as whole units, Christ's public-ministry framework within each Gospel is **observed to be the same** and to consist of <u>Jesus and</u>: John the Baptist, his temptations in the desert, his Galilean ministry, his journey to and ministry in Jerusalem, his passion death and resurrection. Many more particulars support the sense of **sameness** in the Synoptics, but under closer scrutiny, - **differences**, major and minor, begin to emerge.

Differences

When starting the Gospel according to Luke after finishing Mark's account, one is immediately struck by **Luke's** opening foreword and the newness and beauty of Luke's **infancy account** which occupies two full chapters. In a major way Luke's beginning was **sharply different** from Mark's immediate plunge into the start of Jesus' public ministry with no comment about Jesus' birth or origin. **Matthew** also starts with a two-chapter **infancy account** that corresponds with Luke's account on a few critical points but also includes episodes untouched by Luke.[2] In fact, the **differences** between the infancy accounts of Matthew and Luke are **so pronounced** as to convince most scholars that Luke never saw

---

2. Matthew has: the **W**ise men, the **I**nnocents slaughtered, the **S**tar, flight into **E**gypt; [the mnemonic **WISE** helps to remember them]. None of these items is present in Luke's account.

-198-

Matthew's text and the finisher [called a redactor] of Matthew's Gospel never saw Luke's text.

In many other instances Matthew and Luke have data **common** to their Gospels, but not found in Mark, for example, the beatitudes, infancy accounts,and the Lord's prayer. Further, in these two entries common to Luke and Matthew, each evangelist presents them with **differences** in both quantity and context. In another instance, the very important **Last Supper** account of the eucharist's origin, Matthew and Mark are almost identical, while Luke, although substantially similar, nevertheless emphasizes the new covenant **differently.**

When we step back from the comparison of the texts to view the synoptic narratives historically, we would expect that three different authors, writing independently about the same person, would come up with three different presentations. We expect **the differences.** Lives of Lincoln by different authors are quite different. And since the narratives are about the same public person, we would expect some, but not all, of the same events to be spoken about. But we would hardly expect similar sentences with the same words in the same word order! Yet, different authors will present the Gettysburg Address with the same words in the same order. Lincoln wrote the original. Thus, the Gettysburg Address was **already a written piece of literature before** the modern biographers even started their work. In other words each author would be using the original or a copy of it. Jesus didn't write his **Sermon on the Mount.** Newspapers and reporters didn't even exist to copy down such things. Matthew added much of Jesus' public teaching within its framework to give it the character of an inaugural address; whereas Luke narrowed it down to its central message; Mark didn't even allude to it. The **puzzle** of trying to discover how and why the synoptic Gospels presented Christ's words and deeds with gaps, samenesses and differences such as these is called **the synoptic problem.**

As mentioned, one expects differences, but one does not expect word-for-word **sameness** in the ordinary prose of the synoptic authors; this is a **surprising element.** Some scholars used to think that the Jewish tenacious memory of tradition offered a solution. But, when other scholars pointed out that Jesus' very important words at the Last Supper are presented in such a way that the Matthew/Mark duo are different from the Luke/Paul[4] duo, the tenacious memory theory was abandoned. Much later, it was theorized that the Matthew/Mark duo appeared to represent a **Jewish-Christian** influence and probably manifested the **Jerusalem liturgy** in the Last Supper text; whereas the other duo, Luke (a gentile) and Paul who saw himself as Apostle to the Gentiles, reflected the **Gentile-Christian** emphasis on the **new covenant** which probably characterized the liturgy of the heavily Gentile-Christian community in **Antioch.**

Liturgical reflections shed light on this part of the synoptic problem. No overall solution has as yet been been found to the synoptic problem as a whole, but the work of many scholars continues to throw light on at least parts of the problem.[5] At this point scholars have applied methods known as: Literary Criticism, Source criticism, Text Criticism, Form Criticism and Redaction Criticism in their efforts to analyze the Sacred Scriptures. One scholar working on the Synoptic problem, **Pere L. Vaganay,** took Christian historical tradition into account in his search for an overall view of how the Synoptic Gospels **became so interrelated.** Vaganay's hypothesis[6] helps to give one a bird's-eye view of the work. I will adapt his hypothesis, oversimplify it, apply numbers of verses to it and try to diagram it. To preserve Vaganay's reputation for excellence, i will refer to my paraphrased model only as "the Theory".

Jesus is the starting point. He chose his twelve disciples whose individual names are indicated in the diagram by a first capital letter. **The 12** (after Matthias replaced Judas) are sources of the Gospel's **common oral tradition;** within the thirty to forty years of Apostles' oral proclamation of the Gospel many items were undoubtedly written down. Highlighted initials indicate

---

4.   Luke's account of Jesus' institution of the Eucharist is so close to Paul's (1 Cor 11:22-26) that scholars think both writers are expressing the same tradition.
5.   The Jerusalem Bible, (Garden City, New York: Doubleday & Company, Inc., 1966), "Introduction to the Synoptic Gospels", p.5.
6.   Pere L. Vaganay's hypothesis is spelled out in much greater detail and with the identification of many of the texts in question in The Jerusalem Bible, pp.5-14. Vaganay's original work is titled Le Probleme Synoptique (Paris: Desclee, 1954).

particular apostolic sources of Gospel material. Next, "the Theory" examines the ancient Christian history written by the scholarly Bishop **Eusebius** about the year 324; the book is named <u>Historia Ecclesiastica</u> (abbreviated <u>H.E.</u>). One of the many earlier authors it quotes is **Papias**, the Bishop of Hieropolis, who died about 130. Papias says that Matthew wrote first in Aramaic [let **MTaram** symbolizes this work]. Papias also says that many translated **MTaram** into Greek [let MtG_1, MtG_2, MtG_3 stands for these translations]. Next,"the Theory" notes that Matthew and Luke have **235 verses** in common which neither copied from the other. Mark has none of these 235 verses thus they had to come from some other supplementary source in Aramaic. "The Theory calls this supplementary source a Supplementary Collection [let C stand for this Aramaic collection of Gospel data and C_1, C_2, C_3, etc. stand for their Greek translations of it]. Now "this Theory" looks at the individual evangelists.

Mark: 661 verses

Papias reported that Mark was **Peter's interpreter** and that he wrote accurately. Thus, in "the Theory" being examined Peter and Aramaic Matthew are the sufficient sources of the **661 verses** contained in Mark's Gospel.

Luke: 1149 verses

Mark and Luke have **366 verses** in common; **Luke**, a convert, indicates that many wrote about these Gospel matters before he did. From Luke's own statement, scholars are convinced that Mark wrote before Luke and that Luke copied from Mark the **366 verses** he wanted to use. "the Theory" next holds that Luke took **235 verses** from a source such as C_1 and that Luke obtained his remaining **548 verses** from his <u>own research</u> and from a source such as MtG_3. These four sources would be adequate to sum up and to account for the **1149 verses** in Luke's Gospel.

Matthew: 1068 verses

Matthew has **601 verses** in common with Mark. "The Theory" assumes that both Mark and the final Greek Matthew [abbreviated as **Matt**] got these verses from different Greek translations of Aramaic Matthew, i.e. from MtG_1, MtG_2, MtG_3. "The Theory" holds that Matthew took the **235 verses** in common with Luke from the same pool of info as Luke but in a different translation C_3. Finally, Matthew has **232 verses** exclusive to himself. Thus,

Matthew's verses add up to the **sum of 1068** and are sufficient to account for the quantity of verses in Matthew's Gospel. "The theory" also acknowledges that the finisher of Matthew's Gospel probably also had a copy of Mark's Gospel available to him.

1. The following is an oversimplified version of how one works toward a solution of the synoptic problem.

2. This hypothesis takes into account all that **historical documents** say [this is its special strong point] about the Gospels as well as what is discernible from the fullest study of the text from literary, philological, textual, etc. studies.

3. The bottom termination-point of the connecting lines [when they are put in place] will indicate the **sources** flowing into each Gospel according to this hypothesis.

The **diagram** follows with the lines flowing down from Christ as the origin to the last repository of the Gospel data. [Draw lines from **Peter** and **Mtaram** to Mark; then circle **336 verses** with a line-arrow to Luke; arrows can deliver **235 verses** from C_1 and C_3 to the proper numbers of Luke and Matt respectively. Little arrows on either side of Luke's **548 verses** can serve to represent material coming from his **own research** and from MtG_3 to finish Luke's needs. MtG_2 can bring **601 verses** down to **Matt**; **232 verses** can be supplied from the Apostolic line of sources; a dotted line can be used to connect Mark's **336 +265** as a secondary source for Matt's **601 verses**.]

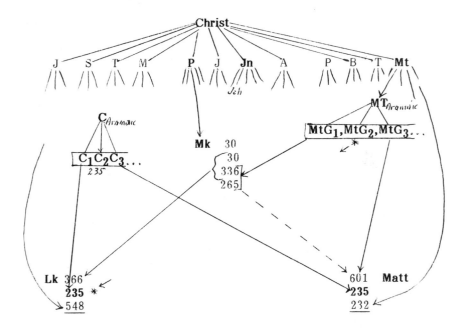

[Caution: "This Theory" **merely gives an idea** which moves toward solving the synoptic problem. The actual work (of analyzing the verbal and thought relationships of the synoptic Gospels) is exceedingly more complex; every verse of each synoptic Gospel must be accounted for. Alternatives, other than the few supplied here, are demanded by the Greek variations of the texts; for example, the Greek of Matthew's Gospel is freshly written, it is neither a direct copy of Mark nor of any stilted Greek translation of the Aramaic Matthew mentioned by Papias.]

Appendix 9: I & II Thessalonians

The town of **Thessalonika** (now called Salonika) is a seaport on the Northwest corner of the blue Aegean Sea. In the first century it was the Roman capitol of Macedonia. The famous Egnatian Way from the Bosphorus to the Adriatic passed through this city. A still-standing, later massive Roman arch marks the entrance to the city through which the missionaries, **Paul, Silas and Timothy,** walked in the year 49. One inscription on the great arched gate identified the "local magistrates '**politarchs**' (a very unusual title)" which supports Luke's use of the title in Acts 17:6.[1] Chapter 17 of Acts describes the circumstances which the missionaries encountered when they started their second new Christian community in Europe.

Shortly before this, their first European foundation had been in **Philippi**, 100 miles to the east, where they had been beaten and jailed for their efforts. Undaunted by their troubles the missionaries trekked about 20 miles a day from Philippi to Thessalonika's entrance. Luke says nothing about setting up Christian communities in Amphipolis & Appolonia, two towns along the Egnatian way on either side of the mountain pass through which the cobblestone Roman road passed.

Thessalonika: seaport, military center and capitol of the Roman province of Macedonia, was home to a mixture of peoples. Macedonians, Greeks, Roman military personel, Jews, and others flourished there. Stoics, Epicureans, various mystery-rite (Eleusinian, Dionysian, Isis & Osiris, etc.) devotees, believers in the state gods and Jews practiced their **religion** there. The missionaries waited for the Sabbath, the Jewish day of synagogue worship; then Paul addressed the synagogue's congregation, composed of Jews and prospective gentile converts [called **God-fearers**]. They went there on three successive sabbaths to proclaim vigorously that **Jesus, risen from the dead, is the Messiah** of Jewish expectation.

On the third sabbath the synagogue erupted; some Jews believed them, a number of God-fearers believed, but influential opponents wanted the missionaries, especially Paul, punished for

---

1. A.M. Hunter, Introducing the New Testament, 3rd ed. (Philadelphia: Westminster Press, 1972), p.142.

disrupting their peaceful synagogue and life. Soon, they wanted Paul, the leader, jailed and even killed! The convert, **Jason**, offered his home as a center for the new Christian Community which Paul calls an **ecclesia** (1 Thes 1:1). In about three months the missionaries got out of the town and went about thirty miles southwest to **Beroea** where, at first, they enjoyed great success among both Jews and god-fearers. Later, influential Thessalonians intruded and stirred the town to violence against Paul who escaped by sea to **Athens** (Acts 18). There, Paul, worried about the Thessalonian converts, sent young Timothy back to check on their situation and faith. Paul was in **Corinth** when Timothy returned with the good and bad news. The year was 50/51; Paul decided to write his **first** letter to the **Thessalonians.** The converts, although suffering opposition as a newly formed group in Thessalonika, were courageous in the faith. However, Some of them were having trouble giving up their pagan sexual practices; others were afraid that loved ones who died before Christ's Second Coming (= **the Parousia**) would not share in the resurrection.

1 Thessalonians

In this first, still extant New Testatment writing, Paul, following the letter-form of the first century [1.sender; 2.addressee; 3.greetings], wrote:

> From Paul, Silvanas (=Silas) and Timothy to the **ekklesia** in Thessalonika which is **in** God the Father and the Lord Jesus Christ: wishing you grace and peace.

By the year 50, only twenty years after Christ's Passion, Death and Resurrecton (PD&R), the term **ekklesia** was already the common name [needing no explanation] for the Christian community being set up in each new town. The Greek word, ekklesia, comes from the Hebrew word, **kahal** which signifies "those called out and brought into community by **the Word of God**". In other words the **kahal = ekklesia = the community brought into being by the Word of God.** Paul's expressions **in God** and **in Christ** were also realities he had already taught the new Christians in the few weeks of his initial instruction. He now used them as fully familiar expressions.

He thanked God that they had given up **idolatry** and were courageously living their new faith in Christ (ch 1). Paul's attention is focused on the Gentile converts, not the Jewish converts. He doesn't cite Jewish men of God like Abraham, Moses, or David, nor does he mention the Temple, the Torah or the Mosaic Covenant; he "makes no use of the Old Testament."[2]

His enemies must have impugned his motives, because (2:1-12) he strongly rejects the charge of 'self-seeking'. In **2:13** Paul points out that God communicates to us in human language, that the **Word of God** is contained in his inspired words. Paul writes:

We thank God constantly that in receiving **his message** from us, you took it not as the word of man, but as it truly is, the **Word of God....**

He wanted to visit them again (ch.3). But he thought it better to send **Timothy** to them while remaining alone in **Athens.** He urged them to live and grow in integrity in preparation for the **Parousia,** the end-time presence of the risen Christ with them.

Paul keeps his moral exhortations for the end of his letters. In chapter 4 Paul urges: avoid greed and sins against morality; **God called us to holiness,** not immorality.[3] Rejection of these instructions is a rejection of God; we exhort you to grow in goodness and avoid idleness.

Finally, Paul says that those still alive at Christ's Second Coming (= **the Parousia**) will have no advantage over your loved ones who have died before the glorious event. In chapter 5 Paul says no one knows when the Parousia will come, but it will be as sudden as labor pains for an expectant mother. Be alert! God has destined us **for acquiring salvation through our Lord Jesus Christ.** He died for us **that** together **we might live with him.** Before his ending he says rejoice! Respect and esteem those in authority in the Lord; seek each other's good.

2 Thessalonians

Some time after this first letter was received, early expectation of the Parousia seems to have gotten out of hand. Some exegetes think it was only a couple of months later and that Paul himself

---

2. Edgar Krentz, "Roman Hellenism and Paul's Gospel", The Bible Today, vol 26, no. 6 (Collegeville: The Liturgical Press, Nov., 1988) p. 329; [hereafter T.B.T., date and page].
3. Charles Giblin, "The Heartening Apocalyptic of Second Thessalonians", T.B.T., Nov. 1988, p. 352.

wrote it; other critics think it was years and that this second letter to the Thessalonians was written by a disciple of Paul who updated and applied Paul's thinking to the feverish anxiety about the end of the world.[4] Apparently some of the new Christians figured: if the end (called the **eschaton**) is near why store food or why work for the future; in fact why work? Others thought: lets have a 'good time' before it comes! It was a kind of eschatological fever; - what would New Yorkers do if they thought the world was going to end on next January 1st?

[Brief paraphrase.] In any event Paul or the disciple in his name said **we do not know when** the end (the eschaton or the glorious Day of the Lord) is going to be. Peacefully go about your work and planing. He cited a penalty for those refusing to work. Further, he emphasized the joyful hope with which their lives were guided by the very one whose parousia they were awaiting.[5]

Further (ch.2), using the apocalyptic type of writing then flourishing, the author sought to calm down their anxiety, he said signs of the parousia would be a prior mass religious **apostasy**; a **man of lawlessness** (perhaps like a satanic messiah?) will **enthrone himself** and claim to be God. Paul had told them all this already. Some kind of **a restraint** is holding back the lawless leader. He cannot do his evil before his appointed time. **The Time** is not yet! Stand firm! Keep the traditions we taught you whether by word of mouth or letter. Don't be deceived! Await God's glorious day in calmness while living your everyday life in accord with God's will.

Finally (ch.3) pray; avoid idleness and disunity. Correct the disorderly. If anyone refuses to obey, avoid him to help him come to his senses. May the Lord of Peace give you peace. (Paul ends

---

4. Charles Giblin, "The Heartening Apocalyptic of Second Thessalonians", T.B.T., Nov. 1988, p. 350; 2nd Thes is commonly held to be deuterocanonical; Giblin names it "a pseudepigraph".
5. Giblin, op.cit., 352, Giblin limits parousia thus: "...the parousia means first and foremost the final union of risen or transformed Christians with Jesus and with all the saints in heaven on the day of the general resurrection from the dead".

the letter in his own handwriting as a sign of genuineness, - to frustrate efforts at forgery.)[6]

Reflection: The Word of God produces **Community (ekklesia)**

In studying the Thessalonian epistles notice that a **new community** has just come into existence. Read A̲c̲t̲s̲ (ch. 17) for a background description to Paul's letters. Pagan Greek and Roman communities were living there; a Jewish community big enough to support a synagogue was there. In their midst Paul is founding a new community. **God-fearers** (= non-Jews who believed in monotheism, the decalogue & Jewish worship of the one God, but hesitated to become full Jewish converts) were in the Synagogue where Paul proclaimed the **kerygma** (= the Passion, Death & Resurrection of Christ for all). Try to analyze the characteristics of this new community. It is a united community of persons, not just clustered individuals as in a bus or subway. This gives an idea of its genus or general classification. Paul tells them that love (not hate or hostility) must characterize them (1 Thes 2:1; 4:9.). Thus, it is a c̲o̲m̲m̲u̲n̲i̲t̲y̲ ̲o̲f̲ ̲l̲o̲v̲e̲.

Notice that **(a) belief in Christ** distinguishes the new group, not social, political, economic or other interests. Those who fully believe in Christ know that they in some way belong to Christ. Their community belongs to Christ (1 Thes 1:11); it is C̲h̲r̲i̲s̲t̲'̲s̲ c̲o̲m̲m̲u̲n̲i̲t̲y̲. Also, **(b)** Christ **redeemed** this community of persons (2 Thes 3:1; 3:15); it is a r̲e̲d̲e̲e̲m̲e̲d̲ ̲c̲o̲m̲m̲u̲n̲i̲t̲y̲. Further, this community is supposed to make itself **(c) pleasing to God** (the Father) as Jesus did, i.e. it is serious about personal integrity (1 Thes 4:3); it feels the Christian obligation of s̲e̲e̲k̲i̲n̲g̲ ̲i̲n̲t̲e̲g̲r̲i̲t̲y̲. Finally, this community is moving toward a **joyful final end** (eschaton) with Christ; it is an **(d) eschatological** c̲o̲m̲m̲u̲n̲i̲t̲y̲ (1 Thes 2:16).

Adding up this genus with the discovered characteristics, one can arrive at a beginning or tentative definition of this new community which Paul calls an **ecclesia** (in 1 Thes 1:1). The definition form would look something like this:

---

6. This ending tends to support the defenders of Paul's direct authorship, rather than those saying it is Paul's thought in the words of a disciple.

The new Ecclesia = (a) + (b) + (c) + (d) + genus.

Thus, the **ecclesia = Christ's redeemed, integrity-seeking, eschatological community of love.** At least 4 or 5 more essential characteristics of the new life in Christ are contained in this first extant Christian document. Did you notice the amazing new two-word prepositional expression which Paul uses?[7] The new community isin some mysterious way so united to the risdn Christ that Paul can say they are **"in Christ"**. One Scripture scholar, R.F.Collins, says that for Paul, Christ's new church is "a gathering together of people 'in the Lord Jesus Christ.'"[8]

---

7.   Dictionary of the Bible, John L. McKenzie, Bruce, Milwaukee, 1965, p.436.
8.   R.F.Collins, "The Lord Jesus Christ", T.B.T., Nov. 1988, p.342.

Questions

1. Which came first in the Christian era: New Testament Scripture or the living Tradition?
2. Name 3 items of specifically Christian belief contained in the letter(s)?
3. Do the letters affirm or imply any knowledge of other Christian beliefs that Paul already taught the Thessalonians: a)Trinity? b)Christ's resurrection?
4. Who gave Paul the authority to preach to the Thessalonians?
5. What is Paul's principal motive in proclaiming the Gospel?
6. What does Paul declare to be his "pride and joy"?
7. What did Paul warn the Thessalonians to expect when they became disciples of Christ?
8. What is this thing: the ekklesia that Paul identifies them as. Does he use the expressions inside of or those outside of it?
9. Did Paul exercise any authority, or give any orders?
10. Is there any indication of authority in this brand new community of Christians?
11. Other Questions?

Appendix 10

In New Testament: Jesus' Resurrection

The five places where **the resurrection of Jesus** is rather fully cited are: first, St Paul's letter to the Corinthians, then later at the ends of the four Gospel accounts about 70 A.D. Mark, about 80/85 Matthew and Luke, about 95 John. Scholars think that Paul wrote his first letter to the Corinthians in 56/57 A.D. This letter (or epistle) is the **earliest extant writing** we have that testifies in a direct and formal way to Christ's resurrection. It is a very important witness to Christian belief in the resurrection.[1] Prior letters by Paul (1 Thessalonians 50/51, Galatians in the early 50s), and many other New Testament references (also early),[2] mention Christ's resurrection but only briefly and in passing. On the other hand, chapter 15, verses 3-8 of 1st Corinthians, (written about 25 years after Jesus rose from the dead), focuses **explicitly on Christ's resurrection"**

> For I handed on to you as of first importance **what I also received**: that Christ died for our sins in accordance with the scriptures; that he was buried; that he was **raised on the third day** in accordance with the scriptures; that he appeared to **Kephas** [Peter], then to **the Twelve.** After that, he appeared to more than **five hundred brothers at once,** most of whom are still living, though some have fallen asleep. After that he appeared to **James,** then to **all the apostles.** Last of all, as to one born abnormally, he appeared **to me.**

The four points: "death, burial, resurrection and appearance" are **the core** of the Apostles' early oral proclamation which Paul received from others; these points are embedded in the above quotation and in the four Gospel accounts.[3] Even earlier than

---

1. Frederick Cwiekowski, The Beginnings of the Church, (New York: Paulist Press, 1988), p.110; [hereafter quoted as Cwiekowski, Beginnings, and page.]
2. John L. McKenzie, Dictionary of the Bible, (Milwaukee: The Bruce Publishing Company, 1965), "resurrection".
3. Joseph A. Fitzmyer, The Gospel According To Luke, (Garden City, New York: Doubleday & Company, Inc. 1985), p. 1533; [Hereafter, Fitzmyer, Luke and page.]

this developed 4-point core was the dramatic announcement of Jesus' resurrection from the tomb: **He has been raised! He is not here!** This affirmation is referred to as the "praeconium pascale" (the pascal proclamation).[4]

Very interestingly, Paul says that he is handing on **this list of appearances** which he himself had received. He was converted by the risen Christ himself about five or six years after Jesus rose from the dead; this list of appearances (minus Paul's addition of himself) was already well known throughout the apostolic community. **Paul added** (to the Corinthian list) Christ's Damascus-road appearance to himself; he did it in such a way that the list **seems** to be in chronological order: first Peter and last (5 or 6 years later) Paul. Peter as the prime witness is listed with the Aramaic name (**Kephas or Cephas = rock**) which Jesus had given him during the public ministry. The appearance to 500 at once appears nowhere else in the N.T. writings. When Paul wrote his letter, within the 56/57 year span, most of the 500 who saw the risen Jesus were still alive! Peter's Aramaic name, **Cephas**, is evidence of the list's **Jewish**-Christian origin; further evidence of Jewish background is the fact that the list mentions no women as witnesses, not even Mary, Jesus' mother, or Mary Magdalen whose name is mentioned in Gospel accounts of the resurrection.

The next source, the Gospel according to **Mark**, comes from about the year 70 A.D. (before the destruction of Jerusalem). In the available ending of this Gospel (Mk 16:1-8) the disciples are directed to an **appearance in Galilee**; no actual resurrection appearances are described. Mark 16: 7-8 says:

"You seek Jesus of Nazareth, the cucified. **He has been raised**; he is not here. Behold the place where they laid him. . .he is going before you to **Galilee**; there you will see him as he told you."

The abruptness of Mark's ending has given rise, through the centuries, to different scholarly theories: did Mark intend to end so abruptly; was the brittle end of the original scroll lost; did the last papyrus page of the codex break off before it was copied. In any case, the infant church saw fit to add other endings to Mark's Gospel. The so-called **"longer ending"** (Mk 16:9-20) cites three of Jesus' **resurrection appearances:**to Mary Magdalen, to

---

4. Fitzmyer, Luke, pp. 1534ff.

two disciples walking to the country (to Emmaus?), and to **the Eleven** whom the Risen Jesus commissions: "Go into the whole world and proclaim the gospel to every creature." This "longer ending" also includes instruction to impose "hands on the sick" and a brief notice of the Ascension.

The next source, the Gospel according to **Luke**, mentions **four appearances** of the risen Jesus: 1)to the women at the empty tomb; 2)to the disciples on the road to Emmaus; 3)to Simon (Peter) alone; and 4)to **the Eleven** (apostles) plus others. The appearances to Peter and to the women are merely mentioned; those to the Emmaus duo and to the Eleven (the commissioning makes them **"Apostles"**) are described in some detail.

Next, the Gospel according to **Matthew,** speaking of dawn on the first day of the week [Sunday], has the angel saying to the women (Mary Magdalen and others) who came to embalm Jesus' body:

> "Do not be afraid! I know that you are seeking Jesus the crucified. He is not here, for **he has been raised** just as he said. Come and see the place where he lay. Then go quickly and tell his disciple, 'He has been raised from the dead, and he is going before you **to Galilee**; there you will see him.' Behold, I have told you" (They hastily departed.) "And behold, **Jesus met them** on their way and greeted them. They approached, embraced his feet, and did him homage. The Jesus said to them, "Do not be afraid. Go tell my brothers to go **to Galilee,** and there they will see me."

Matthew notes the report which the Sanhedrin guards at the tomb gave to the Jewish leaders and their pay-off by the Sanhedrin to say that Jesus' disciples stole the body while they slept. Then, this Gospel ends with Jesus **appearing to his eleven disciples** (some still doubting) **in Galilee** and giving them in formal language his great commission.

> "All power in heaven and on earth has been given to me. Go, therefore, and make disciples of all nations, baptizing them in the name of the Father, and of the Son, and of the holy Spirit, teaching them to observe all that I have commanded you. And behold, I am with you always, until the end of the age."

Finally, the Gospel according to **John** describes first a dramatic and thrilling appearance to the weeping Mary Magdalen **at the tomb.** Then, this Gospel narrates Jesus' startling appearance in the midst of the disciples fearfully gathered behind locked doors; Thomas was absent **"on the evening of that first day** of the week."

> **"Jesus came and stood in their midst** and said to them, 'Peace be with you.' When he had said this, he showed them his hands and his side. The disciples rejoiced when they saw the Lord. [Jesus] said to them again, 'Peace be with you. As the Father has sent me, so I send you.' And when he had said this, he breathed on them and said to them, **'Receive the holy Spirit.** Whose sins you forgive are forgiven them, and whose sins you retain are retained.'"

Thomas refused to believe what the others told him. 'Unless I see and touch him , I will not believe'. A **week later** when Thomas was with the others, **Jesus came as before**; he said to Thomas:

> "'Put your finger here and see my hands, and bring your hand and put it into my side, and do not be unbelieving, but believe.' Thomas answered and said to him, **'My Lord and my God!'** Jesus said to him, 'Have you come to believe because you have seen me? **Blessed are those who have not seen and have believed.'"**

John's Gospel says that Jesus "did many other signs" not written here,

> "But these are written **that you may believe** that Jesus is the Messiah, the Son of God **and** that through this belief you may **have life in his name."**

To the original account of John's 20 chapters, a 21st chapter was **later added** like a postscript. Scholarship is unanimous that chapter 21 was added later, but very soon after the original was finished and before any copies were sent to other first-century churches. This chapter describes Jesus meeting with Peter and six other disciples on the shore of the Sea of Galilee (= Sea of Tiberias). This was the important meeting in which Jesus three times addressed Peter alone and commanded him to "Feed my sheep". John 21:14 explicitly notes: "This was now **the third time**

Jesus was revealed to his disciples after being raised from the dead."

A listing gives an overview of what is common and what is different in the accounts:

1 Cor	Mark	Matt	Luke	John
	Galilee			
	(Mk Ending)			
	Magdalen	Magdalen	Women	Magdalen
	Emmaus two		Emmaus two	
Cephas			**Peter**	
The 12[5]	**The 11**	**The 11**	**The 11**	**Disciples (10)**
				The 10+Thos
				Peter+ (Jn 21)
500 (simul)				
James				
All(Apostles)				
Me (Paul)				

The listing helps us to see clearly that none of the inspired **authors** sought to make a **complete listing of all** the resurrection appearances, thus: only Paul listed the 500 at once and James, while the others omitted these; all the Gospels mentioned Magdalen or women, whereas Paul's list omitted all women; John's text **locates** Magdalen at the tomb and Peter at the sea of Galilee, the others do not say where Peter was; Mark, Matthew and John mention Galilee, Luke chooses to tell only the Jerusalem events. Further, **the times** of the appearances seem condensed into one day in some accounts, whereas John has meetings with the Apostles a week apart, while Luke in chapter one of **Acts** (not included in the above listings) says: Jesus

"presented himself alive to them by many proofs after he had suffered, **appearing to them during forty days.**"

---

5. The disciples specially chosen by Jesus became known as **The 12**; This special connection with Israel and its historic 12 tribes appears to be a Jerusalem emphasis. In any event, the expression **The 12**, could signify the official group of the Apostles (as in Paul's quotation of the traditional listing) even though Thomas was absent or Judas had not yet been replaced.

No scholar has been able to correlate all the data in each of the sources so successfully in an historical-critical way as to quiet the objections of critics. One scholar proposed a theory that there was only one big appearance and the rest were spin-off episodes by the evangelists.[6] That theory gained no adherents. Another scholar, trying to reconcile the differing times and the 4-day journey between Jerusalem and Galilee, hypothesized that first Jesus appeared to Mary Magdalen at the tomb, then to Peter in Jerusalem, after that to Peter and some apostles by the sea of Galilee and finally to all the apostles gathered in Jerusalem.[7] Chapter 21 of John's Gospel is very explicit about the appearance to Peter, John and others by the Sea of Galilee: "**This was now the third time** Jesus was revealed to his disciples after being raised from the dead." The hypothesis, still needing close scrutiny, can be seen to fit John 21, but this hypothesis (as paraphrased) neglects the "500 at once" plus James and others. Scholar John McKenzie thinks: "A complete reconciliation of these accounts **in all details** is simply impossible and should not be attempted."[8]

In any event, **historical analysis**, by definition, cannot get at the transcendent risen Lord but only at the witnesses who claimed to have seen him; it has not solved the questions raised. **Non-believers**, frequently neglecting to inform the reader of their belief-status under the guise of "objective research", sometimes use the problem to deny the resurrection itself; this generally implies a denial of Christ's divinity. **Believing scholars**, mostly known by their Church affiliation, recognize that the data is insufficient to solve all the questions that can be raised. Scholars are now more carefully perceiving that **each evangelist limited his choice** to those appearances which were specially adapted to his overall plan (as **Luke** highlighted **Jerusalem** events) or the needs of the community being addressed, (as **Matthew** highlighted the **authority** given to the Apostles). Biblical scholars emphasize "historical criticism's" need to explain the empty tomb. Christian scholars are reminded of the **crucial faith-factor** in St. Paul's strong assertion: "And **if Christ has not been raised**, then empty [too] is our preaching; empty too, your faith"(1 Cor 15:14).

In childhood we may have pictured Jesus as being raised to exactly the way he had been before his suffering and death. The

---

6. Cwiekowski, Beginnings, p. 68.
7. Ibid., pp. 68-69.
8. McKenzie, Dictionary, "Resurrection".

mode of Jesus' risen state (glorified human body and all) is difficult to appreciate. Perhaps our youthful understanding even yearned for Jesus' resurrection **to exactly the way he was** before his passion and death, - without realizing that such a happening would merely be **resuscitation**. But that is not at all what the evangelists have said. The resuscitations of: Jairus' daughter, the widow's son at Nain and Lazarus - to natural, earthly existence are adequate to manifest divine power, but utterly inadequate as models of Jesus' resurrection.[9]

Jesus' **Resurrection** is to an entirely **new way of being**; Jesus was fully himself, but he rose into a life-reality which belongs to **Divine nature**, - to God's way of being. His new state of living **entirely transcends** our ordinary sense-way of seeing, hearing, and feeling here on earth. Because Jesus' **risen state** is an intrinsically divine reality, our purely human tests for earthly things can not get at this towering dimension. We know about it only from Divine revelation in the personal experience of the apostles and others who witnessed it. The apostles, disbelieving the breathless report of the women, found it almost impossible to describe what they themselves shortly afterwards experienced. Uncertainty, awe, confusion, joy, exhilaration marked their initial reactions. Our familiarity with the idea of Christ's resurrection should not dull our appreciation of the electrifying effect experienced by the apostles. St. Paul struggles with words to say: ". . .even if we once knew Christ **according to the flesh**, yet now we know him **so** no longer";(2 Cor 5:15). As theologian, Gerald O'Collins puts it: ". . .the risen Christ. . .can now no longer be experienced as a worldly reality but **belongs fully to the divine realm**. . .". For this very reason the evangelists are insistent on the bed-rock reality of the risen Christ's appearances. Luke says "He presented himself alive to them by many proofs after he suffered,. . ."(Acts 1:3).

In the new transcendent state that the Risen Jesus is in[10], **he has to perform a miracle** to make himself visible, audible and touchable to his chosen Apostles[11] and to everyone else whom

---

9. Fitzmyer, Luke, p. 1538.
10. Gerald O'Collins, S.J., The Resurrection of Jesus Christ, (Valley Forge, Pennsylvania: The Judson Press, 1973) p. 10; [hereafter O'Collins, Resurrection, and page].
11. The risen Jesus **chose** the ones he wanted to be the witnesses of his resurrection.

he intends to witness his resurrection. The evangelists merely stated the fact that the risen Jesus appeared **to some and not to others.** Jesus freely and simply chose those whom he wanted **as witnesses.** In Jesus' appearance to Paul on the Damascus Road, Paul (and Luke in writing about it) recognized that **Paul alone** in his group experienced the risen Christ's presence, none of the others did. The event that radically changed Paul's life was declared; the fact that the others in the group were not able to see the Risen Christ was also stated. Why Paul was chosen and supernaturally enabled to see and hear Christ, and not the others, was and remains Christ's free choice. Thus too, **Jesus had to "enable"** his apostles to see, hear and touch him. This realization helps us to appreciate the astonishment and confusion, and even doubt for some, when the risen Jesus appeared in their midst with the doors being closed. St. Paul struggles to verbalize the resurrection by saying in 1 Cor 15:36ff:

"What you sow is not brought to life unless it dies. And what you sow is **not the body that is to be** but a bare kernel of wheat. . ."
"So also is the resurrection of the dead. It is sown corruptible; it is raised incorruptible. . . .It **is sown a natural body; it is raised a spiritual body.**"

Later, theology will replace the word, "spiritual", with the term, **"supernatural",** in an effort **to sharpen Paul's distinction** between the things of this world (man is by nature spiritual) and the things immediately pertaining to God which are above human nature, i.e. **supernatural** to the purely human order.

Paul further implies the distinction when he tries to express the gifts that God has in store for those who respond positively to his loving invitation and thus will receive **resurrection to eternal life.**

What eye has not seen, and ear has not heard, And what has not entered the human heart, [that is] what God has prepared for those who love him.
This God has revealed to us through the Spirit. (1 Cor 2:9-10)

P.S. Doubt, disbelief and denial faced the infant Church as well as it faces the modern Church. That is why **Matthew** felt he had to address the charge that the Apostles stole the body while the guards slept. The **first letter of John** had to insist on experiencing the real flesh and blood body of Jesus against the heretical

Docetists who denied that Jesus ever had a real body even during his public ministry. **Paul** faced those who thought that their baptism already gave them resurrection-bodies which could commit no sin. He also had to insist on the reality of Jesus' **bodily resurrection** for the Greek converts who, influenced by Plato's philosophy, thought that the resurrection of the soul was enough.

This latter confrontation suggests the modern secular thinking which confuses the culturally-embedded philosophical **body/soul mind–set** we inherited from Greek philosophy with the biblical **semitic mind–set** which underlies the resurrection narratives. The Jews did not have the word or concept for body which the Greeks had. For the Greeks a man was composed of **soma + pseuche** (in English a man = a body/soul composite); For a Jew (using Greek terms) a man consisted of **sarx + hema + pneuma** (in English a man = a flesh & blood & spirit reality). The terms had areas of overlapping but they were not simply interchangeable. For the Athenian Greeks the body was a prison, something they did not want back; note how they reacted to Paul's speech on the Areopagus (Acts 17:18-34).

For the Jews with a different verbal and cultural mind–set, unless the one who went into the tomb got up out of it and was seen and heard and touched alive there was no such thing as resurrection. In fact, the **Sadducees** didn't think it possible; the **Pharisees** believed that God could do it. Luke, in <u>Acts</u>, affirms that many Pharisees were converted; they believed that God had **raised Jesus Christ** after his self-offering on the cross.

Joseph Fitzmyer sees **the modern question** about the resurrection arising from

"attempts to square it with the dichotomy of body and soul . . . common to all modern Western thought. Or it is called in question because of other philosophical difficulties that people have with the idea, born of scientific objections or of modern sophisticated (post-Enlightenment) ways of regarding human existence. But it should be recalled that the **NT writers who formulated the resurrection narratives . . . were scarcely trying to cope with this sort of thinking**. Denials of the "resurrection" were current already in Paul's time (as 1 Cor 15 attests), but not even he was trying to cope with modern problems. . .. Luke too sought to cope with the manifestation of doubt about the resurrection,

but he does it in a less philosophical way than Paul
(see 24:41-43; Acts 1:3a; 10:41)."

Thus, present-day objections to the resurrection are modern
sophisticated twists replacing the ancient objections responded to
by Paul and the Gospel authors. Even when an objection is
answered, **the objector must confront** the basic New Testament
belief: that God can raise the dead to the resurrection life, **that**
Jesus of Nazareth was thus raised, **and that** you and I are inexorably
headed for the same glorious resurrection of unity with God or
the utter frustration of eternal separation.

Appendix 11

Biblical Interpretation in Crisis:[1]
(Digest[2]: Cardinal Ratzinger's lecture/1988)
[Paragraph Numbers[3]

I. Introduction: The Situation and the Problem

a)Where the Problem lies:

1. There is ambivalence in the modern Historical-Critical (abbreviated: **H-C**)[4] method of exegesis; Cardinal Ratzinger quotes a novel in which the **antichrist** is a famous **exegete.**

2. The so-called **Enlightenment**[5] identified **"defined doctrine"** as an **impediment** to correct understanding of the bible itself; it held that only **H-C** would yield strict objectivity to hear again the voice of Jesus.

3. Gradually **H-C's** picture of Scripture became **more & more confused!** a)[6] **H-C** became multi-theoried; b) the bible became inaccessible to ordinary people; c) faith was not a factor in reading it; d) nor was God a factor; e) **only the human** was claimed

---

1. Joseph Cardinal Ratzinger delivered this lecture entitled: "Biblical Interpretation in Crisis: On the Question of the Foundations and Approaches of Exegesis Today" in St. Peter's Lutheran Church (New York) on January 27, 1988. **The Rockford Institute Center on Religion and Society,** headed by Lutheran minister, Rev. Richard J. Neuhaus, sponsored the Ratzinger address to a selected group of scholars.
2. Some parts of the lecture have been condensed; but parts which seemed essential to advance Cardinal Ratzinger's thought have been quoted fully.
3. **Paragraph Numbering** has been added to Ratzinger's text for quick reference to the individual paragraphs of the original.
4. Footnotes in the original were eliminated and abbreviations were used where feasible to condense the address; the complete text with footnotes is available from the Rockford Institute and was later published by Origins, Vol 17: no. 35, Feb. 11, 1988.
5. Highlighting was added to the text; only a very few underlinings were present in the original text.
6. a,b,c's, were occasionally added to aid student analysis of the text.

to be **truly historical**; not the text but what is human underneath the text is all that the bible gives in an **H-C** view.

4. **Counter-reaction** to the **H-C** method set in: a) Some Theologians sought a path as independent as possible from Historical Criticism; or b) others totally rejected **H-C** & sought the Bible itself in its literal purity (fundamentalism); c) another alternative appeared: **H-C** = one part of the interpreter's posture, another part is his understanding within the world of today. After his historical "autopsy", what exegete reawakens the text and how does he make his synthesis?

5. When **Bultmann** used the philosophy of Heidegger as his vehicle, then Heidegger became the essence of Jesus' message. The Bible through Heidegger's philosophy = **Heidegger's commentary** on the Bible. Today, **materialist and feminist exegesis** appear to be seeking their own readings without even being interested in understanding the text itself in the manner in which it was originally intended. A particular agenda has displaced the search for truth in itself; **H-C** may be used as a cloak to hide the new agenda.

b)The Central Problem

6. Many scholars reject radical hermeneutics and apply Historical Criicism with prudence; they seek a better synthesis betw History and Theology. They acknowledge the present lack of a synthesis which accounts for **"the undeniable insights uncovered by the historical method,** while at the same time overcoming **its limitations and disclosing them** in a thoroughly relevant hermeneutic." It will take a generation to do this! A few **first steps** toward the eventual solution are attempted here.

7. a)**Fundamentalism** is useless; b)a merely positivistic ecclesiasticism will not do; c)merely challenging new theories will produce no synthesis; d)eclecticism using Tradition as a norm fails to satisfy & remains arbitrary. **What is needed** is a criticism of **H-C's** foundations, i.e., "a **criticism of criticism.** By this I mean not some exterior analysis, but a criticism based on the inherent potential of all critical thought to analyze itself."

8. "**We need a self-criticism** of the historical method which can expand to an analysis of historical reason itself" (cf. Kant). "The self-critique of historical method would have to begin, it seems, by reading its conclusions in a diachronic manner so that **the appearance of a quasi-clinical scientific certainty is avoided. It**

has been this **appearance of certainty** which has caused its conclusionss to be accepted so far and wide."

9. "In fact, at the heart of the historical critical method lies the **effort to establish** in the field of history a level of methodological precision which would yield conclusions of the **same certainty as in the field of the natural sciences."** Exegetes allow only other exegetes to criticize them; if they so hold to the science-model shouldn't they **remember the Heisenburg principle?** "The outcome of a given experiment is heavily influenced by the point of view of the observer." Applied to History, how does one see it "just as it was"? "The word **'inter-pretation'** gives us a clue to the question itself: every exegesis requires an **'inter',** an entering in and a being **'inter'** or between things; this is the involvement of the interpreter himself. **Pure objectivity is an absurd abstraction.** It is not the uninvolved who comes to knowledge; rather, interest itself is a requirement for the possibility of coming to know."

10. The Q = how become interested such that the self does not drown out the other? How develop an **inner understanding** for the things of the past?

11. Heisenburg's subject/object relationship is important! Further, "physical processes are in the present and repeatable, whereas **historical processes are past and unrepeatable. Moreover,** historical processes deal with the impenetrability and the depths of the **human being himself,** and are thus even more susceptible to the influence of the perceiving subject than natural events." How reconstruct the original historical context from the clues which remain?

12. A **diachronic approach** looks at the last 200 years of exegetical findings; the results are very uneven; the 200-year history is "not simply one of progress from imprecise to precise and objective conclusions. It appears much more as a history of **subjectively reconstructed inter-relationships** whose approaches correspond exactly to the developments of spiritual history. In turn, these developments are **reflected in particular interpretations** of texts. In the diachronic reading of an exegesis, its philosophic presuppositions become quite apparent...these interpretations, which were supposed to be so strictly scientific and purely 'historical', **reflect their own over-riding spirit,** rather than the spirit of times long ago." **H-C** has **its limits** which need honest recognition.

II. Self-Criticism of H-C method (Dibelius & Bultmann Model)

a) The Method's principal elements & their presuppositions:

13. **Reiner Blank's** noteworthy dissertation, "Analysis and Criticism of the Form-Critical Works of Martin Dibelius and Rudolph Bultmann" critiques the **H-C** method. His work neither builds conclusions on conclusions nor constructs hypotheses and then opposes them. "It looks for a way to identify its own foundations and to purify itself by reflection on those foundations." It seeks its own proper space. D&B[7] have been surpassed and corrected in many details, "but it is likewise true that **their basic methodological approaches continue even today to determine the methods and procedures of modern exegesis.** Their essential elements underlie more than their own historical and theological judgements and . . . have widely achieved an authority like unto dogma."

14. D&B wished to overcome the arbitrary exegesis of the prior so-called "Liberal Theology". "This was embued with judgements about what was 'historical' or 'unhistorical'." B&D "sought to establish strict <u>literary</u> criteria" to search out the **pure form** and the rules which governed the development from the initial **forms** to the text as we have it before us today. Dibelius proceeded with the idea that "the secret of history discloses itself as one sheds light on its development." B&D assumed a "series of fundamental presuppositions" which "both [B&D] considered trustworthy beyond question". **(1)**"Both proceed from the **priority of what is preached over the event itself:** in the beginning was **the word.** [Am Anfang war die Predigt.] Everything in the Bible develops from the proclamation. This thesis is so promoted by Bultmann that for him **only the word** can be original: **the word generates the scene.** All **events**, therefore, are already secondary, mythological developments."

15. "And so a **further axiom** is formulated which has remained fundamental for modern exegesis since the time of D&B: **(2)** the notion of **discontinuity.** Not only is there **no continuity** between the pre-Easter and the post-Easter periods, between the pre-Easter Jesus and the formative period of the Church; **discontinuity applies to all phases** of the tradition. This is so much the case that

---

7. D&B will be used as an abbreviation for the names of Dibelius and Bultmann which appear frequently in the text.

Reiner Blank could state, **'Bultmann wanted incoherence at any price.'"**

16. "To these two theories, [1] the pure originality of the simple word and [2] the discontinuity between the particular phases of development, there is joined the further notion that [3] **what is simple is original,** that **what is more complex must be a later development.** This idea affords **an easily applied parameter** to determine the stages of development: the more theologically considered and sophisticated a given text is, the more recent it is, and the simpler something is, the easier it is to reckon it original. The criterion according to which something is considered more or less developed, however, is not at all so evident as it first seems. In fact, **the judgement essentially depends upon the theological values of the individual exegete.** There remains considerable room for arbitrary choice."

17. "First and foremost, one must challenge that basic notion dependent upon a **simplistic transferral of science's evolutionary model to spiritual history.** Spiritual processes do not follow the rule of zoological genealogies. In fact, it is frequently the opposite: after a great breakthrough, generations of descendants may come who reduce what was once a courageous new beginning to an academic commonplace...."

18. "One can easily see how questionable the criteria have been by using a few examples." Who holds that Clement of Rome (c.95 A.D.) is more complex or developed than Paul's epistles (c.50-67 A.D.). Is James (85+?) more advanced than the epistle to the Romans (57)? Etc. Examine also later times: Aquinas (+ 1274) is more advanced than his later commentators; modern Orthodox Lutheranism is more medieval than Luther himself. "Even between great figures there is nothing to support this kind of developmental theory."

19. Gregory the Great simplified Augustine (431 A.D.); Pascal and Descartes: is the one whose thought is more complex, - later? [Of course, not!] "All **judgements based on** the theory of **discontinuity** in the tradition <u>and</u> on the assertion of an evolutionary **priority of the 'simple' over the 'complex'** can thus be immediately called into question as **lacking foundation.**"

20. As to determining what is "<u>simple</u>", form and content are considered separately. The search was for **the original forms.** Dibelius found them in the so-called 'paradigm'...behind the

proclamation. In succession he next posited the 'anecdote'. then the 'legend' and finally the 'myth'.

21 "Bultmann saw the **pure form** in the 'apophthegm': 'The **original** specific **fragment** which would sum things up concisely; interest would be concentrated on the word (spoken by) Jesus at the end of the scene; the details of the situation would lie far from this kind of form; Jesus would never come across as the initiator...**everything not corresponding to this form Bultmann attributed to development.**' The arbitrary nature of these assessements which would characterize theories of development and judgements of authenticity from now on, is only obvious. To be honest, though, one must also say that these theories are not so arbitrary as they may first appear. The designation of the 'pure form' is based on a **loaded idea of what is original**, which we must now put to the test."

22. The **'Word over event'** "thesis conceals two further pairs of opposites: the pitting of word against cult [i.e. worship], and eschatology against apocalyptic. In close harmony with these is the antithesis between judaic and hellenistic." For Bultmann **hellenistic = cosmos, mystical worship of the gods, & cultic piety.** "The consequence is simple: what is hellenistic cannot be palestinian, and therefore it cannot be original. Whatever has to do with cult, cosmos or mystery, must be rejected as a later development. The rejection of **'apocalyptic'.** . . leads to yet another element: the supposed antagonism between the prophetic and the 'legal', and thus between the prophetic and the cosmic and cultic. In the beginning there was no ethics but simply an ethos. What is surely at work here is the by-product of Luther's fundamental distinction: the **dialectic between the law and the gospel.** According to this dialectic, ethics and cult are to be relegated to the realm of the **law,** and put **in dialectical contrast with Jesus,** who as bearer of the Good News, brings the long line of promise to completion, and thus overcomes the law. If we are ever to understand modern exegesis and critique it correctly, we simply must return and reflect anew on **Luther's view** of the relationship betwen the Old and New Testaments. In place of the analogy model which was then current, he substituted a dialectical structure."

23. "However, for **Luther** all of this remained in a very delicate balance, whereas for Dibelius & Bultmann [hereafter **D&B**], the whole degenerates into a developmental scheme of well-nigh

intolerable simplicity, even if this has contributed to its attractiveness."

24 **"With these presuppositions, the picture of Jesus is determined in advance.** Thus Jesus has to be conceived in strongly 'judaic' terms. Anything 'hellenistic' has to be removed from him. All apocalyptic, sacramental, mystical elements have to be pruned away. What remains is a strictly 'eschatological' prophet, who really proclaims nothing of substance. He only cries out 'eschatologically' in expectation of the 'wholly other'. . ."

25. **"From this view** emerged **two challenges** for exegesis: it had to explain **(1)** how one got **from** the un-messianic, un-apocalyptic **prophetic Jesus** to the **apocalyptic community** which worshipped him as Messias; to a community in which were united Jewish eschatology, stoic philosophy and mystery religion in a wondrous syncretism. This is exactly how Bultmann discribed early Christianity."

26. **(2)** "The second challenge consists in **how to connect** the original message of Jesus to Christian living today, thus making it possible to understand his call to us."

27. The first problem is relatively easy [for B&D] to solve in principle; the agent producing the **contents** of the N.T. (esp. the Gospels) is **the "community"**, not individual persons; hellenization & "history of religions" school furthered the analysis.

28. "The second problem was more difficult. Bultmann's approach was his theory of **de-mythologization,** but this did not achieve quite the same success as his theories on form and development."

29. Of interest is **Bultmann** [as exegete] **responsible** "for an ever more solid **consensus** regarding the methodology of scientific exegesis."

b)The philosophic source of the Method.

30. The question arises: **How could B&D's** essential **categories** for judgement: 1)pure form; then opposition: 2)betw Semitic and Greek, 3)betw cultic and prophetic, 4)betw apocalyptic and eschatology, etc., - **present such evidence** to B&D, that they believed they had at their disposal the perfect **instrument for gaining a knowledge of history?** Why is this method used almost automatically today

without questioning its foundations? "But **what was their dominant idea?**"

31. "With this question, the self-critique of the historical method passes over to the **self-criticism of historical reason,** without which our analysis would get stuck in superficialities."

32. 1st in the "History of Religions" school "the **model of evolution** was applied to the analysis of biblical texts." It was "an effort to use the **methods and models of natural science on** the study of **history.** Bultmann laid hold of this notion in a more general way and thus attributed to the so-called scientific world-view a kind of dogmatic character. Thus, for example, **for him, the non-historicity of the miracle stories was no question whatever anymore. The only thing** one **needed** to do yet was to **explain how these miracle stories came about.** On one hand the introduction of the scientific world-view was indeterminate and not well thought out. On the other hand, it offered an absolute rule for distingishing between what could have been and what had to explained only by development. To this latter category belonged everthing which is not met with in common daily experience. **There could only be what there always is.** For everything else, therefore, historical processes are invented, whose reconstruction became the particular challange [sic] of exegesis."

33. A further step is needed to get at the foundation of the [B&D] categories of judgment. "The real philosophic **presupposition of the whole system** seems to me to lie in the philosophic turning point proposed by Immannuel Kant. According to him, **the voice of being in itself cannot be heard by human beings.** Man can hear it only indirectly, in the postulates of the practical reason, which have remained, as it were, the small opening through which he can make contact with the real, that is, his eternal destiny. For the rest, as far as the content of his intellectual life is concerned, he must limit himself to the realm of the categories [split from their residence in being]. Thence comes the **restriction to the positive,** to the empirical, to the 'exact' science, which by definition excludes the appearance of what is 'wholly other', or the one who is wholly other, or a new initiative from another plane."

34. "In theological terms, this means that **revelation must recede into** the pure formality of **the eschatological** stance, which corresponds to the Kantian split. As far as everything else is concerned, it all needs to be 'explained'. What might otherwise

seem like a **direct proclamation of the divine, can only be myth,** whose laws of development can be discovered. It is **with this basic conviction that Bultmann, with the majority of modern exegetes, read the Bible.** He is certain that it cannot be the way it is depicted in the bible, and he looks for methods to prove the way it really had to be. To that extent there lies **in modern exegesis a reduction of history into philosophy,** a revision of history by means of philosophy."

35. "The real question before us then is, can one read the bible any other way? Or perhaps better, **must one agree with the philosophy which requires this kind of reading?** At its core, the debate about modern exegesis is **not a dispute among historians: it is rather a philosophical debate.** Only in this way can it be carried on correctly. Otherwise it is like a battle in a mist. Such a struggle cannot be conducted casually, nor can it be won with a few suggestions. It will demand, as I have already intimated, the attentive and critical commitment of an entire generation. It cannot simply retreat. . . neither can it renounce the insights of the great believers of the past and pretend that the history of thought seriously began only with Kant."

36. "In my opinion the more recent debate about Biblical hermeneutics suffers from just such a narrowing of our horizon. One can hardly dismiss the exegesis of the Fathers by calling it mere 'allegory' or set aside the philosophy of the Middle Ages by branding it as 'pre-critical'."

III. The basic elements of a new synthesis.

37. Positive side of the problem: "how join its [**H-C's**] tools with a better philosophy which would entail fewer drawbacks foreign to the text, which would be less arbitrary, and which would offer greater possibilities for a true listening to the text itself. **The positive task is without a doubt even more difficult than the critical one. . . .** [May I suggest] where the main road lies and how it is to be found."

38. 3.1 "Gregory of Nyssa called upon the rationalist Eunomius not to confuse theology with the science of nature, [Theology is not physics.] 'The **mystery of theology is one thing,' he said, 'the scientific investigation of nature is quite another.'** One cannot then 'encompass the unembraceable nature of God in the palm of a child's hand.'"

39. "Modern exegesis, as we have seen, completely relegated God to the incomprehensible, the other worldly and the inexpressible in order to be able to treat the Biblical text itself as an entirely worldly reality according to natural scientific methods."

40. "Contrary to the [Scriptural] text itself, phusiologein [physics-type thinking] is practiced. As a 'critical science', [H-C] claims an exactness and certitude similar to natural science. This is a false claim because it is based upon a misunderstanding of the depth and dynamism of the word. Only when one takes from the word its own proper character as word and then stretches it onto the screen of some basic hypothesis can one subject it to such exact rules. Romano **Guardini** commented in this regard on the **false certainty of modern exegesis**, which he said, 'has produced very significant individual results, but has lost sight of its own particular object and generally has **ceased being theology**'. The sublime thought of **Gregory of Nyssa** remains a true guidepost today: '...these gliding and glittering lights of **God's word** which sparkle over the eyes of the soul...[draw us close to] the thoughts of God...'"

41. "Thus the word should not be submitted to just any kind of enthusiasm. Rather, preparation is required to open us up to the inner dynamism of the word. This is possible only when there is a certain **'sym-pathia' for understanding**, a readiness to learn something new, to allow oneself to be taken along a new road. It is not the closed hand which is required, but the opened eye..."

42. "**3.2** Thus the exegete should not approaach the text with a ready-made philosophy, nor in accordance with the dictates of a so-called modern or 'scientific' world-view, which determines in advance what man may or may not be. He may **not exclude a priori** that (almighty) God could speak in human words in the world. He may **not exclude** that God Himself could enter into and work in human history, however improbable such a thing might at first appear."

43. "[The exegete] must be ready to learn from the extraordinary. He must be ready to accept that the truly original may occur in history, something which cannot be derived from precedents, but which opens up of itself. He may not deny to humanity the ability to be responsive beyond the categories of pure reason, and to reach beyond ourselves toward the open and endless truth of being."

44. "**3.3** We must likewise **re–examine the relationship between event and word. For Dibelius, Bultmann and the mainstream** of modern exegesis, the event is the irrational element. It lies in the realm of mere facticity, which is a mixture of accident and necessity. The fact, as such, therefore, cannot be a bearer of meaning. [For D&B] Meaning lies **only in the word,** and where events might seem to bear meaning, they are to be considered as illustrations of the word to which they have to be referred. There is, however, no evidence in reality to support them [i.e.the words (in the D&B theory)]. Such evidence is admissible [by D&B] only under the **presupposition** that the principle of scientific method, namely that **every effect** which occurs can be **explained in terms of purely immanent relationships** within the operation itself, is not only valid methodologically but is true in and of itself. Thus, [according to D&B's logic] in reality there would be only 'accident and necessity', nothing else, and one may only look upon these elements [i.e.events] as brute [meaningless] facts."

45. "But, what is useful as a methodological principle for the natural sciences is a forgone banality as a philosophical principle; and **as a theological principle it is a contradiction.** (How can any or all of God's activity be considered either as accidental or necessary?) It is here, for the sake of scientific curiosity, too, that we must experiment with the precise contrary of this principle, namely that things can indeed be otherwise."

46. "To put it another way: the event itself can be a 'word', in accord with the Biblical terminology itself. From this flow **two important rules for interpretation:**

47. "**a)** First, **both word and event** have to be considered **equally original,** if one wishes to remain true to the biblical perspective. The dualism which banishes the event into wordlessness, that is meaninglessness, would rob the word of its power to convey meaning as well, for it would then stand in a world without meaning."

48. "It also **leads to a Docetic Christology** in which the reality, that is the concrete fleshy existence of Christ and especially of man, is removed from the realm of meaning. Thus the essence of the Biblical witness fails of its purpose."

49. "**b)** Secondly, such a dualism splits the Biblical word off from creation and **would substitute** the principle of **discontinuity** for the **organic continuity of meaning** which exists between the Old

and New Testaments. When the continuity between word and event is allowed to disappear, there can no longer be any unity within the Scripture itself. A **New Testament**, cut off from the Old, is automatically abolished since it **exists, as its very title suggests, because of the unity of both.** Therefore the principle of discontinuity must be counterbalanced by the interior claim of the Biblical text itself, according to the principle of the analogia scripturae: the mechanical principle must be balanced by the teleological principle."

50. "Certainly texts must **first** of all be traced back to their historical origins and interpreted in their proper historical context. But then, in a **second** exegetical operation, one must look at them also in the light of the total movement of history and **in light of history's central event, Jesus Christ.** Only the combination of both these methods will yield understanding of the Bible. If the first exegetical operation by the Fathers and in the Middle Ages is found to be lacking, so too is the second since it easily falls into arbitrariness."

51. "Thus, the first [i.e.,**H–C** all by itself] was fruitless, but the rejection of any coherence of meaning leads to an opinionated methodology. To recognize the inner self-transcendence of the historical word, and thus the inner correctness of **subsequent re-readings in which event and meaning are gradually interwoven**, is the **task of interpretation** properly so-called, for which appropriate methods can and must be found. In this connection, the exegetical maxim of Thomas Aquinas is quite to the point:'The duty of every good interpreter is to contemplate not the words, but the sense of the words.'"

52 "**3.4** In the last hundred years, exegesis has had many **great achievements**, but it has brought forth **great errors as well.** These latter, moreover, have in some measure grown to the stature of academic dogmas. To criticize them at all would be taken by many as tantamount to sacrilege, especially if it were to be done by a non-exegete. Nevertheless, so prominent an exegete as **Heinrich Schlier** previously warned his colleagues: 'Do not squander your time on trivialities.' **Johann Gnilka** gave concrete expression to this warning when he reacted against an exaggerated emphasis by the history of traditions school. Along the same lines, **I would like to express the following hopes**:"

53. "**a)** The time seems to have arrived for a new and thorough reflection on exegetical method. Scientific exegesis must

recognize the philosophic element present in a great number of its ground rules, and it must then reconsider the results which are based on these rules."

54.   "**b)** Exegesis can no longer be studied in a[n] unilinear, synchronic fashion, as is the case with scientific findings which do not depend upon their history, but only upon the precision of their data. **Exegesis** must recognize itself as **an historical discipline.** Its history belongs to itself. In a critical arrangement of its respective positions within the totality of its own history, it will be able, on the one hand, to recognize the relativity of its own judgements, (where, for example, errors may have crept in.) On the other hand, it will be in a better position to achieve an insight into **our real, if always imperfect, comprehension** of the Biblical word."

55.   "**c)** Philological and scientific literary methods are and will remain critically important for a proper exegesis. But for their actual application to the work of criticism – just as for an examination of their claims – an understanding of the philosophic implications of the interpretative process is required. The self-critical study of its own history **must also imply an examination of the essential philosophic alternatives for human thought.** Thus, it is not sufficient to scan simply the last one hundred and fifty years. The great outlines of patristic and medieval thought must also be brought into the discussion. It is equally indispensible to reflect on the fundamental judgements made by the Reformers and the critical importance they have had in the history of exegesis."

56.   "**d)** What we **need now** are **not new hypotheses** on the Sitz im Leben, on possible sources or on the subsequent process of handing down the material. What we do need is **a critical look at the exegetical landscape we now have,** so that we may **return to the text and distinguish** between those hypotheses which are helpful and those which are not. Only under these conditions can a new and fruitful collaboration between exegesis and systematic theology begin. And only in this way will exegesis be of real help in understanding the Bible."

57.   "**e)** Finally, **the exegete must realize that he does not stand** in some neutral area, **above or outside history and the Church.** Such a presumed immediacy regarding the purely historical can only lead to dead-ends. The first presupposition of all exegesis is that it accepts the Bible as a book. In so doing, it [i.e, exegesis]

has already chosen a place for itself, which does not simply follow from the study of literature. It has identified this particular literature as the product of a coherent history, and this history as the proper space for coming to understanding. If it [exegesis] wishes **to be theology,** it must take a further step. It must recognize that **the faith of the Church** is **that form of** 'sympathia' without which the bible remains a closed book. **It must** come to **acknowledge this faith as a hermeneutic,** the space of understanding, which does not do dogmatic violence to the Bible, but precisely allows the solitary possibility for the Bible to be itself."

Glossary

Agraphon an authentic saying of Christ which located in the New Testament outside of the Gospels (cf. Acts 20:35).

Anawim the devout poor with few material possessions, but confident in their dependence on God.

Antichrist The Chief enemy of Christ symbolizing in 1 John and 2 John the one at the end-time who seeks to destroy Christ and take his place. This apocalyptic enemy will be destroyed at Christ's 2nd coming.

Apocalypse A Greek word meaning **revelation** or uncovering; Apocalyptic is the adjective applied to writings which reveal the hidden meaning of events through which God is governing history and leading his people. Such writings flourished from 2nd century B.C. to 2nd century A.D.

Apocrypha Certain Jewish and Christian writings which made some pretension to divine authority, but which were not accepted as inspired. ex. the so-called Gospel of Thomas.

Apostasy The state of one who renounces and rejects the faith he previously believed. One who publicly renounces his faith to save his life or gain public acclaim or office is an apostate.

Apostle comes from the Greek **apo + stello** = "I send out"; in the N.T. it signifies one who is sent out with a commission to proclaim the Good News. Jesus first chose particular disciples. Certainly, at a point later in his public ministry, Jesus identified certain of his disciples to be **"the 12"**. Later still the Gospels proclaim that Jesus gave the specific 12, not everybody, a **commission** which carried with it obligations, rights, powers and authority, in a word, made them **his apostles**. Further, Jesus chose **one of these apostles**, Peter, and gave him a commission and obligations with reference to the other apostles and to his entire flock.

Beatitudes These are the expressions in Matthew's Gospel which begin with: "Blessed (or Happy) are they who. . ."

Blasphemy An insult to God or his name; mocking the sacredness due to God. The Sanhedrin accused Jesus of blasphemy because he identified divine properties with himself.

Breaking of the bread this expression is used in Acts 2:42; 20:11 to signify the liturgy of the **eucharist**; cf. also Luke 24:30.

Brothers of the Lord The Aramaic word **ah** had meanings such as cousin, relative, nephew, half-brother, brother and other meanings; Greek-speaking semites gave the same meanings to adelphos and adelphe including niece, half-sister, etc. James, Joseph, Jude and others were somehow "related" to the Lord without being blood-brothers.

Canon This Greek word means a measure, a rule or a norm. In scripture studies its technical meaning is the list of those books accepted by the Church [in official acts in 367, Council of Trent (1545-1563) and other acts] and **believed** by Christians to be **inspired by God.**

Christ is the English word for Christos which is Greek for the Hebrew term **Messiah.** The Hebrew word signifies "anointed". he high priest was anointed as was the king giving them a special relationship to God. The awaited Messiah would in some way restore Israel. By the year 50 A.D. **Christ** had become a proper name identifying **Jesus.**

Christology The theological study of who Christ is, his humanity and divinity and his relationship to God, the Father, and all other human beings.

Covenant This word signifies a **treaty** or an **agreement,** as a binding treaty sworn to by kings of equal strength. A treaty between radically unequal authorities such as between God and Israel was by analogy also called an agreement. Here the term **covenant** carried a special note of sacredness because only God can bind himself and God never fails his side of the agreement.

Deacon from the Greek word **diakonein** meaning to serve; the original **deacons** were ordained by the Apostles (Acts 6 ff.) for functions, such as preaching and baptizing within the Christian community.

Dead Sea Scrolls The manuscripts of the **Essene** community located **Qumran** on the Northwest shore of the Dead Sea; among them were found, in whole or part, most of the Old Testament books.

Deutero-canonical The first New Testament writings which were acknowledged as canonical were referred to as **proto-**canonical; the writings later acknowledged as canonical were called **deutero-**canonical. James, 2nd Peter, 2nd & 3rd John, Jude, Hebrews and the Apocalypse are sometimes cited as deutero-canonical.

Diaspora the settlement of Jews abroad, i.e. outside of Palestine; it is also called the dispersion.

Diptych a literary arrangement in which the material is presented as a sort of picture composed of two panals; Luke 2: Birth of Baptist | Birth of Jesus.

Docetism the word comes from the Latin **docet** meaning "it appears";the error comes from those who claimed that Christ did not have a real human nature and body, but only **appeared** to be a man.

Ekklesia is the Greek word for the aramaic word **kahal**; in Latin the word is **ecclesia**; in Italian it is **Chiesa**; in German **Kirche**; in English **Church.**

Eschaton This is the Greek term used to refer to the **end** of the world as we know it. Its adjective referring to the end-time is **eschatological.**

Essenes An ascetical community of Jewish men living a celibate, monastic type of life; they had a monastary-like settlement at **Qumran** located on the northwest shore of the **Dead Sea.** Their sacred scrolls, containing most of the Old Testament were discovered in 1947.

Exegesis The study which seeks the author's meaning of a scriptural passage; its opposite term is **eisegesis** which means putting a meaning **into** the passage not acceptable to the inspired author.

Form criticism an analytic study of the New Testament which seeks to reconstruct imaginatively the way in which the words and deeds of Christ were verbally formulated during the **oral stage** before being commited to writing by the evangelists. It considers the liturgical, missionary, didactic and polemical life-situations in which the Gospel was proclaimed and explained.

Glory This technical term in Scripture signifies a manifestation of the divine transcendence; God's presence is manifested by his **"glory"**. God elevates an individual human nature to share his divine life by **glorifying** it. John 17:5 "Now **glorify** me, Father, with you, with the **glory** I had with you **before the world began.**" Jesus intends to incorporate his Apostles and those who join them into his **glory**, - his **life in eternity.**

God-fearer Technical term describing a gentile who accepted the belief of Jewish monotheism, cult of sabbath worship, and code of the **Torah** (10 commandments, kosher laws, etc.), but would not accept circumcision or full incorporation into Judaiasm.

Hellenism This term refers to the overlay of Greek (Hellenic) culture, language and attitudes on the culture of another nation or people. Alexander the Great so influenced the Mediterranean world that Greek was its common spoken language for five centuries. The 27 New Testament books are written in koine (common) Greek.

Hermeneutics the study of the **principles and rules** for interpreting Scripture and the process by which the rules are properly applied.

Herodians The people in Palestine who supported and sought the favor of the ruling Herod and his family.

Incarnation identifies the belief that the eternal Son of God came among human beings in human nature the same as theirs; he came "in flesh" (in carne).

Kerygma means in Greek a proclamation; it is the term used in Scripture to signify the proclamation of the "passion, death and resurrection of Christ for all".

Midrash the highlighting of a biblical text or event to show its meaning for the present. For example, the Magis' gifts of gold, frankincense and myhrr, whether given to the Christ-child or not, signify the gentiles coming to the savior.

Parable a small literary unit in which some truth is presented in terms of a concrete image to which the truth can be compared; thus, a **seed** can be used as an image of the **word of God.**

Parousia this word signifies **presence**; it is generally reserved to mean Christ's second coming and his presence at the end-time.

"People of God" Dt 7:6 here and elsewhere God made Israel his "chosen people" provided they kept his word, his Torah. Lv 20:24 this covenant people is to be holy and set apart. Christ, the Son, established a new covenant and renewed a remnant to be the **People of God**; but it is not 'of the flesh' involving circumcision or nationalism. 1 Peter 2:10 identifies the Christians thus: **"you are God's People".**

Pericope a small **unit-section** of the text, like a parable or a cure, **cut out** or isolated for special attention. Many such small units are found in Scripture, especially the Gospels.

Proselyte an alien living in a country not his own; applied in a religious sense to a Gentile who became a Jew or vice versa. Thus, one who is a full convert to another religion. **Proselytism** is the process of seeking converts.

Publican One who paid money to the Roman Government for the right to collect taxes from the other citizens. For Jews it meant defilement from subordination to, and contact with, pagans to exact money (often excessive) from the "people of God".

Redaction refers to a **reworking** of a text; for example Luke **reworked** or reshaped some traditional Jewish material probably from Mark's Gospel to make it more readily understandable to gentile readers. **Redaction Critics** are those exegetes who closely examine the writing stage of the Biblical documents (esp. the Gospels) to discover the way each inspired author moulded the traditional data to fulfill the purpose he had in mind.

Ritual purity Lv 7:19-21 One who was purified for worship according to the Mosaic Law. Contact with certain things or persons made one **unclean** (Nm 19); certain washings, rites, etc. made one clean again. The concept was related to worship rather than chastity.

Samaritans were the people who lived in the territory of **Samaria** located between Judea and Galilee. Historically, many came from Jews who had intermarried with idol-worshipping pagans. The **Pentateuch** was sacred to them; they once had a temple on Mt. Gerizim which the Judeans had destroyed.

Septuagint The **Greek Translation** of the Old Testament done by Jewish scholars approximately between the years 200 B.C. to 50 B.C. Tradition indicated that 70 scholars accomplished it, hence Roman numeral seventy **LXX** is used as a symbol for it.

Syncretism the result achieved when the principles or doctrines on one religion are inserted into another religion.

Torah means the "way of life" or "law" (from God) for the Jewish people; for the Sadducees it was equivalent to the **Pentateuch**; Pharisees held that the Torah depended on the **Pentateuch + the Prophets + the Writings,** in other words on the **whole Old Testament**.

Triptych a literary arrangement in which the material is presented as a sort of picture composed of three panals.

Zealots Some 1st century Jews who thought that any means (assassination, etc.) of getting the pagan Romans out of Palestine were legitimate. They were mostly younger men of fighting age led by older men who, despite their awareness of great military inferiority, fanatically felt that God would drive the Romans out. The Zealots' posture and acts

precipitated the bloody Jewish-Roman war which destroyed
Jerusalem in the year 70 A.D.

"Fish with Bread and Wine. The Food of Life symbolized by the Eucharist and
the feeding of the five thousand (John 6) with allusion to the ichtys (fish) symbol.
Crypts of Lucina, Catacomb of Calixtus. Shortly after 200."
(A ECW 42)   Atlas 9 & Early Christian World - Von der Meer & Mohrmann